EAT UP
SLIM DOWN

ANNUAL
RECIPES
2 0 0 9

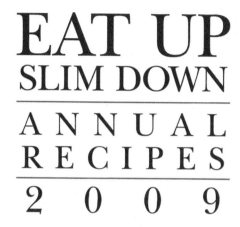

EAT UP
SLIM DOWN

ANNUAL
RECIPES
2 0 0 9

195 Simply Delicious Recipes
for Permanent Weight Loss

RODALE

Printed in the United States of America
Rodale Inc. makes every effort to use acid-free ∞, recycled paper ♲.

Interior design by Kristen Morgan Downey
Interior photograpy credits appear on page 345.
Front cover recipe: Luscious Blueberry Creme (page 279)

ISBN-13 978-1-59486-999-0
ISBN-10 1-59486-999-5

2 4 6 8 10 9 7 5 3 1 hardcover

We inspire and enable people to improve their lives and the world around them

For more of our products visit **rodalestore.com** or call 800-848-4735

CONTENTS

SPECIAL
THANKS

In grateful appreciation to all the contestants
in the Eat Up Slim Down Recipe contest,
we would like to thank all the readers of
www. prevention.com who were kind enough
to share their delicious recipes, clever tips, and
inspiring stories of weight loss. We salute you
and wish you continued success.

And sincere, heartfelt thanks to the five
weight loss winners who shared their stories
with us in personal profiles: Katie Ciaria,
Joanne Giannini, Maureen Harris, Kimberly
Justus, and Bonne Marano.

ACKNOWLEDGMENTS

A very special thank you to everyone who had a hand in creating *Eat Up Slim Down Annual Recipes 2009.*

Carol Angstadt
Jill Armus
Marisa Bardach
JoAnn Brader
John Carpitella
Kristen Morgan Downey
Anne Egan
Rachelle Laliberte
Marilyn Hauptly
Mitch Mandel
Leah McLaughlin
Joan Parkin
Stacy Petrakovitch
Jean Rogers
Pam Simpson
Shea Zukowski

CONTRIBUTORS

This book includes many of the delicious and creative recipes sent to us by weight loss winners across the United States and beyond. The number of recipes we received was so great, it was a difficult task to choose which ones appear here. But after a careful selection process and many long hours in our test kitchen, we managed to whittle it down. Here are this year's recipe contributors. We salute their innovate efforts in the kitchen and hope you'll enjoy using their recipes to reach your own weight loss goals.

INTRODUCTION

Welcome to another year of *Eat Up Slim Down*, the cookbook that proves good food and weight loss can go hand in hand! If there's one thing we know from the hundreds of letters and emails we receive from *Prevention* readers every month, having just the right recipe is one of the most essential ingredients for weight loss success.

That's why we're proud to bring you the eighth year of *Eat Up Slim Down*, a wonderful collection of delicious dishes and weight loss news that's sure to help wherever you are on your journey to a thinner, new you. Looking for a good place to start? Check out the first chapter, aptly titled Weight Loss News We Can All Use. Here you'll find six reliable ways to

tune in to your hunger cues as well as advice on how to create meals that will leave you feeling truly satisfied. And because getting the best mix of nutrients is even more challenging when you're cutting back calories, we've also included a helpful quiz to test your nutrition IQ. Use it to help you spot the best ways to get the most out of all your everyday food choices. Throughout the book, you'll also find plenty of "Shopping Savvy" sidebars that feature great new ingredients to try—after all, having a well-stocked pantry makes it so much easier to enjoy a variety of dishes from week to week.

Plus, this year we're proud to bring you more recipes that ever! We've compiled close to 200 recipes, many from readers around the country who couldn't wait to share the dishes that have worked for them. Every recipe has been put through the paces in our test kitchen in Emmaus, Pennsylvania, to ensure you'll have great results in the kitchen. Truth be told, after all the taste testing was through, we had a hard time picking a favorite dish—and we bet you probably will, too.

So if you need some new dishes to jazz up your regular routine, be sure to check out the Baked Italian–Style Stuffed Tomatoes on page 256 sent to us by DeAnna Piper from Rice Lake, Wisconsin. Her dish draws from a classic recipe for stuffed peppers and retrofits it with another summer food we should all enjoy more often, tomatoes. And if you're a fan of Asian food, you'll surely want to try Susan Riley's Tangy and Nutty Thai Chicken Pizza on page 153. This exciting recipe features a delicious homemade peanut sauce and just the right blend of chicken, bell pepper, carrots, and peanuts on top—all the classic Thai

ingredients expertly reinvented in an American favorite. Perfection!

Perhaps you're the type of dieter who finds it easier to stay on track when you have a good dessert to look forward to. If so, the Banana Walnut Torte on page 290, sent to us by Jean Gottfried of Upper Sandusky, Ohio is sure to please. She created this tender fruit-filled cake topped with luscious dark chocolate and walnuts for family gatherings—and it has only 217 calories per serving!

Looking for some more inspiration? Turn to the "It Worked for Me" weight loss stories, complete with before and after photos, to read how five real women were able to change their eating habits and reach their weight loss goals. As you travel toward your own goals, think about taking your own before-and-after pictures if you haven't already. And let us know what you think of this year's collection—we'd love to hear what works for you!

WEIGHT LOSS NEWS WE ALL CAN USE

Are you looking to lose weight but tired of turning to diet plans that dictate every morsel? You're not alone. Not only are such plans time-consuming and tedious, but most people find them tough to carry out over the long haul. Sooner or later (and most likely sooner), you may be tempted to toss the rule book. So if that's the case, how much do you really need a prescribed program to lose those pounds?

The really good news in weight loss is that, yes, you *can* do it yourself! The trick is to tune in to your own body's hunger signals so you eat only when you need—and no more than you need—to eat. Read on for a dozen easy-to-follow eat-right strategies to find out how you can make them work for you.

6 Ways to Tune In to Hunger

"Hunger is a physical cue that you need energy," says Dawn Jackson Blatner, RD, dietitian at the Northwestern Memorial Hospital Wellness Institute in Chicago.

However, hunger can also be your best diet ally. If you listen to your body, you'll instinctively feed it the right amount. But fall out of touch and hunger becomes diet enemy number one: You may eat more than you need or get too hungry and stoke out-of-control cravings.

Nutrition experts share these six tips that teach you to spot hunger and eat to stay satisfied—so you control calories and shed pounds without "dieting."

IDENTIFY YOUR SPOT ON THE HUNGER SCALE

Do you really know what hunger feels like? Before you can rein it in, you must learn to recognize the physical cues that signal a true need for nourishment. Prior to eating, use this to help figure out your true food needs.

- **Starving:** An uncomfortable, empty feeling that may be accompanied by light-headedness or jitteriness caused by low blood sugar levels from lack of food. Binge risk: high.
- **Hungry:** Your next meal is on your mind. If you don't eat within the hour, you enter dangerous "starving" territory.
- **Moderately hungry:** Your stomach may be growling, and you're planning how you'll put an end to that nagging feeling. This is optimal eating time.
- **Satisfied:** You're satiated, not full but not hungry either. You're relaxed and comfortable and can wait to nosh.
- **Full:** If you're still eating, it's more out of momentum than actual hunger. Your belly feels slightly bloated, and the food doesn't taste as good as it did in the first few bites.
- **Stuffed:** You feel uncomfortable and might even have mild heartburn from your stomach acids creeping back up into your esophagus.

DIY STRATEGY: Eat when you are "moderately hungry" or "hungry." At these stages, you've used most of the energy from your last meal or snack, but you haven't yet hit the point where you will be driven to binge.

REFUEL EVERY 4 HOURS

Still can't tell what true hunger feels like? Set your watch. Moderate to full-fledged hunger (the ideal window for eating) is most likely to hit 4 to 5 hours after a balanced meal. Waiting too long to eat can send you on an emergency hunt for energy—and the willpower to make healthful choices plummets. When researchers in the United Kingdom asked workers to choose a snack just after lunch,

POWER PEANUTS

Want to make a simple, good-for-you snack even more healthful? Try boiled peanuts. This Southern specialty (available widely in those states and at nutsonline.com) has up to four times the disease-fighting phyto-chemicals of its dry-roasted, oil-roasted, and raw counterparts, according to Alabama A&M University food scientists. Researchers say that when whole peanuts are boiled in water, the kernels may absorb antioxidants from the shell (it's removed early on in other processing methods); heat may also help release these powerful compounds.

70 percent picked foods such as candy bars and potato chips; the percentage shot up to 92 percent when workers chose snacks in the late afternoon.

"Regular eating keeps blood sugar and energy stable, which prevents you from feeling an extreme need for fuel," explains Kate Geagan, RD, a Park City, Utah–based registered dietitian.

DIY STRATEGY: Have a 150-calorie snack to hold you over if you're feeling hungry between meals. Munch on whole foods such as fruit and unsalted nuts—they tend to contain more fiber and water, so you fill up on fewer calories. Bonus: They're loaded with disease-fighting nutrients. But in order to avoid temptation away from home, try packing healthful, portable snacks such as string cheese and dried fruit in your purse, desk drawer, or glove compartment.

EAT BREAKFAST WITHOUT FAIL

A recent study published in the *British Journal of Nutrition* tracked the diets of nearly 900 adults and found that when people ate more fat, protein, and carbohydrates in the morning, they stayed satisfied and ate less over the course of the day than those who ate their bigger meals later on.

Along the same lines 78 percent of successful dieters have breakfast every day, according to the National Weight Control Registry, a database of more than 5,000 people who've lost more than 30 pounds and kept the weight off for at least a year.

Unfortunately, the reality is that many Americans do the exact opposite and start off on an empty stomach: In one recent survey, consumers reported that even when they eat in

SKIM OR SOY?

Fat-free milk has earned a reputation as a fat fighter. Now a study finds its calcium-fortified cousin soy milk works just as well. In the study, published in the *Journal of the American Dietetic Association,* nutritionists at Northern Illinois University put 14 women on a reduced-calorie diet that included 3 cups of either fat-free or soy milk daily (everyone got the same amount of calories, protein, fat, calcium, and vitamin D). After 8 weeks, both groups lost about the same number of pounds and percentage of body fat. They also shrank their bellies by the same amount. Aim to get 1,000 to 1,200 milligrams of calcium a day; if you choose soy, be sure it's fortified with at least 30 percent of the daily value of calcium per serving.

the morning, the meal is a full breakfast only about one-third of the time.

DIY STRATEGY: Aim to breakfast on a minimum of 250 calories every day. Strapped for time? Prepare breakfast before bed (cut fruit and portion out some yogurt) or stash single-serving boxes of whole grain cereal or packets of instant oatmeal and shelf-stable fat-free milk or soy milk at work to eat when you arrive. Can't stomach food so early? Eat a late breakfast. "Don't force anything," says John de Castro, PhD, a behavioral researcher and dean of the College of Humanities and Social Sciences at Sam Houston State University in Huntsville, Texas. "Just wait awhile and eat at

9:00, 10:00, or even 11:00 a.m. It will help you stay in control later in the day."

BUILD LOW-CAL, HIGH-VOLUME MEALS

Solid foods that have a high fluid content can help you suppress hunger. "When we eat foods with a high water content like fruits and vegetables, versus low-water-content foods like crackers and pretzels, we get bigger portions for fewer calories," says Barbara Rolls, PhD, author of *The Volumetrics Eating Plan* and a professor of nutritional sciences at Pennsylvania State University. Bottom line: You consume more food but cut calories at the same time. Dr. Rolls has found a similar effect in foods with a lot of air. In a recent study, people ate 21 percent fewer calories of an air-puffed cheese snack compared with a denser one.

DIY STRATEGY: Eat fewer calories by eating more food. Start dinner with a salad or make it into your meal (be sure to include protein such as lean meat or beans). Choose fresh fruit over dried: For around the same amount of calories, you can have a whole cup of grapes or a measly 3 tablespoons of raisins. Boost the volume of a low-cal frozen dinner by adding extra veggies such as steamed broccoli or freshly chopped tomatoes and bagged baby spinach.

MUNCH FIBER ALL DAY LONG

Fiber can help you feel full faster and for longer. Because the body processes a fiber-rich meal more slowly, it may help you stay satisfied long after eating. Fiber-packed foods are also higher in volume, which means they can fill you up so you eat fewer calories. One review recently published in the *Journal of the American Dietetic Association* linked a high intake of cereal fiber with lower body mass index—and reduced risk of type 2 diabetes and heart disease.

DIY STRATEGY: Aim to get at least 25 grams of fiber a day. Include produce such as apples and carrots—naturally high in fiber—in each meal and snack and replace some or all of your regular bread, pasta, and rice with whole-grain versions. Reach for fiber-filled cereals any time of day, too. Three we like: Fiber One Honey Clusters (14 grams per 1¼ cups), Nature's Path Optimum Slim Cereal (11 grams per 1 cup), and Vermont Morning Multi-Grain Hot Cereal (8 grams per ½ cup).

SIDESTEP DAILY DIET SLIPUPS

Problem: There's no time in the morning for breakfast, so you grab a muffin or doughnut.

Solution: Zap a packet of instant oatmeal with low-fat milk as soon as you wake up. Take bites between showering, dressing, and putting on makeup. Bring an apple or banana to eat in the car.

Problem: You've underestimated how long your errands would take; you're now ready for lunch but stuck in traffic.

Solution: Dig into your glove compartment for the high-fiber, protein-packed bar you keep there for such emergencies. When you reach your destination, eat a lighter-than-normal lunch to compensate for the extra calories.

Problem: It's late afternoon and you're low on energy. The office vending machine is calling your name.

Solution: Stash single-serving packages of nuts and dried fruit in your desk and plan to munch a few hours after lunch—when you feel moderate hunger.

Problem: You're going out for a late dinner with your girlfriends, but it's only 5:00 p.m. and you're already hungry.

Solution: Have a 150- to 200-calorie snack such as yogurt with some fruit or celery and 2 tablespoons of peanut butter a couple of hours before your dinner date.

Problem: It's past your normal bedtime and now your stomach is growling.

Solution: Grab a fiber-filled piece of low-calorie fruit such as a juicy apple or pear instead of, or at least before, diving into the cookie jar.

FOODS THAT FIGHT FAT

Add these items to your shopping list to curb your appetite, burn fat, and put you on the road to a slimmer you.

Oatmeal. A 2006 study found that the fiber in the rolled grain curbs your appetite without a truckload of calories—the perfect combo to help you eat less and lose weight.

Vegetable juice. Consider this a calorie-cutting cocktail: Have a glass before mealtime and you'll eat up to 135 fewer calories later, according to scientists at Pennsylvania State University.

Nuts. Add a few very small servings of your favorite variety to your diet—the fiber and good fat in nuts make them very filling, so your weight stays steady, say researchers at Loma Linda University.

Fat-free milk. Several studies have shown a link between calcium and body fat: As calcium intake increases, body fat decreases. And one study showed that two servings of dairy every day may reduce the risk of gaining weight by as much as 70 percent.

Green tea. Compounds in this type of tea may help boost your body's metabolism and fat-burning abilities, according to studies.

INCLUDE HEALTHY PROTEIN AT EACH MEAL

When researchers at Purdue University asked 46 dieting women to eat either 30 percent or 18 percent of their calories from protein, the high-protein eaters felt more satisfied and less hungry. Plus, over the course of 12 weeks, the women preserved more lean body mass, which includes calorie-burning muscle.

DIY STRATEGY: Boost your protein intake. Have a serving of lean protein such as egg whites, chunk light tuna, or skinless chicken at each meal. A serving of meat is about the size of a deck of cards or the palm of your hand—not including your fingers. Build beans into your meals. Black beans, chickpeas, and edamame (whole soybeans) are low in fat, high in fiber, and packed with protein.

6 Secrets of the Naturally Slim

Chances are, you know someone who seems to effortlessly follow the above strategies—and more. We all have that one thin friend—the one who's never bullied into submission by the bread basket, and when she says, "I'll just have a bite," she does just that without a second glance at the goodies left behind. Is she for real?

Turns out, research shows that thin people simply don't think about food the same way as, well, the rest of us. "Thin people have a relaxed relationship with food," explains David L. Katz, MD, an associate professor adjunct in public health at Yale University. "Those who are overweight, however, tend to be preoccupied by it. They focus on how much or how often they eat, or they attach labels like 'good' and 'bad' to certain foods. As a result, mealtime is always on the brain." Below, weight loss experts explore the mysterious minds of the "naturally" slim to offer you even more slim-down tips. Here's how you can act the part.

DON'T USE FOOD TO CURE THE BLUES

It's not that thin women are immune to emotional eating, says Kara Gallagher, PhD, a weight loss expert based in Louisville. But they tend to recognize when they're doing it and stop.

DIY STRATEGY: Add the word *halt* to your vocabulary, says Dr. Gallagher. More than just a command (as in "stop eating that entire sleeve of cookies"), it's an acronym that stands for "hungry, angry, lonely, or tired"—the four most common triggers for emotional eating. If you're truly hungry, choose a balanced snack, such as a handful of nuts, to tide you over until your next meal. But if you're angry, lonely, or tired, seek an alternative calorie-free solution to your emotional need. Blow off steam by going for a run or just jumping around—the heartbeat boost will help dissipate your anger. Lonely? Call a friend, e-mail your kid, or walk to the park or mall. Being around others will make you feel more connected to your community (even if you don't bump into anyone you know). If you're tired, for heaven's sake, sleep!

Think *halt* and chances are your emotional need to nosh will pass. "People give in to cravings because they think the cravings will build in intensity until they become overwhelming, but that's not true," says Cynthia Bulik, PhD, author of *Runaway Eating* and director of the Eating Disorders Program at

WARM UP TO FROZEN FRUITS

The farmers' market may be closed for the season, but you can still fit frozen fruits into your meals. Add these summer favorites to warm recipes year-round for a healthy dose of nutrients with minimal calories.

First Microwave	Then Add To
Berries	Your morning oatmeal with a dusting of nutmeg
Cherries	Warm brown rice pudding garnished with slivered almonds
Mangoes	Baked fish or a sweet potato after combining with lime juice and honey
Peaches	Slices of toasted oat bread or whole-grain waffles spread with fat-free ricotta sprinkled with cinnamon and cloves

the University of North Carolina at Chapel Hill. Cravings behave like waves: They build, crest, and then disappear. If you "surf the urge," you have a better chance of beating it altogether, she says.

EAT MORE FRUIT

Lean people have, on average, one more serving of fruit and eat more fiber and less fat per day than overweight people, reports a 2006 study published in the *Journal of the American Dietetic Association*.

DIY STRATEGY: Start tinkering. Examine your diet for ways to add whole fruits (not juices) to your meals and snacks. Aim for two or three servings per day. Sprinkle berries over your cereal or on your yogurt. Add sliced pears to your turkey sandwich or bake an apple for dessert. Keep a bowl of fruit on your kitchen table or desk to motivate you to think fruit first, vending machine never.

BE A CREATURE OF HABIT

Any dietitian will tell you that a varied diet is good—but too much variety can backfire, says Dr. Katz, author of *The Flavor Point Diet*. Studies have shown that too many tastes and textures encourage you to overeat, he explains. "Thin people have what I call a food groove—the majority of their meals consist of well-planned staples," says Judith S. Beck, PhD, author of *The Beck Diet Solution*. "There are a few surprises thrown in, but for the most part, their diets are fairly predictable."

MAKE SMART CHOICES ALL DAY

It's easier than you think. Just remember a few key tips every time you eat.

- Opt for whole fruit over juice—and for a snack. One cup of orange juice has more than 2½ times the calories of a tangerine, and the tangerine is totally portion controlled. A baseball-size portion of fresh fruit provides about 50 to 100 calories, the amount in only three pretzel twists.

- Make veggies half the bulk of your meals. Produce contains a lot of water, which makes it naturally low in calories.

- Always measure these foods: rice, cereal, peanut butter, and oil. They're hard to eyeball and are calorie dense. A heaping cup of rice has 25 percent more calories than a level one.

- Have only one high-fat food per meal. High-fat foods (such as full-fat dressing, nuts, croutons, or cheese) pack more calories into a smaller serving, which adds up quickly.

- Pick "slippery" salad dressings such as oil and vinegar or reduced-fat vinaigrette. They coat your salad more easily than thick ones like blue cheese or Russian, so you can use less.

WINNING HABITS OF SUCCESSFUL LOSERS

Researchers predict that 75 percent of US adults will be overweight by 2015. The good news: This trend is reversible. Data from the National Weight Control Registry reveals the three most commonly shared behaviors of successful "losers."

1. Exercise, on average, about 1 hour per day (90 percent)

2. Weigh themselves at least once a week (75 percent)

3. Watch less than 10 hours of TV per week (62 percent)

DIY STRATEGY: Try to be as consistent as possible with your major meals—have cereal for breakfast, a salad at lunch, and so forth. It's okay to add grilled chicken to the salad one day and tuna the next, but by sticking to a loosely prescribed meal schedule, you limit the opportunities to overindulge.

BECOME A STUDY IN SELF-CONTROL

Researchers at Tufts University found that the biggest predictor of weight gain among women in their fifties and sixties was their level of disinhibition, or unrestrained behavior. Women with low disinhibition (in other words, a finely tuned sense of restraint) had the lowest body mass index. High disinhibition (i.e., low restraint) was linked to an adult weight gain of as much as 33 pounds.

DIY STRATEGY: Prepare for moments when your disinhibition is likely to be higher—such as when you're in a festive atmosphere with a large group of friends. If you're at a party, tell yourself you'll take one of every fourth passed hors d'oeuvre. If you're out at dinner, order an appetizer portion and share dessert. Or if you're stressed—another low-restraint moment—make sure you have a source of crunchy snacks (like fruit or carrot sticks) at the ready.

BE A MOVER AND SHAKER

On average, slim people are on their feet an extra $2\frac{1}{2}$ hours per day—which can help burn off 33 pounds a year, according to a study from the Mayo Clinic in Rochester, Minnesota.

DIY STRATEGY: Try a reality check. Studies have shown that people often overestimate how active they really are, says Dr. Gallagher. Most people actually spend 16 to 20 hours a day just sitting. Wear a pedometer on an

(continued on page 14)

WHAT'S YOUR NUTRITION IQ?

You're no slouch: You know a calorie from a carbohydrate and consider nutrition labels required reading. But are you eating the right foods to help you not only lose weight but build bone and protect your heart? Answer these questions to see if you're making the best choices to safeguard your health for life.

Q: You're stuck in a breakfast meeting and starving. Which would be the lowest-calorie choice from the tray of baked goodies?

A. Blueberry muffin

B. Butter croissant

C. Cinnamon chip scone

Answer: B. All that air inside makes the sinful-sounding croissant (about 355 calories) much less calorie dense than the scone (470) or muffin (500). If you're trying to lose weight, capping breakfast at about 400 calories is smart—even smarter would be bringing a healthy snack to munch on during mealtime meetings, such as peanut butter on whole wheat or a bag of nuts and dry whole-grain cereal.

Q: Now that manufacturers have filtered trans fats out of many foods, they're replacing partially hydrogenated oils with other types. Which of these should you be avoiding, too?

A. Soybean oil

B. Palm oil

C. Corn oil

Answer: B. Tropical oils—such as palm and coconut—are usually solid at room temperature, so they give products about the same shelf life that trans fats provide. That's great for food makers, not so great for your heart: Palm oil is 51 percent saturated fat; coconut oil, more than 90 percent. Just like trans fats, saturated fat boosts levels of "bad" cholesterol and raises your risk of heart disease. Scan ingredient lists for liquid olive or canola oils instead; they're low in saturated fat and high in heart-healthy monounsaturated fat. Nonhydrogenated corn, soybean, and safflower oils also make good trans-free substitutes.

Q: "Organic" and "natural" on a label mean basically the same thing—true or false?

Answer: False. For a label to earn a USDA-certified organic seal, it must meet specific government standards— organic meat, poultry, and dairy come from animals that aren't given hor- mones or antibiotics, and organic crops are grown without using most conventional fertilizers, synthetic pesticides, or bioengineering. *Natural,* on the other hand, is loosely defined as not containing synthetic preservatives or artificial color or flavor; the term is not regulated. Though many foods labeled "natural" are healthy, some, like all-natural soda and chips, are still loaded with calories and sugar.

Q: You need potassium to keep your metabolism revved and muscles strong. Which of these offers the most?

A. One medium baked sweet potato

B. A cup of fat-free yogurt

C. One medium banana

Answer: A. It contains 542 milligrams of the mineral; the yogurt has 475 and the banana, 422. Other potassium-rich foods to help you reach the recommended 4,700 milligrams per day (amounts listed in milligrams per cup): tomato sauce (811), orange juice (496), and cantaloupe (427).

Q: Which ground meat makes the healthiest low-fat burger?

A. Ground beef

B. Ground turkey

C. Ground chicken

Answer: They all can (if you choose wisely). For ground beef, look for 90 to 95 percent lean on the label, which equates to less than 10 grams of fat per 3.5-ounce serving. Just a few percentage points lower can make a big difference—85 percent lean beef packs a whopping 18 grams of fat per serving, or about the same as a McDonald's Quarter Pounder. With turkey and chicken, ground breast is better than regular (because the high-fat skin doesn't get processed in), and extra-lean is best, with less than 5 grams of fat per serving.

Q: Of these fast-food sandwiches, which has more calories than a Big Mac?

A. Wendy's Chicken Club

B. Arby's Roast Turkey & Swiss

C. McDonald's Premium Grilled Chicken Classic

Answer: B. Sure, it sounds healthy, but with its supersize slabs of bread, you get 725 calories, 8 grams of saturated fat, and more than a full day's worth of sodium! Order it without the mayo to make it healthier and save half for the next day.

Q: If you must have chips, which of these is the most nutritious?

A. Banana chips

B. Veggie chips

C. Potato chips

(continued)

Answer: B. Veggie chips made from real vegetables are the best of the bunch, with only about 150 calories per serving. (Some not-so-healthy varieties contain mostly flour and food coloring, so check the ingredient list.) Potato chips take a surprise second, with the same calories per handful as veggie chips and lots of choices with little (or no) saturated or trans fats. Banana chips should be skipped altogether: A serving is loaded with 10 grams of fat, nearly all of which is saturated.

Q: You'll lose 5 pounds in 3 months if you skip your daily dose of this popular coffee-shop drink:

  A. Small cappuccino

  B. Small light Frappuccino

  C. Small vanilla latte

Answer: C. At 190 calories, a vanilla latte is heftier than the cappuccino or light Frappuccino (about 90 calories each). Skim 60 calories off your latte by requesting fat-free milk and just two pumps of syrup. For more tricks to cut 100 calories, visit prevention.com/100calories.

Q: Calcium is key to building bones, but which of these dairy foods is not a good source?

  A. Cottage cheese

  B. Yogurt smoothie

  C. Fat-free milk

Answer: A. The combination of low calories and high protein makes cottage cheese the perfect waist-friendly food. But during processing, up to 75 percent of the calcium drains away, leaving each $\frac{1}{2}$-cup serving with only 70 milligrams of calcium—less than half of what you get in the same amount of fat-free milk. To meet your daily calcium needs (1,000 milligrams for age 50 and younger; 1,200 for age 51 and older), choose foods with 20 to 30 percent of the daily value (200 to 300 milligrams) listed on the label.

Q: Which salty snack contains the most sodium?

  A. One sourdough pretzel

  B. 17 salt-and-vinegar potato chips

  C. A quarter cup of salted peanuts

Answer: A. Just one sourdough pretzel tips the sodium scale at 500 milligrams; eat three and you've hit your limit for the day if you're over age 50. (The chips have 380 milligrams and the nuts only 115.) A food is considered low sodium if it contains 140 milligrams or less per serving. If you have slightly elevated blood pressure, pay close attention to sodium counts: Cutting back may lower your risk of cardiovascular disease by up to 25 percent, according to a recent study in the *British Medical Journal*.

Q: Which of these salad toppings will set you back the most calories?

A. Roasted almonds

B. Butter-garlic croutons

C. Crispy chicken

Answer: C. Tossing in a few crispy chicken strips adds 330 calories and 17 grams of fat. Opt for grilled chicken (at only 150 calories and 4 grams of fat) and pile on mandarin oranges and cherry tomatoes (for added volume and vitamins). Enjoy ¼ cup of nuts on occasion (though high in calories, they offer good-for-you fats). But skip the croutons and crispy noodles altogether; they're just empty calories. Find ways to make more of your favorite meals healthier at prevention. com/mealbalancer.

Q: Which of these swaps is worth making?

A. Brown sugar for white

B. Sea salt for table salt

C. Light olive oil for regular

Answer: None of them—and here's why: Brown sugar has just as many calories as white (about 16 per teaspoon) and gets processed by your body the same way. Molasses gives brown sugar its color and adds a little bit of magnesium and calcium but not enough to make a difference. Though natural, sea salt or bay salt contains the same amount of sodium per ¼ teaspoon (about 575 milligrams). Light olive oil refers to the color, flavor, and aroma, but in terms of fat per tablespoon, both light and regular have about 14 grams. Bottom line: Use what suits your palate; just watch your portions.

Q: Drinking VitaminWater is a good substitute for taking a daily multivitamin—true or false?

Answer: False. Most flavors of Vitamin-Water contain only a few water-soluble vitamins like C and B vitamins and a couple of minerals (the Multi-V Vitamin-Water has the most, with 11 vitamins and minerals). A basic multi, on the other hand, offers about 20 nutrients. If you're under age 50, look for a standard women's formula—it will contain certain essentials you need more of, like iron and B$_{12}$. (If you're older, choose an over-50 women's formula.)

Q: Which type of calorie turns into fat faster?

A. Carb

B. Protein

C. Fat

Answer: None of them. It doesn't matter where calories come from—if you eat too many, they get converted to fat at the same rate.

average day and see how close you get to the recommended 10,000 steps (about 5 miles, burning about 500 calories). Your day should combine 30 minutes of structured exercise with a variety of healthy habits, such as taking the stairs instead of the elevator or mopping the floor with extra vigor. To see how many calories your activities burn, check the exercise calculator at caloriecontrol.org.

SNOOZE TO LOSE

Slim folks sleep 2 more hours per week, compared with overweight people, says a study from Eastern Virginia Medical School in

Norfolk. Researchers theorize that a lack of shut-eye is linked to lower levels of appetite-suppressing hormones like leptin and higher levels of the appetite-boosting hormone ghrelin. In a University of Chicago study, a few sleepless nights were enough to drop levels of leptin by 18 percent and raise levels of ghrelin by about 30 percent. Those changes alone caused appetite to kick into overdrive, and cravings for starchy foods like cookies, potato chips, and bread jumped by 45 percent.

DIY STRATEGY: Break it down. Two extra hours of sleep a week is only 17 more minutes a day—a lot more manageable, even for the most packed of schedules. Start there and slowly work toward 8 hours of snooze time a night—the right amount for most adults.

10 WAYS TO GET A HANDLE ON HUNGER

It's a typical Tuesday at the Food and Brand Lab at Cornell University in Ithaca, New York, and director Brian Wansink, PhD, has invited some guests for lunch. The women think their free meal is a thank-you for testing the sound quality of iPods. But Dr. Wansink, one of the nation's few psychologists specializing in food marketing and eating behavior, has something else up his sleeve.

His grad students greet the guests, show them into the kitchen, and describe their lunch buffet: Royal Italian Bolognese, haricots verts, crusty bread with butter, and a beverage. Everyone eagerly starts serving themselves, not suspecting that they're being bamboozled by a scientific prank worthy of *Candid Camera*. Behind a one-way mirror, Dr. Wansink is watching them from his office as hidden cameras record all. Scales, hidden under dish towels on the counter, weigh how much food each person takes. "They're buying it," he says with a huge grin.

What they're buying is what they've been told—it's an elegant thank-you meal. But like anything that happens in Dr. Wansink's lab, nothing is what it seems. That Royal Italian Bolognese? It's really Beefaroni. The haricots verts? Canned green beans. This experiment is part of a larger test to see if people eat bigger portions when the food has evocative names. It's just one of hundreds he's conducted over the past 20 years to answer the most critical question for dieters: Why do we eat as much as we do?

Dr. Wansink chronicles decades of his work in his recent book *Mindless Eating: Why We Eat More Than We Think*. His research often involves gathering folks together for food and a flick or in another festive setting, situations that can lead otherwise sensible eaters to send caution—and calories—to the wind. Here, he shares 10 top eat-smarter tricks that really work—and other experts also weigh in on how to rethink habits that lead to overeating, especially when you let your guard down with friends and on weekends.

1. Create Stop Signs

In one experiment, Dr. Wansink invited more than 100 women to view a video and rate it—but the real goal was to find out how many potato chips they'd eat while watching the TV. Everyone received a full canister of chips, but only one group got ordinary Pringles. The other groups got doctored packages: Either every ninth or every thirteenth chip was dyed red. Those with the regular Pringles ate 23 on average, while those with a dyed chip ate 10 or 15, respectively.

WHAT'S GOING ON? Mindless munching. "The women got caught up in the video—not paying attention to how much they were eating—until something broke their rhythm," says Dr. Wansink. In this case, it was the red potato chip, but you can create your own natural break.

"I portion out a snack on a plate or in a plastic bag and leave the rest in the kitchen," says Dr. Wansink. "I may get up for seconds, but I'll have to make a conscious effort to do so." (And as some of his other studies show, you're far less likely to go back for more if you have to walk a couple of steps for it than if you have the package in front of you.) If you absolutely must dig your hand into a bag, pick up single-serve packages, such as Nabisco's 100 Calorie Packs or Orville Redenbacher's Mini Bags, which contain 110-calorie portions of popcorn.

Be especially diligent on weekends. A University of North Carolina at Chapel Hill study revealed that adults take in an extra 222 calories—nearly 15 percent of the number of

BEAT THE MUNCHIES AT THE MOVIES

If you're settling in for an evening with a tear-jerker DVD, prepare for a major snack attack, say University of Mississippi researchers. Their 30 subjects munched 28 percent more buttered popcorn—or 115 extra calories' worth—while watching the sentimental film *Love Story* than they did during the comedy *Sweet Home Alabama.* "The study subjects were probably using the food to boost their sad mood," says study author Nitika Garg, PhD. Not that there's anything wrong with that, but you could always order that popcorn plain.

5 "HEALTHY" FOODS TO AVOID

1. **Wheat pancakes:** Ounce for ounce, pancakes made with buckwheat and whole wheat flour have the same number of calories as the plain old buttermilk type. Instead, save calories by skipping the butter and syrup.

2. **Taco salad:** If you eat the edible shell, you'll consume nearly twice as many calories as if you eat the salad alone. Reduce temptation—order yours on a regular plate.

3. **Soup in a bread bowl:** The same theory applies to soup—the edible bowl adds more than 550 calories to your total count. Opting for oyster crackers is a little better, but a half cup is still 96 additional calories.

4. **Vegetable quesadilla:** It has about the same number of calories as the chicken version; the reason is often the cheese, so ask the server to hold half.

5. **Fish sandwich:** Even without the tartar sauce, a breaded fish patty at a fast-food restaurant has more calories than a bacon cheeseburger. Go for whatever is grilled.

calories an average woman needs each day—over the course of the weekend (including Friday). The need for a reward is human nature, says Stephen Gullo, PhD, author of *The Thin Commandments Diet*. And for many, that "something special" is food. Choose one portion-controlled item that requires you to leave the house, such as a cup of lobster bisque from your favorite eatery or a small, fresh pastry from the bakery. "It's more rewarding to have a nice treat than to waste calories on regular things you can have anytime, like potato chips or cookies," says Dr. Gullo. Doing something special works, too: Catch that must-see museum exhibit, get a massage at the spa, or buy a flattering pair of yoga pants.

2. Ignore the Health Halo

Using a setup similar to the chips-and-clip event, Dr. Wansink asked another 100 or so women to his lab to watch a video and gave them same-size packages of low-fat granola to nosh on. The trick: Only half were labeled low-fat—and the women who got those ate 49 percent more (an extra 84 calories) than those whose bags bore no health claim.

WHAT'S GOING ON? "Many people think low-fat means low-cal," he explains. "We assume that if a food is healthy in one way, it's good for us in all ways." That's how we get tricked by what Dr. Wansink calls health halos—the growing number of claims on food packaging trumpeting the lack of fat, the gobs of fiber, or the illness that the food prevents. Although all of these assertions may be true, it's calories that count if you're trying to lose weight. After all, a trans-free doughnut still contains about 200 calories more than you can probably afford. So bypass such claims and head straight to the calorie info on the label to determine if a food really is diet friendly.

Case in point: One variety of oatmeal-raisin cookie has 107 calories and 9 grams of sugar, and the fat-free version of the same brand has 106 calories *plus* 14 grams of sugar. "The terms *fat-free* or *sugar-free* can create a green light effect, triggering people to eat more," says Cynthia Sass, MPH, RD, *Prevention*'s nutrition director. In fact, researchers at Cornell University found that overweight people who choose low-fat versions of snack foods rather than the regular versions consume on average twice as many calories. So go for reasonable amounts of the real thing—if you adore ice cream, have a small scoop of premium. "You won't stick to a diet that doesn't include your favorites," says David Grotto, RD, a spokesperson for the American Dietetic Association. Life's too short for forbidden foods.

3. Fixate on Fullness

In another sneaky study by Dr. Wansink, 54 college students showed up to rate the quality of cafeteria food. Instead, each was served an 18-ounce bowl of Campbell's tomato soup. Some bowls were rigged to food-grade rubber tubing that snaked under the table and connected to a 6-quart soup vat that constantly refilled the bowl (surprisingly, only one student caught on to the bottomless-bowl-of-soup trick). After 20 minutes, students with the automatically refilling bowls ate an average of

TALK ABOUT INFLATION

Restaurants' expanding portion sizes are a major obstacle to maintaining a healthy weight. People eat about 300 more calories at lunch when served a large portion, says a University of Minnesota study. We ordered takeout and then weighed and measured it in our own kitchen to see how inflated restaurant servings compare with the ideal sizes (below). Your solution: Downsize what you eat (and ask for a doggie bag); if you do enjoy a heavy restaurant dish, make your next meal lighter.

Serving Size	Meat, Fish, Poultry	Grains (rice, pasta, couscous)	Fat (butter, oil, salad dressing)	Cheese
Correct portion	3 oz = deck of cards or your palm	$\frac{1}{2}$ c = computer mouse	1 Tbsp = thumb tip	1 oz = 4 dice
Restaurant serving	Steak dinner = 4 portions!	Rice with Chinese takeout = 4 portions!	1 packet salad dressing = 4 portions!	1 slice NY-style pizza = 2 portions!

15 ounces of soup, while the other students consumed about 9 ounces—a 135-calorie difference.

WHAT'S GOING ON? Most people will eat what's put in front of them, stopping or slowing down only when a bowl is almost empty or when most of the food on a plate is gone. Hunger doesn't enter into it. "I think the stomach has three settings," says Dr. Wansink. "They're 'I'm stuffed,' 'I'm full, but I could eat more,' and 'I'm starving.' Your goal is to recognize when you're full and not eat more." Don't rely on the amount of food left on your plate to signal when you're full. Instead, listen to your body's cues.

4. Leave the Mess

Dr. Wansink is a real party animal. For one study, he invited 53 guests to a sports bar for a Super Bowl bash, during which he served free chicken wings and soft drinks. Waitresses were told to take away wing remnants from only half of the tables. The guests at the clean tables ate seven chicken wings on average—two more than those whose tables held the visual proof of what they'd eaten.

WHAT'S GOING ON? Unless you can see the damage, you're not going to remember how much you ate—and you'll eat more. A cluttered, messy table reminds you that you've eaten plenty. "Whether you're eating chicken wings or cookies, you'll have less if you see evidence of what you've already eaten," says Dr. Wansink. "At dinner parties, my wife and I often don't

clear empty wine bottles from the table so we don't overindulge."

In fact, when you eat with friends, you consume 50 percent more than you do alone, found a Pennsylvania State University study. Researchers suspect that it's not the food but a tendency to lengthen the meal to keep the good times going—that's how you end up with the eye-popping evidence of overindulgence. Instead, shift your notion of fun to nonfood activities. You likely have a few favorites that don't involve eating—build on these until you shift the balance from drinks and dinner to window-shopping or visiting a new art exhibit. If you do want to grab a bite, stick to lunch—it's easier to eat light, and you probably won't order cocktails.

5. Hide Your Treats

During Administrative Professionals Week one year, Dr. Wansink and another researcher gave out clear or white candy dishes filled with 30 Hershey's Kisses to the secretarial staff at the University of Illinois at Urbana-Champaign, where he was once simultaneously professor of business administration, nutritional science, advertising, and agricultural and consumer economics. A tag explained that the candy was a personal gift and requested that the employee keep it on her desk and not share it. The ulterior motive: finding out whether the recipients would eat more from the bowls in which they could see the candy. Every night for 2 weeks, after the staff went home, Dr. Wansink went from office to office, counting Kisses and refilling dishes. Those who got a clear dish ate eight pieces of candy every day, but those who got an opaque dish had about four—more than a 100-calorie difference.

WHAT'S GOING ON? "We eat with our eyes," explains Dr. Wansink. "Having food in plain sight tempts people to eat every time they look at it." But surprisingly, that doesn't mean he wants you to keep your kitchen and office junk-food free. "That only makes you feel deprived," he says. "When you're feeling deprived, your diet is doomed." Instead, keep small amounts of your favorite treats in the house, but store them out of sight and out of easy reach—in an opaque container on a high shelf, at the back of the pantry, or in a distant room. "I stash a couple of bottles of Coke in my

4 DAYS TO A NEW YOU

Behavioral researchers know that to make a change in your lifestyle, you need to give yourself an adjustment period of at least 4 days. Get over that hump and you're more than halfway to realizing success.

Martha Beck, PhD, has put this knowledge to use for dieters in her book *The Four Day Win: End Your Diet War and Achieve Thinner Peace*. Instead of drastically slashing your calorie intake, cut back by about 10 calories and then give yourself at least 3 days to mentally and physically adjust to the change, advises Dr. Beck. By day 4, you'll hardly feel hungry, and that's what she calls a 4-day win.

Her plan involves stringing together five 4-day rounds in which you eat a little less during each consecutive cycle. Adding an extra day at the end brings you to 3 weeks—the point at which your new reduced-calorie eating plan will officially become a hard-to-break habit, psychology studies show. Stay at that intake level until you reach your goal weight. If you plateau before then, begin another 21-day plan to cut your intake further and start dropping pounds again.

refrigerator in the basement," says Dr. Wansink. "It's a hassle to run down there and get it when I want a bottle, so I don't do it that often." Conversely, keep healthy snacks where you can see and grab them. When you get a sugar jones, you can reach for that luscious pear on your desk or a banana from the glass bowl on the dining room table.

6. Pour Smarter

Dr. Wansink and his crew went into bars in Philadelphia and asked the bartenders to pour a standard 1$\frac{1}{2}$-ounce shot of whiskey or rum into either a tall, skinny 11-ounce highball glass or a short, fat 11-ounce tumbler. The pros were on target for the highball glasses but overpoured by 37 percent into the tumblers—even when they were asked to take their time. The point: "If bartenders can't pour the right amount, what hope do you have?" says Dr. Wansink.

WHAT'S GOING ON? It's a trick of the eye—we tend to perceive objects that are tall as larger than short, squat ones. That means you're more likely to fill a low, wide juice glass to the brim but stop about halfway for the tall highball glass, even if they hold the same amount of liquid. So replace any short, wide glasses with tall, slim ones. Likewise, balloon-like red wine glasses can trick you into serving yourself more than the recommended 5 ounces a day. "My wife wasn't happy about it, but we got rid

of all the red wine glasses that we received for our wedding," says Dr. Wansink. (There are no juice glasses in his house either.)

Another good reason to go light on libations: "Alcohol breaks down inhibitions, so it's harder to make healthy food choices when you do sit down," says Gary Foster, PhD, director of the Center for Obesity Research and Education at Temple University in Philadelphia. A glass of Cabernet and a few handfuls of mixed nuts while making dinner or waiting to be seated can add up to more than 600 calories—and that's even before the appetizer. Instead, have the wine with your meal and save added calories by swapping fries for veggies or sharing the lower-cal sorbet, not the chocolate cake. Choose high-quality drinks you'll want to savor, such as vintage wine or single malt scotch, over high-cal fruity concoctions and sub in one or two club sodas with lime.

7. Know Where You Overeat

When moviegoers in Chicago went to a 1:00 p.m. flick, Dr. Wansink and his colleagues offered them free medium or large buckets of popcorn in exchange for answering "concession-related" questions after the film. But this treat was a trick—the popcorn was stale. Most people reported that it tasted bad. Despite that and the fact that they'd eaten lunch before the movie, the average patron consumed more than 250 calories' worth of stale popcorn—more if they received a large container.

WHAT'S GOING ON? You may be more influenced by where you are (at the movies), what you're doing (sitting in the dark, watching an engrossing flick), and what the people you're with are doing (also chomping away) than by the taste and quality of the food in front of you

SWEET TOOTH? SMARTER SUBS

Overeating fattening foods that are low in nutrients (like candy) might damage your heart as much as your waistline. When Boston University researchers tracked the diets of nearly 1,300 heart disease–free women, they found that those who ate lots of empty calories had a significant increase in the thickness of their carotid artery walls, a predictor of cardiovascular disease, compared with women who favored nutrient-rich foods. Satisfy your sweet tooth and protect your ticker with these tasty substitutes.

Empty-Calorie Snack	Instead Try
Bag of fruity gummy candy	½ c unsweetened mixed dried fruit (like apples, nectarines, figs)
Slice of apple pie	One diced apple tossed with 2 tsp brown sugar and apple pie spices, microwaved and topped with toasted oats
Milk chocolate candy bar	Two medium strawberries dipped in dark chocolate
Fast-food cinnamon roll	Packet of instant plain oatmeal, prepared and topped with 1 Tbsp pecans, 1 tsp cinnamon, and 1 tsp maple syrup

or your own hunger. That's why you'll have popcorn at the movies, hot dogs at the ballpark, and ice cream on a hot summer night, no matter how they taste or how full you are. If you find that you're tempted, have a bottle of water or some sugar-free gum as a substitute.

Also, remember that not every outing or event may be splurge-worthy. Healthy eating doesn't have an on/off switch; it's a way of life, says nutritionist Grotto. He encourages his clients to treat themselves during the week, maybe with a light beer one night or a child's-size ice cream cone another, so they're not feeling deprived and desperate enough to polish off a half-pint of ice cream on Friday night for 500 calories. If you blow it, don't wait until Monday to get back on track; start at your next meal or snack. Besides, giving yourself free rein on the weekend can reactivate

negative eating patterns that are bound to carry over into the following week, says Dr. Gullo. Keep it up and extra pounds are almost guaranteed.

8. Serve Small

Forty graduate students showed up for a Super Bowl party that Dr. Wansink threw on the pretense that he was studying the new commercials. The real deal: His crew weighed how much Chex Mix guests took from either half-gallon or gallon bowls by using a scale hidden under a tablecloth. The students who served themselves from the gallon bowl took 53 percent more than those who served themselves from the smaller bowl.

WHAT'S GOING ON? "We use background objects as a benchmark for estimating size," says Dr. Wansink. "If all the serving bowls are big, what ends up on our plate is a big portion." That's why you should stick to serving bowls that hold just 4 to 6 cups of food.

Scale down everything else while you're at it: Portion out the food with a tablespoon rather than a much-larger serving spoon, and as Dr. Wansink did, switch to salad plates in place of Frisbee-size dinnerware.

9. Keep Snacks Simple

PTA parents attending a special meeting to view a video each received a bag of M&M's. Though the bags were the same size, the contents were different: Some contained 7 colors, while others had 10. Those with the most colorful candies ate a whopping 43 more candies than those whose bags held 7 hues. **WHAT'S GOING ON?** "When there's a variety of foods—even if the difference is as subtle as the color of M&M's—people want to try them all," Dr. Wansink says. "So they end up eating more—a lot more, in fact."

Use variety to your advantage. Keep seven or eight different kinds of fruits and veggies in the house rather than three or four. Look for prepackaged produce that offers variety. But when it comes to high-cal, high-fat treats, keep choices to a minimum. If you must have M&M's, stock up on holiday versions, which usually contain only two or three colors.

Be prepared so you're not tempted by the array of edibles at drive-thrus and food courts, too. Between errands, quality time with the kids, grocery shopping, and household chores, some days it's easy to slack off on your regular diet-and-exercise schedule.

And remember that to make a real difference part of developing healthy habits for life is about adapting, says Dr. Foster. It just takes a

(continued on page 26)

SMALLER FRUIT, BIGGER BENEFITS

You know it's wise to downsize snacks so you eat less bad stuff, like unhealthy fat and sugar. More surprising: When it comes to produce, smaller may be superior nutritionally.

As fruits and vegetables grow larger, their vitamins, minerals, and other health-boosting compounds significantly diminish, according to a recent report issued by the Organic Center, a nonprofit organization that gathers science on the health benefits of organics.

But that's not all: Taste and aroma decrease as well. Although the losses occur in organically grown produce as well as conventional, organic items tend to be smaller in general— making shopping those aisles a way to maximize your nutrient intake.

THE NO-GAIN GUIDE TO VACATION DINING

While all the advice in this chapter is useful any time of year, other strategies may be even more helpful to keep in mind when planning your vacation—after all, you've earned the right to indulge, but the trick is to not undo all the health gains you've made the rest of the year. Here are some simple strategies that let you have your cake, fruity drink, or burger—without gaining an ounce.

IN THE CAR

Driving all day cuts your average daily calorie burn by 400. Follow these tips to help readjust your intake (from your normal 1,800 calories to 1,400, for example) and bypass the thousands of junk-food-filled rest stops along US highways.

- **Drink up.** "The recirculated air in a car can make you thirsty, which you might mistake for hunger," says Charles Stuart Platkin, MPH, founder of dietdetective.com. Keep plenty of water on hand.

- **Seek fresh food.** Although a handful of drive-thrus sit right off the highway, a grocery store—with many more good-for-you options—is probably only a few minutes farther; there you can get a healthy meal—turkey on whole wheat from the deli, an apple, and fat-free yogurt—for less than 350 calories. Or pick up a copy of *Healthy Highways,* a guide to more than 1,900 nutritious eateries across the United States. Download updates at healthyhighways.com before you depart to help you plan your meal stops.

- **Pack healthy snacks.** Load a cooler with low-cal, protein-rich foods, such as apple slices and peanut butter—the protein keeps you fuller longer.

AT A CAMPSITE

Fresh air, stories around the fire, and dinners under the stars: For most of us, that's the perfect recipe for a weekend in the woods. Here, the right ingredients to make it healthier.

- **Trade the dogs, swap the s'mores.** Instead of all-beef, get turkey, veggie, or tofu hot dogs—all lower in fat. And to shave many calories off dessert, try this tweaked s'mores recipe: Break off a 100-calorie portion of Hershey's Dark chocolate or a Cadbury Thins Premium Dark chocolate bar and wrap it in foil with one large marshmallow and a sliced banana; roast a few minutes over the fire, then grab a spoon.

- **Make a fish stop.** Swing by a grocery store on the way to the grounds for a piece of trout or salmon. (You don't have to catch it—unless you want to.) Season with olive oil, salt, and pepper and serve with easy-to-prepare dehydrated vegetables (harmonyhousefoods.com has a great selection). For simple outdoor grilling, get the Coleman Fold 'n Go Propane InstaStart Stove ($80, fuel sold separately; available at sporting goods stores). With two separate skillets, you can make the fish in one and veggies in the other.

- **Fuel up for hikes; snack lightly for strolls.** Pack some sustenance if you're heading out for 2- or 3-mile stretches. Easy-to-tote fruit-and-nut bars such as Lärabar (starting at 190 calories, 9 grams fat) or Clif Nectar (starting at 150 calories, 5 grams fat) provide the energy you need, and you'll burn off the calories. For less strenuous exercise, stick to fruit or a few almonds.

ON A CRUISE

With pizza served at 3:00 p.m., dinner at 6:00 p.m., and a 24-hour dessert cart, most cruises are one big, endless buffet. "Just because they feed you 18 times a day doesn't mean you have to eat 18 times a day," says Davida F. Kruger, MSN, author of *The Diabetes Travel Guide*. Try to follow your at-home eating schedule, as well as these tips.

- **Rein in the rum runners.** Enjoy your favorite fruity concoction with lunch or a glass of wine with dinner, but when you're lounging by the pool, strolling the deck, or playing a midnight game of poker, order an alcohol-free fruit smoothie in a 5-ounce martini glass for about 90 calories or a seltzer spiked with juice and lime for around 30.

- **Scan the menus.** Several cruise lines provide meals low in calories and fat: Cunard's Queen Mary 2 offers gourmet options prepared by Canyon Ranch Spa chefs, including tortilla soup with pico de gallo (85 calories, 5 grams fat) and spinach and roasted beet salad (110 calories, 4 grams fat). Crystal Cruises has low-carb ice cream, and Silversea Cruises offers iced key lime cheesecake and peach crumb cobbler at less than 200 calories each.

- **Always use the salad plate.** Be it for the breakfast bar, lunch buffet, or dinner entrée, this tried-and-true trick will help keep your portions in control. Use it to eat a salad before each meal, too—another way to cut your total calories.

few adjustments: Toss a low-cal energy bar or apple into your purse before hitting the mall so you're not tempted by the food court; if you know you're going to be on the road all afternoon, have a later breakfast; or if restaurant reservations aren't until late, snack on string cheese and whole-grain crackers to hold you over and then order lean fish or meat and vegetables for dinner.

10. Rate the Taste

Guests at the Spice Box in Illinois—a testing ground for wannabe chefs—received a free glass of wine with their meals, courtesy of Dr. Wansink. Tables on the right side of the room were offered their drink from "a new winery in California"; the left side got theirs from "a new winery in North Dakota." Except

THE SECRET TO ONLINE DIET SUCCESS

The key to losing weight online is to seek out a site that offers a human touch. Researchers from the University of North Carolina gave 192 overweight adults access to a weight loss Web site; a third of them also had e-mail access to a behavioral weight counselor, and a third received automated reminders when they logged on. After 3 months, those who got either type of extra assistance had lost 12 to 13 pounds, while the no-counseling group lost about half that much. At 6 months, weight loss had slowed for the dieters getting the automated messages. But dieters with access to a live person had lost an average of 16 pounds—10 more than the no-counseling group.

Personal feedback makes dieters feel accountable, says Lynn Grieger, RD, a dietitian and wellness coach in Vermont. "Without it, people tend to lose interest in logging on." Many sites offer this service as a premium, but you can also enlist a therapist or a registered dietitian. Try sending a weekly message about your progress to your counselor of choice and ask her to e-mail you encouragement—and to check in if she doesn't hear from you.

for this wording, both labels were identical. In reality, all of the wine was the ultracheap Charles Shaw brand—often referred to as Two-Buck Chuck—from Trader Joe's. All guests could order whatever they wanted off the same menu. Those who received the California wine ate, on average, 11 percent more of their food than those who got the North Dakota vintage.

WHAT'S GOING ON? "Once patrons saw the wine was from California, they said to themselves, *This meal is going to be good,*" says Dr. Wansink. "And once they concluded that, their experience lined up to confirm their expectations."

A great rating, fancy tableware, a prestigious label—or a free glass of wine or appetizer—doesn't guarantee quality. Imagine you're a restaurant reviewer and critically examine the flavor of whatever you eat. If you don't care for the dish, don't finish it. And if your whole meal has been only so-so, don't take a chance on dessert. Ask yourself, *Is this really worth the calories?* If it isn't, stop eating.

And what about those women who ate the fake Bolognese for lunch? The diners who thought the Beefaroni was a gourmet feast ate considerably more than those who were told that lunch came from a can. One woman even said, "It was the best lunch I had all week."

THE LATEST TOOLS FOR HEALTHIER COOKING

Kitchen gadgets are like toys for grown-ups: Finding the right one can turn rushed, in-a-rut dinner prep into a healthy adventure. Once you see how a cleverly designed grater or nonstick pan can transform your usual meal into a nutrient-rich, calorie-shy sensation, you'll be inspired to play and make your own delicious creations. To help you find your next five-star buy, we turned to those who know—nutritionists, cooking instructors, food writers, and even celebrity chefs. Then we added our own two cents to help you make even better use of your new purchases to notch up nutrition and slash fat and calories in your own favorite recipes. Here, their picks and our tricks for the essential kitchen toys to make cooking easier, tastier, healthier, and—of course—more fun.

Inspire Creativity

FOODIE'S FAVE: KitchenAid Artisan Series 5-Quart Mixer ($300; attachments, $65 to $100; shopkitchenaid.com)

"I love this mixer! I make my own whole wheat spaghetti with the pasta maker add-on. I create low-sugar fruit sorbets thanks to the ice cream maker attachment. The food grinder addition is fantastic for making healthy grass-fed beef burgers. And, of course, it's great for making doughs and batters quickly."

—Scott Uehlein, corporate chef for Canyon Ranch resorts, SpaClubs, and living communities

TASTY TIDBIT: Talk about a beautiful transformation: Overripe, mushy fruits take on an elegant new life when used in homemade sorbet. Use the ripest, most fragrant fruit you can find when you make this light, refreshing frozen dessert that's ideal for the dairy averse. Sorbet differs from sherbet and ice cream in that it is made without milk products, eggs, or gelatin.

EAT TO SPEED METABOLISM

Many women think they've permanently lowered their body's calorie-burning ability from years of yo-yo dieting. The truth: Cutting calories affects your metabolism only in the short term. An often-cited study published in the *Journal of the American Dietetic Association* tracked overweight women who had dieted on and off for 18 years. They found that the metabolism dip experienced after severe calorie restriction is only temporary. Once women go back to eating enough to maintain a healthy body weight, their calorie-burning ability usually returns to normal. For maximum weight loss, cut excess calories without eliminating too many, and forestall small dips in metabolism throughout the day with these eat-smart tips.

Don't: Under- or overestimate your calorie needs. Check out prevention.com/ healthtracker to calculate the perfect daily energy budget for you.

Do: Eat every 3 to 5 hours. Your body needs regular fuel, and balanced meals spaced no more than 5 hours apart keep your metabolism running smoothly. You don't need a full meal—a 150- to 200-calorie snack will do.

Don't: Save up for one big splurge. Your body uses calories over the course of the day and will store a onetime surplus as fat. Prepare for treats by eating regularly but having slightly less than at normal meals.

Bake Better

FOODIE'S FAVE: Regency Non-Stick Parchment Paper ($3.50; laprimashops.com)

> "I bake fish in parchment paper. As it cooks in its own steam, the flavors meld and deepen so there's hardly any need to add oil or butter. Just wrap ingredients tightly in the center and tuck the sides underneath to form a pouch."
>
> —Clotilde Dusoulier, creator of chocolateandzucchini.com

TASTY TIDBIT: The French name for steaming food in a paper package—*en papillote*—comes from the word for "butterfly," *papillon*. This refers to the traditional heart shape of the paper before it is folded and sealed around the food. Although parchment paper is the classic wrapper, foil can be used instead. This cooking method is perfect for delicate foods such as fish, chicken, or vegetables because it gently steams the food, locking in moisture and flavor. Another bonus: Food can be wrapped en papillote and stored in the refrigerator for several hours before it is cooked, making it convenient for entertaining.

Calculate Calories Instantly

FOODIE'S FAVE: Salter Nutri-Weigh Dietary Scale ($100; chefsresource.com)

> "Not only does this scale weigh food, it analyzes its nutritional content by portion size so you can see the calories, protein, carbs, sugar, fat, sodium, and more."
>
> —Thomas Griffiths, certified master chef and professor at the Culinary Institute of America in Hyde Park, NY

TASTY TIDBIT: Sometimes we forget that calories do add up (an extra 100 here, another 200 there!) throughout the course of a day—

TRY THE QUIET DIET

Eating in front of the television or while working at your computer seems like a good idea at the time, but it may actually leave you hungry.

UK researchers found that women who dined while distracted wanted to consume more once they were finished. Those who ate in silence, however, felt satisfied with their food.

Instead, take time to dine out in peace. Your waistline will thank you.

and can sabotage the best of weight loss efforts. In fact, an extra 100 calories consumed each day can result in going up a dress size by the end of the year. That's why it's important to remember that every calorie counts—and you can use this high-tech scale to stay on track.

Meanwhile, consider the caloric differences among even healthy foods: A $\frac{1}{2}$ cup serving of strawberries has 23 calories, while a medium banana has more than 100, and an orange has almost half the calories of a glass of OJ. Per 1 cup, raw spinach has 7 calories and boiled eggplant contains 35; mashed sweet potato packs 249. Two cups of air-popped popcorn has the same number of calories as three little whole wheat crackers.

Sneak In More Veggies

FOODIE'S FAVE: Aluminum grater ($17.25; korin.com)

"I use an oroshigane, a Japanese-style grater, on all sorts of ingredients, especially radishes, ginger, carrots, Japanese yams, and daikon. It shreds much more finely and smoothly than a standard grater. I can use the thin slices in sauces and in meat and fish dishes."

—Masaharu Morimoto, Iron Chef on Food Network's *Iron Chef America*

TASTY TIDBIT: With its distinctive gnarled and branched roots, ginger is prized for the clean, fresh taste it gives to many foods. Its pleasantly pungent flavor—an essential of Asian cooking—comes from naturally occurring chemical irritants that also create a warm sensation on the tongue. Try a topping of freshly grated ginger to add zip (but not calories) to cooked vegetables such as yams, carrots, or collard greens. It's also excellent in soups and stews, and it is a good choice for seafood because it neutralizes "fishy" odors. To flavor 1 pound of vegetables, tofu, or seafood, use 1 to 2 teaspoons grated gingerroot. (There's no need to peel ginger before grating it.)

Find In-Season Eats

FOODIE'S FAVE: *Culinary Artistry* ($30; amazon.com)

"This is the best reference book I've used. It has an extensive chart that shows exactly when fruits, vegetables, and meats are at their peak. Sticking to the seasons ensures that food is at its best flavor, price, and, most important, nutritional value."

—Scott Giambastiani, executive chef at Café-7 and Café Moma, serving organic meals to thousands of employees at Google in Mountain View, CA

TASTY TIDBIT: It's hard to beat going local for the freshest foods. Don't live near a farmers' market? Try a health food store. Whole Foods, for example, aims to dedicate 20 percent of its

LOW-CAL FILL-UPS

High-satiety snacks—packed with protein or monounsaturated fat—will tide you over between meals for very few calories. Case in point: 1 ounce of string cheese (80 calories) or peanuts (160 calories) will keep hunger at bay.

DIETERS: PROTECT YOUR BONES

Cutting calories? A startling recent Rutgers University analysis has found that dieting could hurt your bones. In fact, after just 6 months of trying to drop weight, research subjects' bones were up to 3 percent less dense.

"Most dieters have no idea that their skeletons may be losing weight, too," says Sue Shapses, PhD, RD, a Rutgers nutrition researcher. "Calorie cutting causes shifts in three hormones—parathyroid, estrogen, and cortisol—that may make it harder for your body to absorb calcium from food and supplements. Her bone-rescuing tips:

- **Know your calcium goal.** The recommended daily goal is 1,000 to 1,200 milligrams, but Dr. Shapses says women over age 50 should aim for at least 1,500 milligrams to offset lower absorption rates while dieting.

- **Think food first.** Calcium is sometimes such an obvious challenge for dieters because its commonly abundant in many calorie-dense foods: Think rich, creamy cheese and you get the picture. But try to include three servings of these calorie bargains every day: fat-free milk, 285 milligrams of calcium, 77 calories in 8 ounces; and low-fat yogurt, 243 milligrams of calcium, 80 calories in 6 ounces. If necessary, add a supplement of 500 milligrams of calcium citrate (the best-absorbed form) or calcium carbonate (with meals for better uptake) to hit your goal.

- **Don't forget other essential bone builders, including vitamin D:** milk (98 IU per serving), salmon (360 IU), and fortified cereal (40 IU). And take a multivitamin always, but especially while dieting. Make sure it has bone-building vitamin K, magnesium, and vitamin D as cholecalciferol (vitamin D_3).

produce section to locally grown fruits and veggies. Buying local has its advantages: Because the distance from the farm to your plate is shorter, it's good for the planet (fewer carbon emissions are created in transit), and the food is more nutrient packed than varieties from distant lands. Pennsylvania State University scientists discovered that even when spinach was properly stored, it lost nearly 50 percent of its nutrients in 8 days' time. But aside from nutrition, local produce is simply fresher and tastier, says Marion Nestle, PhD, MPH, a professor of nutrition, food studies, and public health at New York University and author of *What to Eat*. That means you're more likely to eat several servings by day's end rather than tossing out limp, tasteless produce that you never touched.

Grind the Healthiest Rub

FOODIE'S FAVE: Krups GX4100 Coffee, Herb, and Spice Mill ($30; krupsonlinestore.com)

"My grinder isn't just for coffee; I use it for spices, too. I throw in toasted whole cumin, cardamom seeds, a little bit of turmeric, chili powder, ginger paste, and freshly pressed garlic; grind 'em up; and voilà, I've got an aromatic, healthy rub. It makes everything—even bland chicken breasts—special. Plus, cumin is loaded with iron; turmeric and ginger have been shown to help prevent cancer; and garlic is great for a healthy heart."

—Leah McLaughlin, *Prevention*'s brand editor

TASTY TIDBIT: To grind whole spices, place about 1 tablespoon of the spice in a grinder and grind to a fine powder. Use it immediately, such as in a spice rub. It's a great way to infuse flavor—without fat—into meats that will be grilled, broiled, or even baked. Massage the dry spice mix into the meat (a dry rub). Or

make a paste by combining the spice mix with a little bit of oil, which helps the seasoning adhere to the meat. Rub any of the following seasoning blends into beef, pork, lamb, or chicken. Wrap the meat in plastic and refrigerate for several hours before cooking.

Tropical spice rub: Combine 2 teaspoons *each* dried cilantro, garlic powder, and salt and 1 teaspoon *each* ground black pepper, ground cumin, and ground oregano. Makes 3 tablespoons.

Middle East spice rub: Combine 2 teaspoons ground black pepper; $1\frac{1}{2}$ teaspoons ground cumin; 1 teaspoon *each* ground coriander and salt; $\frac{1}{2}$ teaspoon ground cardamom; and $\frac{1}{4}$ teaspoon ground cloves. Makes about 2 tablespoons.

ALL ABOUT OLIVE OIL

• **What it is:** Fruity, peppery oil made from crushed olives. The first pressing—called extra virgin—is generally the most expensive olive oil; pure is the next, less pricey olive oil. Light or extra light is filtered to produce a milder flavor, but the fat and calories remain the same (13.5 grams of fat and 119 calories per tablespoon).

• **Why it's healthy:** It's full of heart-healthy monounsaturated fat (10 grams per tablespoon), which lowers "bad" LDL cholesterol and raises "good" HDL cholesterol, and polyphenol antioxidants, which fight cancer and heart disease.

• **How to buy:** Choose a size you'll use within 2 months. As the container empties, it fills with oxygen; the olive oil starts to oxidize, or deteriorate, and eventually tastes stale, like wet cardboard.

• **Opt for dark glass.** It protects the olive oil from light, another source of flavor-sapping oxidation.

• **Splurge for taste.** Buy extra virgin if you want to emphasize the oil's flavor, as in dressings or marinades; use pure for sautéing or stir-frying.

• **Insider advice:** Store opened bottles in a dark, cool place, such as the back of a pantry or your fridge—though oil stored there may cloud, it will clear at room temperature.

Control the Fat

FOODIE'S FAVE: Misto Oil Sprayer ($10; misto.com)

"Instead of pouring gobs of oil into my pan, I spritz a light coating of olive oil with my nonaerosol sprayer. If I'm sautéing or baking, I'll spray grapeseed oil—you can find it at the grocery store—which works great for really high temperatures. Using the sprayer allows me to cook with 100 percent pure oils without the addition of alcohol, lecithin, or methyl silicone found in some store-bought sprays."

—Dawn Jackson Blatner, RD, dietitian at the Northwestern Memorial Hospital Wellness Institute in Chicago

TASTY TIDBIT: Use a mister to spray veggies with herb-infused oil before roasting—you'll add flavor and nutrition in mere seconds.

Two more ways to prevent calorie overload when cooking with oil:

1. Measure with a teaspoon. You may think you use oil sparingly, but this is the only way to know for sure.

2. Omit the oil when you are making your own vinaigrette. Mix in 1 teaspoon (measure it!) just before dressing your salad so you know exactly how much you're getting.

STAY SLIM WITH HIM

Your husband's weight—not his sparkling eyes or sense of humor—may have been what drew you to him, finds new research in the *American Journal of Clinical Nutrition*. Couples tend to share similar body fat levels when they meet—and are likely to stay that way over the years. Similarly, other research shows that if one partner improves his or her habits, the other may follow suit. Here are a few ways you both can live healthfully ever after.

- **Bond over breakfast.** Many studies show that breakfast eaters are less likely to be overweight than those who skip their morning meal. Set aside 15 minutes to eat together before you head out the door.

- **Avoid snacking together.** Just because one of you is a snacker doesn't mean that you both have to be. Stop and consider whether you're actually hungry or just "eating with company" before digging in and encourage him to do the same. (Keep in mind that men generally require more calories than women do.)

- **Preplan your portions.** If dinner at home means lingering over a long meal at the dining room table, dole out a portion before you sit down and leave any extras in the kitchen. With the extras out of sight, you'll both be less likely to overeat.

- **Break up the takeout.** If one of you craves a hearty meal (like pizza), but the other wants something a bit lighter (like sushi), place orders at two different restaurants and eat at home as a couple.

- **Make one meal two ways.** Buy groceries for a shared meal that you can each personalize to your liking and to that day's caloric needs. (The same basic ingredients can be used to make a burrito or a lower-calorie Tex-Mex salad.)

- **Stretch your drink.** Men can usually tolerate more alcohol—and calories. Instead of joining him for seconds, have seltzer with a dash of orange juice and a squeeze of lime. Or ask for half wine and half seltzer and join in both rounds. Encourage him to stop after two (the amount the USDA says men can drink healthfully).

Upgrade Your Grilling

FOODIE'S FAVE: Calphalon One Nonstick Square Grill Pan ($50; williams-sonoma.com)

> "The nonstick surface of my grill pan means I don't have to add a lot of oil—and any excess I do use drips into the grooves, away from my meal. And grilling indoors keeps my food from being exposed to carcinogens. The excessive heat of the outdoor barbecue can create these cancer-causing chemicals."
>
> —Ellie Krieger, RD, host of Food Network's *Healthy Appetite*

TASTY TIDBIT: Mad for marinades when grilling meat? To save calories, use about ½ cup of marinade for every pound of meat—that's enough to properly coat without excess. Watch out for bottled blends—some are essentially liquid salt or sugar with a little garlic thrown in.

To scout out more healthful marinades, scan labels for these key components: natural acidic ingredients (vinegar, wine, tomatoes, fruit juices), which tenderize meat, make it easier to digest, and slow the growth of harmful bacteria; and antioxidant-rich ingredients (herbs, spices, fruit and vegetable purees, honey), which act as anti-agers and disease-fighters but may also counteract some risks associated with outdoor grilling. When meat is heated to a high temperature, cancer-causing substances called heterocyclic amines, or HCAs, are formed. But according to the American Institute for Cancer Research, briefly marinating may reduce HCAs by as much as 99 percent. Scientists at Kansas State University found that marinated steaks had 87 percent fewer HCAs, a reduction that correlated directly with the amount of antioxidants present in the sauce.

(continued on page 40)

DROP 3 POUNDS WITHOUT TRYING

Put that cola down! And head for the sink instead: Dieters who swap sugary beverages for water lose an extra 3 pounds a year, on average, compared with those who continue to chug the sweet stuff. That's according to researchers from the Children's Hospital and Research Center in Oakland, California, who looked at 240 overweight women. Sure, cutting out soda saves calories, but it's possible that water helps rev your metabolism because well-hydrated cells may process carbs and fat more efficiently.

7 WAYS TO CHOP, SAUTÉ, AND STIR YOUR WAY TO BETTER HEALTH

Stocked up on leafy greens? Super. Did you know that sautéing them in a bit of olive oil instead of steaming them will help you absorb up to five times as much of the vision-protecting antioxidant beta-carotene? Buying healthy food is just the first step toward a better diet; preparing it correctly can make or break your nutrient bank. Keep reading for even more surprising nutrition-enhancing prep tips.

1. FIRE UP HEART PROTECTION

Heating lycopene-rich tomatoes instigates a chemical change that makes the heart-healthy nutrient much easier for your body to absorb. Try halving Roma tomatoes lengthwise; arrange on a baking sheet, drizzle with olive oil, and season with salt and pepper. Broil for 15 to 20 minutes, until slightly shriveled. Adding canned crushed tomatoes or tomato paste to recipes works, too. (They were heated during processing.)

2. MAXIMIZE CANCER PREVENTION

High temperatures destroy allinase, garlic's most important cancer-fighting and immunity-boosting enzyme. After chopping, let crushed garlic stand for about 10 to 15 minutes before adding it to a sizzling pan. This allows the pungent herb to generate compounds that blunt the damaging effects of heat, report scientists at Pennsylvania State University and the National Cancer Institute. No time to spare? You can always enjoy raw garlic. Try rubbing it on toasted bread and topping the bread with chopped tomato and onion and a dash of olive oil for a simple bruschetta.

3. GET 10 TIMES THE IRON

Cooking with tomatoes, apples, or lemons? Heat acidic foods like these in a cast-iron pot or skillet to spike the amount of the energy-boosting iron you absorb by more than 2,000 percent, suggests a Texas Tech University study. "Some iron from the skillet leaches into the food, but the particles are small enough that you won't be able to see or taste them—and it's perfectly safe," says Cynthia Sass, MPH, RD, *Prevention*'s nutrition director. Bonus tip: You don't have to pull out a pan; coupling certain iron-rich foods with high-acid ones gives a tenfold boost to your iron absorption. "While the iron in red meat is easily absorbed on its own, the type of iron found in beans, grains, and veggies isn't," Sass says. When making a spinach salad, toss in mango slices to increase the iron payoff. Other healthy combos: beans and tomato sauce or cereal and strawberries.

4. STRENGTHEN EYES AND BONES

Adding avocado, nuts, olive oil, olives, or another healthy monounsaturated fat source to red, green, orange, and yellow fruits and veggies increases the amount of fat-soluble vitamins, such as A, E, and K. These nutrients boost vision, improve immunity, and protect against stroke and osteoporosis, respectively. "Fat acts as a transporter for them," explains Sass. The same strategy works for carotenoids, the compounds that give tomatoes and carrots their bright hues. Proof: A recent study from the Ohio State University Comprehensive Cancer Center found that men and women who ate salsa containing chunks of avocado absorbed 4.4 times as much lycopene and 2.6 times as much beta-carotene as those who enjoyed plain salsa.

5. STOCK UP ON CALCIUM

If you're preparing homemade chicken soup, it's smart to add a hint of lemon juice, vinegar, or tomato to the mix. Pairing a slightly acidic broth with on-the-bone chicken can up the soup's calcium content by 64 percent, according to researchers at Harvard University and Beth Israel Hospital in Boston. (This stock dissolves the bone's calcium more easily than a nonacidic one would.) Bonus tip: Other research that was referenced in the Harvard/Beth Israel study has shown that slathering spareribs with an acidic vinegar-based barbecue sauce will dramatically increase the calcium content.

6. RETAIN KEY NUTRIENTS

Save yourself some time—and some key nutrients—by not peeling eggplant, apples, potatoes, and other produce before using. "The peel itself is a natural barrier against nutrient loss, and many vitamins and minerals are found in the outer skin or just below it," says Roberta Larson Duyff, RD, author of the *American Dietetic Association Complete Food and Nutrition Guide.* Yam skin is loaded with fiber, and zucchini's full of lutein, which may help prevent age-related macular degeneration, for example. (Remove grit and pathogens with cold, running water and a vegetable brush.) Bonus tip: Add citrus zest to your favorite recipes. A University of Arizona study linked eating limonene—a compound in lemon, lime, and orange peel—to a 34 percent reduction in skin cancer.

7. DOUBLE THE ANTIOXIDANTS

Dressing your salad with herbs can more than double its cancer-fighting punch, according to a recent Italian study. When compared with garden salads made with no added herbs, those featuring lemon balm and marjoram had up to 200 percent more antioxidants per serving. Spices such as ginger and cumin also upped the antioxidant quotient.

Make Safety Simple

FOODIE'S FAVE: ThermoWorks Thermapen ($110; bakerscatalogue.com)

> "This thermometer is a favorite in our test kitchen because it's so easy to use and gives the quickest, most accurate read. And the long 4 1/2-inch metal probe makes it perfect for checking large roasts. We always know exactly when our food is done and safe to eat."
>
> —Christopher Kimball, host of the PBS cooking show *America's Test Kitchen* and creator of *Cook's Illustrated* magazine

TASTY TIDBIT: Think that if a burger looks well done, it must be germ free? Kansas State University research shows the eyeball method doesn't work—a meat thermometer is the only way to tell if it's been cooked to a safe 160°F. Thawed meat can turn a little brown, so it might look done before it really is, while some lean burgers might still look pink when they hit 160°F. To check a burger's doneness, insert the thermometer into the center of the meat and chow down only if the reading is 160°F or higher. Bacteria can't multiply above 150°F or below 40°F. Complete cooking is the only way to ensure that all potentially harmful bacteria have been killed. For other meats: Cook chicken with bone in until the thermometer registers 170°F, chicken without bone until the thermometer registers 160°F, turkey breast until the thermometer registers 170°F, other turkey (ground or whole) until the thermometer registers 165°F, and fish until it flakes easily. Stay extra safe: If the food's not hot enough and you have to cook it longer, be sure to wash the thermometer before you test

LOW-CAL FOODS THAT FILL YOU UP

Bulking up your meals with water-rich fruits and vegetables is a proven waistline slimmer. Pennsylvania State University scientists found that women who added lots of low-cal produce to a low-fat diet lost more weight than women who simply cut fat. So, even if your diet is already pretty healthy, adding extra fruits and veggies still helps you feel fuller. The reason: Produce is rich in moisture and fiber. Try these flavorful finds.

Produce Pick	Calories/Cup	Percent Water
Cabbage, shredded	17	93
Radishes, sliced	19	95
Spaghetti squash	31	92
Kale, chopped	34	83
Brussels sprouts, whole	38	86
Cranberries, whole	44	87

the meat again to avoid cross-contamination.

And don't taste-test foods before they're cooked, especially pork, fish, and eggs.

Snack Smarter

FOODIE'S FAVE: Oxo Apple Slicer ($11; surlatable.com)

> "I core and divide whole apples and ripe pears into slices, then eat them as a snack or use as a topping on oatmeal, yogurt, or cottage cheese. If I didn't have this handy tool, I swear my fruit would sit around uneaten for weeks!"
>
> —Gloria McVeigh,
> *Prevention*'s nutrition news editor

TASTY TIDBIT: Can an apple a day keep the doctor away? No guarantees—but men who ate the most apples and other foods high in quercetin had 60 percent less lung cancer, 25 percent less asthma, and 20 percent less diabetes and heart disease deaths in a Finnish study. Was the positive effect due to the quercetin-rich foods? "If yes, then one apple a day may be enough to get these benefits," says Paul Knekt, PhD, nutrition researcher at the National Public Health Institute in Helsinki. (Other major quercetin sources are onions, cabbage, and berries. Count on apples—and pears—to keep the pounds away, too: One

3 MUST-HAVE TOOLS

Forget the pricey butcher block peppered with a dozen knives; you only really need two sharp ones. "It may sound counterintuitive, but the sharper the knife, the safer it is," says Katherine Polenz, culinary skills development instructor at the Culinary Institute of America. Dull blades make you exert more force, which can lead to accidents.

1. A chef's knife is a great all-purpose knife—use it for chopping, slicing, and mincing most foods. Look for one made of high-carbon, no-stain steel, such as the 8-inch Wüsthof Grand Prix II Chef's Knife ($99; cookswarehouse.com).

2. Also, get a paring knife, like the Forschner Fibrox 4-inch Paring Knife ($14; amazon.com), for delicate tasks such as peeling tomatoes or cucumbers.

3. To get the most out of your cutlery, use a steel blade sharpener before cutting to refresh the edge.

medium apple with its peel has just 70 calories and 3 grams of filling fiber; a medium pear packs 5 grams of fiber in 96 calories.

Keep More Nutrients

FOODIE'S FAVE: Sharp Stainless Steel Microwave model R-315JS ($115; amazon.com)

> "Microwaving vegetables is the easiest way to steam them. I like to put sliced broccoli, asparagus, onion, pumpkin, and shiitake and enoki mushrooms in a bowl, season with salt and pepper, add a dash of sake, cover with plastic wrap, and microwave for 6 minutes. Since I don't add water, vegetables steam in their own juices and don't lose any nutrients."
>
> —Nobu Matsuhisa, chef and owner of 15 restaurants worldwide and author of the cookbook *Nobu West*

TASTY TIDBIT: Out of fresh veggies? Unwrap one box (10 ounces) of any frozen vegetable, place it on a microwavable plate, and microwave it on high power for 4 to 5 minutes, turning the box once. You won't shortchange yourself nutritionally—believe it or not, frozen produce is even more nutrient packed. That's because the moment produce is picked, it starts to lose nutrients, but freezing slows that loss. A 2007 study found that the vitamin C content of fresh broccoli plummeted 56 percent in 7 days but dipped just 10 percent in a year's time when frozen at -4°F. Skip packages with added sauces and seasonings, which make fat, sodium, and sugar levels skyrocket. Though some manufacturers claim their sauce is light or low fat, that doesn't mean it's healthy. A 10-ounce package of broccoli in low-fat white Cheddar cheese sauce provides nearly 15 times as much sodium as an entire 12-ounce bag of plain broccoli florets.

Make Soup Less Salty

FOODIE'S FAVE: All-Clad Stainless 8-Quart Stockpot ($280; cooking.com)

> "A large stockpot is essential to making chicken, fish, and vegetable stocks from scratch. I use the stock as a base for healthy soups or to poach meat and seafood, which eliminates the need to cook in any oil or fat. And I use a lot less salt than canned broths or stocks."
>
> —Curtis Stone, star of the TLC reality series *Take Home Chef*

TASTY TIDBIT: You probably know that having soup as an appetizer will help fill you up so you naturally eat less. Now it seems that a bowl between meals is better than other snacks at controlling your hunger. When 24 women ate

three different snacks that contained the same ingredients and calories—chicken rice casserole, the casserole with a glass of water, or a soup made with the casserole and water—the soup curbed their appetite the best. They reported less hunger and ate 80 fewer calories at a meal 2 hours later.

Part of the satisfaction you get from having broth-based soup is that you can eat a large portion while still sparing calories. "Your mouth likes the extra food, your brain is turned on by knowing you're having more, and now it seems that your stomach stays full longer than we expected. All work together to keep you satisfied," says study author Barbara Rolls, PhD, author of *The Volumetrics Eating Plan* and a professor of nutritional sciences at Pennsylvania State University. For fast and filling snacks, keep a 100-calorie cup of instant beef noodle or vegetable soup in your briefcase. When the weather is warmer, try chilled soup such as strawberry or gazpacho. They seem to work just as well as hot versions, says Dr. Rolls.

BREAKFASTS

Zesty Spinach Omelet

—Terry Sanchez Allison, Tiki Island, Texas

82
Calories

"I was inspired to make this recipe because I wanted a lot of protein in one serving but didn't want a bland omelet. The jalapeños brought just the right amount of zestiness."

Total time: 20 minutes

- 2 **tablespoons chopped onion**
- 2 **tablespoons chopped red bell pepper, plus more for garnish (optional)**
- 2 **tablespoons chopped mushroom**
- 1 **cup fresh spinach**
- 1 **tablespoon chopped jalapeño pepper (wear plastic gloves when handling)**
- 1 **tablespoon shredded mozzarella cheese, divided**
- 2 **egg whites, lightly beaten**

HEAT a medium nonstick skillet coated with cooking spray over medium heat. Cook the onion for 2 minutes, or until softened. Stir in the bell pepper and mushroom; cook for 2 minutes, or until tender. Add the spinach and cook, covered, for 2 minutes, or until wilted. Stir in the jalapeño. Transfer the vegetables to a plate. Sprinkle with half of the mozzarella and cover with a lid to keep warm.

POUR the egg whites into the same skillet coated with cooking spray. Cook until the eggs are just set in the center, tilting the skillet and lifting the edges of the omelet with a spatula to let the uncooked portion flow underneath, about 3 minutes. Sprinkle the remaining mozzarella and the vegetables over half of the omelet. Fold the omelet over the filling and transfer to a plate. Garnish with bell pepper, if using.

Makes 1 serving

Per serving: 82 calories, 10 g protein, 7 g carbohydrate, 2 g fat, 1 g saturated fat, 6 mg cholesterol, 195 mg sodium, 2 g fiber

Avocado Breakfast Muffin

—Darla Jo Smela, Alanson, Michigan

"This is a simple but amazingly delicious breakfast sandwich!"

343 Calories

Total time: 10 minutes

- ¼ ripe avocado, mashed
- 1 whole wheat or multigrain English muffin, split and toasted
- 1 egg
- 1 slice Canadian bacon or extra-thin sliced deli ham
- ½ slice reduced-fat Colby-Jack cheese

SPREAD the avocado over the bottom half of the muffin. Place on a plate; set aside.

HEAT a small nonstick skillet coated with butter-flavored cooking spray over medium heat. Crack the egg into the skillet and cook for 3 minutes, or until the egg white is solid. Gently slide a spatula under the egg to break the yolk, using the spatula to keep the yolk beneath the white.

PLACE the bacon and cheese over the egg; cook for 2 minutes, or until the cheese melts. Slide the egg mixture onto the muffin with avocado. Top with the remaining muffin half.

Makes 1 serving

Per serving: 343 calories, 22 g protein, 31 g carbohydrate, 16 g fat, 4 g saturated fat,* 229 mg cholesterol, 800 mg sodium,* 7 g fiber

*Limit saturated fat to 10 percent of total calories—about 17 grams per day for most women—and sodium intake to less than 2,300 milligrams.

Vegetable Cheese Roll

This rolled omelet is so simple to prepare, yet it makes a stunning presentation at a weekend brunch. The secret is lining the baking pan with wax paper, which makes it easier to roll the omelet after baking.

171 Calories

Total time: 35 minutes

- 4 cups frozen cut leaf spinach
- 4 eggs, separated
- 1 cup shredded fat-free mozzarella cheese
- ¼ cup grated Parmesan cheese
- ¼ cup fat-free plain yogurt

PREHEAT the oven to 400°F. Coat a jelly roll pan with cooking spray and line with a large sheet of wax paper.

RINSE the spinach in a colander under hot running water for 30 seconds. Squeeze any excess water from the spinach. Stir together the spinach and egg yolks in a medium bowl.

BEAT the egg whites in a large bowl with an electric mixer until stiff peaks form. Fold the egg whites into the spinach mixture. Spread evenly in the prepared pan. Cover with foil. Bake for 20 minutes, or until firm.

STIR together the mozzarella, Parmesan, and yogurt in a small bowl. Turn the omelet onto a clean sheet of wax paper; peel off the lining. Spread evenly with the cheese mixture. Roll up the omelet starting with a narrow end. Cut into 8 slices.

Makes 8 servings

Per serving: 171 calories, 20 g protein, 6 g carbohydrate, 6.5 g fat, 2.5 g saturated fat, 221 mg cholesterol, 485 mg sodium, 2 g fiber

NUTRITION NEWS TO USE

Eat an egg—No offense meant to carrots, but research shows eggs are an even better source of the eye-friendly antioxidants known as carotenoids. Eating an egg a day increases blood levels of lutein (by 26 percent) and zeaxanthin (by 38 percent) without raising cholesterol or triglyceride levels.

Vegetable Skillet Frittata

158 Calories

This family brunch favorite is rendered lighter with a combination of whole eggs and egg whites as well as plenty of vegetables and seasonings.

Total time: 30 minutes

- 1 cup low-fat cottage cheese
- 2 eggs
- 4 egg whites
- ¼ cup reduced-sodium chicken broth
- 1 cup chopped onions
- 1 cup sliced green beans
- 1 cup chopped broccoli
- ¼ cup shredded carrot
- 2 cloves garlic, minced
- ½ teaspoon ground black pepper
- ⅛ teaspoon salt
- ⅓ cup shredded reduced-fat sharp Cheddar cheese

COMBINE the cottage cheese, eggs, and egg whites in a blender or food processor. Pulse until very smooth. Set aside.

BRING the broth and onions to a boil in a large nonstick skillet over medium-high heat. Cook for 5 minutes, or until the onions soften. Add the beans, broccoli, carrot, and garlic; cover and continue cooking for 2 minutes, or until broccoli is bright green. Season with the pepper and salt. Add the egg mixture and cheese. Reduce the heat to low. Cover and cook for 15 minutes, or until the eggs are set. Cut into wedges.

Makes 4 servings

Per serving: 158 calories, 17 g protein, 12 g carbohydrate, 5 g fat, 2.5 g saturated fat, 117 mg cholesterol, 495 mg sodium, 3 g fiber

Herbed Turkey and Vegetable Hash

199 Calories

Low-fat turkey replaces heavy corned beef in this hash. For brunch, serve it with a green salad and a poached fruit dessert. If you have fresh parsley on hand, sprinkle some over the dish before serving.

Total time: 20 minutes

- 1 teaspoon olive oil
- 1 pound turkey breast, cut into 1" cubes
- ¼ cup apple juice
- 3 cups frozen shredded potatoes
- 1 small onion, chopped
- 1 zucchini, halved lengthwise and cut into ¼" slices
- 1 teaspoon dried sage
- ¼ teaspoon dried thyme
- ¼ teaspoon salt
- ⅛ teaspoon ground red pepper
- ½ cup fat-free sour cream

HEAT the oil in a large nonstick skillet coated with cooking spray over medium-high heat. Cook the turkey, stirring, for 3 minutes, or until the turkey is no longer pink in the center. Transfer to a plate; cover to keep warm.

ADD the apple juice to the skillet. Boil, scraping to loosen any browned bits from the bottom. Stir in the potatoes, onion, zucchini, sage, and thyme and cook, stirring, for 8 minutes, or until the onions are tender. Stir in the salt, red pepper, and turkey. Serve with the sour cream.

Makes 6 servings

Per serving: 199 calories, 22 g protein, 24 g carbohydrate, 2 g fat, 0.5 g saturated fat, 30 mg cholesterol, 218 mg sodium, 2 g fiber

Peanut Butter Oatmeal Breakfast

441 Calories

—Cristen Dutcher, Marietta, Georgia

"This recipe is fast and easy on busy mornings and fills me up on days when I know I'll have to eat a late lunch. I enjoy it with a glass of orange juice."

Total time: 5 minutes

- ½ cup quick-cooking oats
- ¾ cup light vanilla soy milk
- 2 tablespoons creamy peanut butter
- ¼ teaspoon ground cinnamon

STIR together the oats and milk in a small microwavable bowl. Microwave at 1 minute intervals, stirring between intervals, until the oatmeal reaches the desired consistency. Stir in the peanut butter and cinnamon.

Makes 1 serving

Per serving: 441 calories, 17 g protein, 51 g carbohydrate, 21 g fat, 3 g saturated fat, 0 mg cholesterol, 221 mg sodium, 7 g fiber

SHOPPING SAVVY

Raising the Bar

For a grab-and-go breakfast that's as healthy as it is convenient, try Luna Sunrise bars—each one holds the right mix of nutrients to power you through your morning. Made with 70 percent organic ingredients, each bar packs 5 grams of filling fiber (pair it with a piece of fruit for an extra boost), 8 grams of energizing protein, and 35 percent of your daily requirement of bone-building calcium. Choose from four flavors: Blueberry Bliss, Strawberry Crumble (each 170 calories, 4.5 grams fat), Apple Cinnamon (180 calories, 5 grams fat), and Vanilla Almond (180 calories, 4.5 grams fat). Look for Luna Sunrise bars at your supermarket, mass merchandiser, or natural foods store. For later-in-the-day cravings, try new Luna Minis. You get 4 grams of protein in half-size, 80-calorie bars in three of Luna's best-selling chocolate flavors: S'mores, Nutz Over Chocolate, and Caramel Nut Brownie. For more information, visit lunabar.com.

Another sweetly sneaky way to work in a quarter of your DV for calcium without bothering to pour milk: Barbara's Bakery Fruit & Yogurt bars. These moist whole-grain bars are filled with a creamy combo in four flavors: Apple Cinnamon, Blueberry Apple, Cherry Apple, and Strawberry Apple. For more information or to shop online, visit barbarasbakery.com.

Protein Waffle One-Two-Three

182 Calories

—Elena Mortell, Hernando Beach, Florida

"This is a very fast, easy, and nutritious waffle, which I like to serve for breakfast, lunch, or brunch."

Total time: 15 minutes

- 2 **tablespoons rolled oats**
- 1 **egg white**
- 1 **tablespoon vanilla-flavored whey protein powder**
- 3 **tablespoons farmer cheese**
  Pinch of grated orange zest
  Greek yogurt, honey, sliced fruit (optional)

GRIND the oats in a coffee grinder or blender until finely ground; set aside. Preheat a waffle iron for 4 minutes, or according to the manufacturer's instructions. (A drop of water should sizzle and bounce when dropped on the iron.)

MEANWHILE, beat the egg white and protein powder in a medium bowl with an electric mixer on high speed for 2 minutes, or until the powder has dissolved and is incorporated into the egg white.

BEAT in the cheese and orange zest for 2 minutes, or until completely smooth. Stir in the ground oats.

COAT the heated waffle grids with cooking spray just before using. Pour the batter onto the hot iron and cook for 3 to 4 minutes. Serve with the yogurt, honey, and fruit, if using.

Makes 1 serving

Per serving: 182 calories, 22 g protein, 8 g carbohydrate, 5 g fat, 2.5 g saturated fat, 24 mg cholesterol, 258 mg sodium, 1 g fiber

Waffles with Sweet Orange Syrup

Delicious over waffles, this sweet and tangy orange syrup is just as tasty over pancakes or frozen yogurt.

290 Calories

Total time: 20 minutes

- ½ cup orange marmalade
- 2 tablespoons orange juice
- 1½ tablespoons packed brown sugar
- ½ tablespoon lemon juice
- 12 frozen multigrain waffles

COOK the marmalade, orange juice, brown sugar, and lemon juice in a small saucepan over medium-high heat, stirring, for 3 minutes, or until the marmalade melts.

PLACE a fine sieve over a medium bowl. Press the mixture through the sieve with the back of a large spoon or a rubber spatula. Discard any orange rind from the marmalade.

TOAST the waffles as directed. Place 2 waffles on each of 6 plates. Top each waffle with 1 tablespoon of the orange syrup.

Makes 6 servings

Per serving: 290 calories, 7 g protein, 48 g carbohydrate, 9 g fat, 2.5 g saturated fat, 74 mg cholesterol, 280 mg sodium, 2 g fiber

Cornmeal Muffins with Blueberries

152 Calories

Buttermilk and blueberries make these muffins tart and tasty—a nice balance to the natural sweetness of corn and brown sugar.

Total time: 25 minutes + cooling time

- ¾ cup low-fat buttermilk
- ½ cup packed brown sugar
- ½ cup canola oil
- 1 egg
- 1 egg white
- 2 tablespoons unsweetened applesauce
- 1 cup all-purpose flour
- ½ cup yellow cornmeal
- ½ cup blueberries
- 1½ teaspoons baking powder
- 1 teaspoon baking soda
- ½ teaspoon ground cinnamon
- ¼ teaspoon salt

PREHEAT the oven to 400°F. Coat a 12-cup muffin pan with cooking spray.

WHISK together the buttermilk, brown sugar, oil, egg, egg white, and applesauce in a medium bowl.

STIR together the flour, cornmeal, blueberries, baking powder, baking soda, cinnamon, and salt in a large bowl. Stir in the buttermilk mixture just until blended.

SPOON into the muffin cups, filling the cups three-fourths full.

BAKE for 12 to 15 minutes, or until a toothpick inserted in the center of a muffin comes out clean. Cool on a rack in the pan for 2 minutes. Transfer to the rack; cool completely.

Makes 12 servings

Per serving: 152 calories, 3 g protein, 23 g carbohydrate, 6 g fat, 1 g saturated fat, 18 mg cholesterol, 247 mg sodium, 1 g fiber

Breakfast in a Muffin

168 Calories

—Barbara Estabrook, Rhinelander, Wisconsin

"This muffin is packed full of nutrition, and I typically begin my day with one along with fat-free yogurt. It also satisfies my craving for sweets about midday!"

Total time: 40 minutes + cooling time

- 1¼ cups finely crushed whole-grain wheat or bran cereal flakes
- ¾ cup all-purpose flour
- ½ cup stone-ground whole wheat flour
- 2 teaspoons baking powder
- 1 teaspoon ground cinnamon
- ½ teaspoon baking soda
- ½ teaspoon salt
- ½ teaspoon ground ginger
- ¼ teaspoon ground nutmeg
- 1 teaspoon grated orange zest
- 2 egg whites
- 3 tablespoons extra-virgin olive oil
- 1 teaspoon vanilla extract
- ½ cup packed light brown sugar
- ½ cup fat-free plain yogurt
- ¼ cup orange juice
- ⅓ cup golden raisins
- 1¼ cups fresh or frozen blueberries
- 1½ tablespoons coarsely chopped almonds
- 1 tablespoon turbinado sugar

PREHEAT the oven to 400°F. Line a 12-cup muffin pan with paper liners.

WHISK together the cereal, flours, baking powder, cinnamon, baking soda, salt, ginger, nutmeg, and orange zest in a large bowl.

WHISK together the egg whites, oil, and vanilla in a medium bowl. Whisk in the brown sugar, yogurt, and orange juice just until blended. Stir into the dry ingredients just until blended. Fold in the raisins and blueberries. Spoon into the muffin cups, nearly filling the cups.

STIR together the almonds and turbinado sugar in a small bowl. Sprinkle by rounded ½ teaspoons over each muffin.

BAKE for 22 minutes, or until the top of a muffin springs back when lightly touched. Cool on a rack in the pan for 2 minutes. Transfer to the rack; cool completely.

Makes 12 servings

Per serving: 168 calories, 3 g protein, 30 g carbohydrate, 4 g fat, 0.5 g saturated fat, 0 mg cholesterol, 245 mg sodium, 2 g fiber

Brown Sugar–Apple Muffins

161 Calories

Cinnamon-flavored crumbs create a scrumptious streusel topping for these sweet muffins studded with apples, dates, and walnuts.

Total time: 30 minutes + cooling time

TOPPING

- ¼ cup all-purpose flour
- ¼ cup packed brown sugar
- ½ teaspoon ground cinnamon
- 1 tablespoon butter, melted

MUFFINS

- ½ cup chopped apples
- ½ cup chopped dates
- ½ cup low-fat buttermilk
- 3 tablespoons packed brown sugar
- 1 egg
- 2 tablespoons unsweetened applesauce
- 2 tablespoons canola oil
- 1½ cups all-purpose flour
- 1 tablespoon toasted chopped walnuts
- 1 teaspoon baking powder
- 1 teaspoon baking soda

NUTRITION NEWS TO USE

Dried fruits are known to be rich in antioxidants—but some of the less popular types are the most nutritious. Figs and dried plums had the best overall nutrient scores, shows recent research at the University of Scranton. A handful of dried figs (about 1½ ounces) increased the body's ability to neutralize free radicals by 9 percent. That's more than double the increase seen after a cup of green tea.

TO MAKE THE TOPPING:

STIR together the flour, brown sugar, and cinnamon in a small bowl. Mix in the butter until crumbly.

TO MAKE THE MUFFINS:

PREHEAT the oven to 400°F. Coat a 12-cup muffin pan with cooking spray.

STIR together the apples, dates, buttermilk, brown sugar, egg, applesauce, and oil in a medium bowl.

STIR together the flour, walnuts, baking powder, and baking soda in a large bowl. Stir in the apple mixture just until blended. Spoon into the muffin cups, filling the cups three-fourths full. Sprinkle each muffin with 2 teaspoons of the topping.

BAKE for 15 to 18 minutes, or until a toothpick inserted in the center of a muffin comes out clean. Cool on a rack in the pan for 2 minutes. Transfer to the rack; cool completely.

Makes 12 servings

Per serving: 161 calories, 3 g protein, 29 g carbohydrate, 4 g fat, 1 g saturated fat, 19 mg cholesterol, 174 mg sodium, 1 g fiber

Ginger Bran Muffins

214 Calories

These moist muffins hide a healthy punch. Bran flakes contribute fiber, and applesauce eliminates $\frac{1}{2}$ cup of oil. That cuts more than 100 grams of fat in just one recipe!

Total time: 25 minutes + cooling time

- $\frac{1}{2}$ cup applesauce
- $\frac{1}{2}$ cup low-fat buttermilk
- $\frac{1}{3}$ cup molasses
- $\frac{1}{3}$ cup packed brown sugar
- $\frac{1}{4}$ cup canola oil
- 1 egg
- 1 egg white
- 1 teaspoon vanilla extract
- 2 cups all-purpose flour
- $\frac{1}{2}$ cup bran flakes
- $\frac{1}{2}$ cup raisins
- 2 teaspoons ground cinnamon
- 2 teaspoons ground ginger
- 1 teaspoon baking powder
- 1 teaspoon baking soda
- $\frac{1}{2}$ teaspoon ground cloves

PREHEAT the oven to 400°F. Coat a 12-cup muffin pan with cooking spray.

WHISK together the applesauce, buttermilk, molasses, brown sugar, oil, egg, egg white, and vanilla in a medium bowl.

STIR together the flour, bran flakes, raisins, cinnamon, ginger, baking powder, baking soda, and cloves in a large bowl. Stir in the applesauce mixture just until blended.

SPOON into the prepared muffin cups, filling the cups three-fourths full.

BAKE for 20 minutes, or until a toothpick inserted in the center of a muffin comes out clean. Cool on a rack in the pan for 2 minutes. Transfer to the rack; cool completely.

Makes 12 servings

Per serving: 214 calories, 4 g protein, 39 g carbohydrate, 5.5 g fat, 1 g saturated fat, 18 mg cholesterol, 189 mg sodium, 2 g fiber

Cinnamon-Raisin Rolls

251
Calories

If the aroma of sweet rolls at the mall makes you swoon, you'll love these treats. These are stuffed with raisins and sprinkled with cinnamon—and they have a wonderful maple flavor.

Total time: 3 hours

- ¾ cup fat-free milk, warmed to about 115°F
- 2 tablespoons packed brown sugar
- 1 package active dry yeast
- 1¾ cups all-purpose flour
- 1 large orange
- 1 tablespoon ground cinnamon
- ½ teaspoon ground cardamom
- ¾ cup maple syrup
- ¾ cup raisins
- 2 tablespoons finely chopped walnuts
- 2 tablespoons light butter, melted

MIX the milk, brown sugar, and yeast in a large bowl. Let stand in a warm place for 5 minutes, or until foamy. Add 1 cup of the flour and stir well. Cover and set in a warm place for 30 minutes, or until doubled in size. Stir in the remaining ¾ cup flour to make a kneadable dough.

TURN the dough out onto a lightly floured surface. Knead, adding more flour as necessary, for about 10 minutes, or until smooth and elastic. Coat a large bowl with cooking spray. Add the dough and turn to coat all sides. Cover and set in a warm place for 1 hour, or until doubled in size.

COAT a 9" × 9" baking dish with cooking spray. Grate 1 teaspoon orange rind into a small bowl; juice the orange into the bowl. Add the cinnamon, cardamom, and ½ cup of the maple syrup; mix well. Pour into the baking dish, tilting evenly to coat the bottom.

ON a lightly floured surface, roll the dough into a 12" × 10" rectangle; sprinkle with the raisins and walnuts. Roll the dough from the longer side into a cylinder; cut into 9 sections. Arrange the rolls, cut sides down, in the baking dish with the sides touching. Cover and set in a warm place for 30 minutes.

PREHEAT the oven to 350°F. In a small saucepan, combine the butter and the remaining ¼ cup maple syrup. Place over low heat for 1 minute. Pour over the rolls. Bake for 25 to 30 minutes, or until golden brown. Let cool; invert onto a plate and separate the rolls.

Makes 9 servings

Per serving: 251 calories, 4 g protein, 53 g carbohydrate, 3 g fat, 1 g saturated fat, 3 mg cholesterol, 27 mg sodium, 2 g fiber

Cranberry-Walnut Date Bread

128 Calories

Along with other berries, cranberries are a good course of ellagic acid, a cancer-fighting antioxidant.

Total time: 50 minutes + cooling time

- ½ cup fresh or frozen cranberries
- ½ cup chopped dates
- ½ cup low-fat buttermilk
- 3 tablespoons packed brown sugar
- 1 egg
- 2 tablespoons unsweetened applesauce
- 2 tablespoons canola oil
- 1½ cups all-purpose flour
- 1 tablespoon toasted chopped walnuts
- 1 teaspoon baking powder
- 1 teaspoon baking soda

PREHEAT the oven to 400°F. Coat a 9" × 5" loaf pan with cooking spray. Dust the pan with flour and shake out the excess.

STIR together the cranberries, dates, buttermilk, brown sugar, egg, applesauce, and oil in a medium bowl.

STIR together the flour, walnuts, baking powder, and baking soda in a large bowl. Stir in the cranberry mixture just until blended. Pour into the prepared pan.

BAKE for 25 minutes. Reduce the heat to 300°F. Bake for 15 minutes, or until a toothpick inserted in the center of the loaf comes out clean. Cool on a rack for 10 minutes. Remove from the pan and cool completely on the rack.

Makes 16 servings

Per serving: 128 calories, 3 g protein, 22 g carbohydrate, 3 g fat, 0.5 g saturated fat, 18 mg cholesterol, 164 mg sodium, 1 g fiber

Cinnamon-Raisin Bread

209 Calories

Spices permeate this breakfast bread, and a cinnamon-raisin filling spirals through it. Cool thoroughly before slicing, but if you enjoy the warm smell of cinnamon, it's irresistible when toasted.

Total time: 2 hours 35 minutes + cooling time

DOUGH

- 1 cup apple juice
- ½ cup sugar
- 1 tablespoon active dry yeast
- 1 tablespoon ground cinnamon
- 1 teaspoon pumpkin pie spice
- 4 cups all-purpose flour
- 1 tablespoon canola oil

FILLING

- 1 cup raisins
- ¼ cup frozen apple juice concentrate, thawed
- 1 teaspoon ground cinnamon

TO MAKE THE DOUGH:

PLACE the apple juice in a small saucepan. Warm over medium heat to about 110°F. Pour into a large bowl. Stir in the sugar and yeast. Let stand in a warm place for 5 minutes, or until foamy. Stir in the cinnamon, pumpkin pie spice, and 2½ cups of the flour until well blended. Cover and set in a warm place for 30 minutes, or until doubled in size.

STIR in the oil and about 1 cup of flour to make a kneadable dough. Turn the dough out onto a lightly floured surface. Knead, adding up to ½ cup more flour, for 10 minutes, or until smooth and elastic. Coat another large bowl with cooking spray. Add the dough and turn to coat all sides. Cover and set in a warm place for 1 hour, or until doubled in size.

TO MAKE THE FILLING:

STIR together the raisins, apple juice concentrate, and cinnamon in a microwavable bowl. Microwave on medium power for 5 minutes, or until thickened. Set aside to cool.

PREHEAT the oven to 350°F. Coat a 9" × 5" loaf pan with cooking spray. On a lightly floured surface, roll the dough into a 10" × 8" rectangle. Spread the raisin filling over the dough, then roll up starting with the narrow side. Pinch the seams to seal. Place, seam side down, in the prepared pan. Let stand for 5 minutes.

BAKE for 45 minutes, or until golden brown. Remove from the pan and cool on a rack before slicing.

Makes 16 servings

Per serving: 209 calories, 5 g protein, 43 g carbohydrate, 2 g fat, 0 g saturated fat, 0 mg cholesterol, 2 mg sodium, 2 g fiber

Blueberry-Buttermilk Coffee Cake

250 Calories

A great potluck dish, this coffee cake is studded with fruit and is moist from the secret ingredient of mashed banana. It travels well and makes a good dessert for box lunches.

Total time: 1 hour + cooling time

- 1 cup whole wheat flour
- 1 cup all-purpose flour
- 2 teaspoons baking powder
- 2 teaspoons baking soda
- 2 cups fresh or frozen blueberries
- ¾ cup honey
- 1 egg
- 3 egg whites
- ¾ cup low-fat buttermilk
- ½ cup mashed banana
- ⅓ cup baby food prunes
- ¼ cup canola oil
- 1 tablespoon chopped walnuts
- ⅓ cup packed brown sugar

PREHEAT the oven to 350°F. Coat a 13" × 9" baking dish with cooking spray.

MIX the flours, baking powder, and baking soda in a large bowl. Fold in the blueberries.

MIX the honey, egg, egg whites, buttermilk, banana, prunes, and oil in a medium bowl. Add to the flour mixture and stir until just blended.

POUR the batter into the prepared baking dish and smooth the top with a spatula. Sprinkle with the walnuts and brown sugar.

BAKE for 40 to 45 minutes, or until a toothpick inserted in the center comes out clean. Cool before cutting.

Makes 12 servings

Per serving: 250 calories, 5 g protein, 47 g carbohydrate, 6 g fat, 1 g saturated fat, 18 mg cholesterol, 316 mg sodium, 3 g fiber

Cherry Streusel Coffee Cake

240
Calories

This moist and fruity coffee cake will make a great contribution to your next potluck. If you have fresh cherries, by all means use them.

Total time: 55 minutes + cooling time

COFFEE CAKE

- ¾ cup unsweetened applesauce
- ½ cup canola oil
- ¼ cup low-fat buttermilk
- ¼ cup packed brown sugar
- 3 egg whites
- 1 egg
- 2 cups all-purpose flour
- 2 teaspoons baking powder
- 2 teaspoons baking soda
- 2 cups frozen cherries, thawed

TOPPING

- ¼ cup all-purpose flour
- 3 tablespoons packed brown sugar
- ½ teaspoon ground ginger
- ½ teaspoon ground cinnamon
- 1 tablespoon oil

TO MAKE THE COFFEE CAKE:

PREHEAT the oven to 350°F. Coat a 13" × 9" baking dish with cooking spray.

STIR together the applesauce, oil, buttermilk, brown sugar, egg whites, and egg in a medium bowl.

WHISK together the flour, baking powder, and baking soda in a large bowl. Stir in the cherries. Stir in the buttermilk mixture just until blended. Pour into the prepared baking dish.

TO MAKE THE TOPPING:

STIR together the flour, brown sugar, ginger, cinnamon, and oil in a small bowl. Sprinkle over the batter. Bake for 40 to 45 minutes, or until a toothpick inserted in the center comes out clean. Remove from the pan and cool on a rack before slicing.

Makes 12 servings

Per serving: 240 calories, 4 g protein, 31 g carbohydrate, 11 g fat, 1 g saturated fat, 18 mg cholesterol, 320 mg sodium, 1 g fiber

Katie Ciaria

VITAL STATS

WEIGHT LOST:
124 pounds

HEIGHT: 5'0"

WEIGHT NOW:
110 pounds

HEALTH BONUS:
She's added years to her life: She's no longer borderline diabetic.

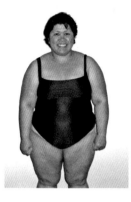

"Sure, I knew I was overweight," says Katie Ciaria. "But over the past 19 years, as I morphed from a 98-pound bride to a 234-pound wife and mom, I thought that fat was my fate." The needle started to tilt after Katie got pregnant. "I ate rich and fattening foods all the time, but my husband made it clear that he loved me no matter what I weighed," she says. "I used his support as an excuse to overeat." She did try to drop the extra weight—but each attempt just left her even heavier.

Her eyes were opened following a 2006 trip home to the Philippines for her parents' 50th anniversary celebration, after which she and her family watched a videotape of the event. "We joked that all the guests who had moved to America had gotten large," she recalls. "Then I came onto the screen—I looked so huge; I couldn't believe it was me. Everyone else kept laughing. I didn't let on that the tears rolling down my cheeks were from hurt."

Within days, Katie saw her doctor and begged for bariatric surgery but was flat-out refused. "Katie, you can do this on your own," the doctor insisted. "I wracked my brain for

something I hadn't tried and settled on Weight Watchers," says Katie. "I started to track what I ate and realized how giant my meals were. It was hard to get used to normal servings, but I never felt deprived as I dropped more than 100 pounds in just over a year."

For example, Katie had to reintroduce her tastebuds to greens. "Before, I thought of broccoli as a miniature tree; now I enjoy it with a little seasoning," she says. "I also ate less rice, which is a huge part of Filipino cuisine. I used to eat way too much. I also stopped frying and now grill, bake, broil, and poach."

"The benefits of my success are amazing," continues Katie. Plus, I'm off my hypertension pills. My doctor was so excited, she practically jumped up and down! I'm indebted to her for believing in me. I'm learning that I, too, can inspire people. The relatives who saw me on that dreadful video now exercise and eat right. They say I'm their role model. If I can do it, anyone can!"

SALADS

Sunny Tofu Salad

307 Calories

—Maryalice Wood, Langley, British Columbia, Canada

"This main course summer salad can be easily adapted using frozen strawberries in the winter. I just thaw them in the raspberry dressing while the tofu is marinating. Serve with hearty multigrain rolls for a delightful nutritious, meatless meal."

Total time: 20 minutes + marinating time

TOFU

- 3 tablespoons light soy sauce
- 1 tablespoon toasted sesame oil
- 1 clove garlic, minced
- 2 cups firm tofu cut into $\frac{1}{2}$" cubes

SALAD

- 4 cups baby spinach leaves
- 4 cups mixed salad greens
- 2 cups sliced strawberries
- 1 can (10 ounces) light mandarin orange segments, drained
- $\frac{1}{2}$ pound snow peas, halved
- $\frac{1}{2}$ cup pecan halves, toasted
- $\frac{1}{2}$ cup raspberry vinaigrette dressing

TO PREPARE THE TOFU:

STIR together the soy sauce, sesame oil, and garlic in a broiler pan. Stir in the tofu, tossing to coat. Set aside for at least 1 hour.

PREHEAT the broiler. Place the tofu 6" from the heat source and broil for 4 to 6 minutes, turning occasionally, until crisp.

TO PREPARE THE SALAD:

TOSS together the spinach, salad greens, strawberries, oranges, and snow peas in a large bowl. Toss the salad with the pecans and vinaigrette. Top with the tofu.

Makes 6 servings

Per serving: 307 calories, 17 g protein, 28 g carbohydrate, 16 g fat, 2 g saturated fat, 0 mg cholesterol, 625 mg sodium,* 7 g fiber

*Limit saturated fat to 10 percent of total calories—about 17 grams per day for most women—and sodium intake to less than 2,300 milligrams.

Asian Harmony Bean and Brown Rice Salad

—Jasmine Buliga, Braintree, Massachusetts

"Rich with healthful vegetables, beans, and rice, this dish is full of great flavor, vibrant color, and wonderful aroma, making it both delicious and satisfying."

Total time: 40 minutes

- ¼ cup orange juice
- ¼ cup prepared green tea, cooled
- ¼ cup rice wine vinegar
- 2 tablespoons honey or agave nectar
- 1 teaspoon grated fresh ginger
- 1 teaspoon minced roasted garlic
- 1 teaspoon ground coriander
- ½ tablespoon toasted sesame oil
- ¼ teaspoon salt
- ¼ teaspoon ground black pepper
- ½ cup olive oil
- 1 can (15.5 ounces) black beans, rinsed and drained
- 2 cups shelled edamame, cooked
- 2 cups cooked brown basmati rice, cooled
- 1 can (8 ounces) sliced water chestnuts, drained and chopped
- ½ cup chopped celery
- ½ cup chopped red bell pepper
- ½ cup slivered almonds
- ¼ cup chopped fresh cilantro

WHISK together the orange juice, tea, vinegar, honey, ginger, garlic, coriander, sesame oil, salt, and pepper in a large bowl. Whisk in the olive oil until emulsified. Stir in the black beans, edamame, rice, water chestnuts, celery, bell pepper, almonds, and cilantro, tossing to coat well.

Makes 8 servings

Per serving: 341 calories, 9 g protein, 33 g carbohydrate, 20 g fat, 2.5 g saturated fat, 0 mg cholesterol, 212 mg sodium, 8 g fiber

NUTRITION NEWS TO USE

Always measure these foods: rice, cereal, peanut butter, and oil. They're hard to eyeball and calorie dense. A heaping cup of rice has 25 percent more calories than a level one.

Black Bean Avocado Salad

207 Calories

—Diane Kretschmer, Ettrick, Wisconsin

"This salad is a great hit at gatherings, and I am always asked for the recipe. Feel free to substitute mild peppers for the jalapeño peppers if you can't take the heat."

Total time: 15 minutes + chilling time

- 2 limes
- ¼ cup olive oil
- 2 avocados, pitted, peeled, and cut into ½" cubes
- 1 can (15 ounces) black beans, rinsed and drained
- 1 can (15 ounces) great Northern beans, rinsed and drained
- 1 cup frozen corn, thawed
- 2 cloves garlic, minced
- 2 jalapeño peppers, seeds removed, chopped (wear plastic gloves when handling)
- 1 red bell pepper, chopped
- 1 pint grape tomatoes, halved
- ½ cup chopped fresh cilantro
- 2 teaspoons ground cumin
  Salt and ground black pepper

ZEST 1 lime into a large bowl. Squeeze the juice of both limes into the same bowl. Whisk in the oil until emulsified. Add the avocados, beans, corn, garlic, jalapeños, bell pepper, tomatoes, cilantro, and cumin, tossing to coat. Season with salt and pepper to taste.

COVER and refrigerate for several hours before serving.

Makes 8 servings

Per serving: 207 calories, 6 g protein, 23 g carbohydrate, 12.5 g fat, 2 g saturated fat, 0 mg cholesterol, 346 mg sodium, 8 g fiber

Beautiful Bean Salad

257
Calories

—Deanne O'Donnell, Greensburg, Pennsylvania

Often requested for parties or picnics, this salad is sure to become a favorite.

Total time: 15 minutes + chilling time

- ⅔ cup olive oil
- ⅓ cup balsamic vinegar
-   Salt and ground black pepper
- 1 can (15 ounces) kidney beans, rinsed and drained
- 1 can (15 ounces) chickpeas, rinsed and drained
- 1 can (15 ounces) black beans, rinsed and drained
- 1 can (15 ounces) navy beans, rinsed and drained
- 1 can (15 ounces) black-eyed peas, rinsed and drained
- 1 can (15 ounces) great Northern beans, rinsed and drained
- 4 plum tomatoes, chopped
- 1 large green bell pepper, finely chopped
- 1 red onion, finely chopped
- 1 rib celery, finely chopped
- ½ cup chopped fresh parsley

WHISK together the oil, vinegar, and salt and pepper to taste in a large bowl until emulsified. Stir in the beans, tomatoes, bell pepper, onion, celery, and parsley, tossing to coat well.

COVER and refrigerate for at least 1 hour before serving.

Makes 12 servings

Per serving: 257 calories, 9 g protein, 29 g carbohydrate, 13 g fat, 2 g saturated fat, 0 mg cholesterol, 545 mg sodium, 8 g fiber

Kale and Lentil Salad

185
Calories

—Debra Olafson, Vancouver, British Columbia

So flavorful, this salad doesn't need added dressing. If you'd like, add some chopped seasonal fruits such as apples, grapes, strawberries, or blueberries.

Total time: 30 minutes

- ½ cup dried green French lentils (do not substitute), picked over and rinsed
- ½ cup chopped red bell pepper
- ½ cup chopped yellow bell pepper
- ½ cup chopped orange bell pepper
- ½ cup chopped zucchini
- 8 cherry tomatoes, quartered
- 8 spears asparagus, chopped
- 10 snap peas or snow peas
- 5 large kale leaves, stemmed and chopped
- ¼ cup crumbled reduced fat feta cheese
- ¼ cup sunflower or pumpkin seeds

COVER the lentils by 2" of water in a medium saucepan and bring to a boil over medium-high heat. Reduce the heat to low, cover, and simmer for 20 minutes, or until just tender. Drain and rinse under cold water.

STIR together the peppers, zucchini, tomatoes, asparagus, peas, and kale in a large bowl. Add the lentils, cheese, and sunflower seeds, tossing until well blended.

Makes 4 servings

Per serving: 185 calories, 12 g protein, 26 g carbohydrate, 5 g fat, 1 g saturated fat, 3 mg cholesterol, 157 mg sodium, 7 g fiber

KITCHEN TIP

You may find this salad is even more flavorful tossed with your favorite low-fat dressing, such as French, Italian, or balsamic vinaigrette.

Barley and Corn Salad

This refreshing, crunchy salad is a great source of fiber—delicious and nutritious!

Total time: 50 minutes

  3 cups reduced-sodium chicken broth
  1 cup uncooked barley
  ¼ teaspoon salt
  2 cups frozen corn, thawed
  ¾ cup frozen green beans, thawed
  1 tablespoon apple juice or water
  ¾ cup sliced radishes
  3 tablespoons lemon juice
  2 tablespoons minced fresh parsley
  2 tablespoons olive oil
  1 tablespoon chopped garlic
  ½ teaspoon dried basil
  ¼ teaspoon ground black pepper

BRING the broth, barley, and salt to a boil in a medium saucepan over medium-high heat. Reduce the heat to low, cover, and simmer for 40 minutes, or until the barley is tender. Let cool.

STIR together the corn, beans, and apple juice in a large nonstick skillet. Cover and bring to a boil over medium-high heat. Drain well. Place in a large bowl. Add the radishes, lemon juice, parsley, oil, garlic, basil, pepper, and barley, tossing to coat well.

Makes 4 servings

Per serving: 312 calories, 9 g protein, 54 g carbohydrate, 8 g fat, 1 g saturated fat, 0 mg cholesterol, 498 mg sodium, 10 g fiber

Hawaiian Barley Salad

—Maryalice Wood, Langley, British Columbia, Canada

Pot barley has been milled to remove some but not all of the outer bran layer. Also known as Scotch barley, milled, or hull-less barley, it's available in health food stores. Pearl barley, a more common form, has been further processed but can be used as a substitute in this recipe.

269 Calories

Total time: 50 minutes + cooling and chilling time

- ½ cup uncooked pot barley
- 1½ cups unsweetened pineapple juice
-   Pinch of salt
- 1 can (12 ounces) crushed pineapple packed in juice
- 1 can (10 ounces) light mandarin oranges, drained
- 1 cup shredded unsweetened coconut
- 1 cup light sour cream
- 1 tablespoon lemon juice
- 2 teaspoons Splenda or other granular sugar substitute
-   Grapes, cherries, or kiwifruit for garnish (optional)

RINSE the barley under cold water and drain. Bring the barley, pineapple juice, and salt to a boil in a medium saucepan over high heat. Reduce the heat to low, cover, and simmer for 35 to 45 minutes, or until tender, stirring occasionally to prevent scorching. Remove from the heat and cool, covered, for 1 hour.

STIR together the pineapple, oranges, coconut, sour cream, lemon juice, Splenda, and the cooled barley in a large bowl. Refrigerate for at least 2 hours to blend flavors. Garnish with grapes, cherries, or kiwifruit, if using.

Makes 6 servings

Per serving: 269 calories, 5 g protein, 42 g carbohydrate, 11 g fat, 9 g saturated fat,* 13 mg cholesterol, 74 mg sodium, 6 g fiber

*Limit saturated fat to 10 percent of total calories—about 17 grams per day for most women—and sodium intake to less than 2,300 milligrams.

Summer Wheat Berry Salad

153 Calories

—Peter Jakubowski, Las Vegas, Nevada

Wheat berries are unprocessed whole wheat kernels that have a nutty flavor and chewy texture. They are great in soups and salads or topped with stir-fried vegetables.

Total time: 1 hour 10 minutes + soaking and chilling time

- ½ cup wheat berries
- 2 cups water
- ½ teaspoon salt, divided
- 10 spears asparagus, cut into 1" pieces
  Juice of 2 limes
- 2 tablespoons spicy brown mustard
- ¼ teaspoon ground black pepper
- 1 can (15 ounces) artichoke hearts, drained
- 1 can (2.5 ounces) sliced black olives, drained
- 1 large tomato, chopped
- ¼ English cucumber, chopped

SOAK the wheat berries in the water overnight. Bring the berries, water, and ¼ teaspoon of the salt to a boil in a medium saucepan over high heat. Reduce the heat to low, cover, and simmer for 1 hour, or until tender. Drain any remaining liquid.

PLACE the asparagus in a bowl with a splash of water and cover with vented plastic wrap. Microwave on high for 1½ minutes. Let stand, covered, for 5 minutes.

WHISK together the lime juice, mustard, pepper, and the remaining ¼ teaspoon salt in a large bowl. Add the artichokes, olives, tomato, cucumber, wheat berries, and asparagus, tossing to coat well. Chill at least 2 hours before serving.

Makes 4 servings

Per serving: 153 calories, 7 g protein, 29 g carbohydrate, 2.5 g fat, 0.5 g saturated fat, 0 mg cholesterol, 890 mg sodium,* 8 g fiber

*Limit saturated fat to 10 percent of total calories—about 17 grams per day for most women—and sodium intake to less than 2,300 milligrams.

Italian Pasta Salad

190
Calories

—Jennifer Halloran, Bloomington, Indiana

Ready in minutes, this zesty salad is a great make-ahead dish for picnics and parties. If the salad seems dry, add ¼ cup more dressing just before serving.

Total time: 30 minutes

- 8 ounces whole-grain spiral pasta
- ½ cup chopped broccoli
- ½ cup chopped carrot
- ½ cup chopped tomato
- ½ cup chopped red bell pepper
- ½ cup chopped onion
- ½ cup shredded low-fat sharp Cheddar cheese
- 1 cup reduced-fat Italian dressing

PREPARE the pasta according to the package directions, omitting any salt. Drain, rinse under cold water, and drain.

STIR together the broccoli, carrot, tomato, pepper, onion, and cheese in a large bowl. Stir in the pasta and dressing, tossing to coat well.

Makes 8 servings

Per serving: 190 calories, 8 g protein, 25 g carbohydrate, 7 g fat, 1.5 g saturated fat, 5 mg cholesterol, 310 mg sodium, 3 g fiber

Bell Pepper Salad

—Nadine Hugley, Detroit, Michigan

Bursting with vibrant color, this salad is nice by itself or served on a bed of greens. Either way it's a tasty change of pace from tossed salads.

171 Calories

Total time: 15 minutes

- 4 boneless, skinless chicken breast halves, cooked and chopped
- 1 red bell pepper, thinly sliced
- 1 yellow bell pepper, thinly sliced
- 1 orange bell pepper, thinly sliced
- 1 onion, thinly sliced
- 1 Golden Delicious apple, chopped
- ⅔ cup light sweet Vidalia onion dressing
- ½ teaspoon ground black pepper
- ¼ teaspoon garlic powder

STIR together the chicken, bell peppers, onion, and apple in a large bowl. Add the dressing, black pepper, and garlic powder, tossing to coat well.

Makes 6 servings

Per serving: 171 calories, 27 g protein, 11 g carbohydrate, 2 g fat, 0.5 g saturated fat, 66 mg cholesterol, 245 mg sodium, 2 g fiber

---

SHOPPING SAVVY

A Filter That Flavors

Whenever you're feeling hungry, drink water first: It may not only quell your cravings but torch calories. A German study found that drinking 50 ounces of cold water can help you burn up to 50 extra calories a day—that's 5 pounds a year—without exercising. Experts attribute the metabolism boost to the extra effort needed to raise the water's temperature to 98.6°F. Prefer a sweeter sip than plain old water? With the new PUR Flavor Option Pitcher, you can pour a glass of plain, filtered tap water—or when the urge strikes, push a button to boost your drink's taste quotient with a blast of zero-calorie strawberry, peach, or raspberry flavoring. The flavor cartridges can be taken in and out so you can switch up flavors. For a store locator, visit purwater.com.

Grapefruit Spinach Salad with Creamy Dressing

—Maryalice Wood, Langley, British Columbia, Canada

"Nothing is more refreshing on a hot summer day than this salad. Pair it with grilled chicken and vegetables, a tall glass of lemonade, and good friends—you'll have it 'made in the shade'!"

Total time: 15 minutes + chilling time

DRESSING

- 2 grapefruit
- 2 teaspoons Dijon mustard
- 1 tablespoon honey
- 1 clove garlic, pressed
- ½ teaspoon lemon pepper seasoning
- ¼ cup fat-free lemon yogurt

SALAD

- 4 cups baby spinach leaves
- 1 cup sliced mushrooms
- ½ red onion, thinly sliced
- 2 tablespoons chopped fresh parsley
- 1 tablespoon bacon bits (optional)

TO MAKE THE DRESSING:

CUT the peel and white pith from the grapefruit. Holding the grapefruit over a medium bowl to catch the juice, cut between the membranes to release the segments and allow them to drop into the bowl. Squeeze the membranes to release any juices into the bowl. Transfer the segments to a plate with a slotted spoon. Reserve 3 tablespoons juice in the bowl. Whisk in the mustard, honey, garlic, and seasoning. Whisk in the yogurt until well combined. Refrigerate for at least 30 minutes for the flavors to blend.

TO MAKE THE SALAD:

DIVIDE the spinach among 4 plates. Top with the mushrooms, onion, and reserved grapefruit sections. Sprinkle with the parsley and bacon bits, if using. Drizzle with dressing just before serving.

Makes 4 servings

Per serving: 114 calories, 3 g protein, 27 g carbohydrate, 0 g fat, 0 g saturated fat, 0 mg cholesterol, 198 mg sodium, 4 g fiber

Creative Cauliflower Salad

162
Calories

—Joan L. Grube, Alexandria, Ohio

Cauliflower replaces potatoes in this take on classic potato salad. Our testers were amazed by how well this version tastes like the real thing from an old-fashioned church supper.

Total time: 50 minutes + chilling time

- **2** large heads cauliflower, cut into florets
- **2** cups fat-free salad dressing or mayonnaise
- **½** cup fat-free half-and-half
- **⅓** cup Splenda or other granular sugar substitute
- **2** tablespoons vinegar
- **2** tablespoons mustard
- **4** scallions, chopped
- **½** cup shredded carrot
- **3** hard-cooked eggs, chopped
- **3** hard-cooked egg whites, chopped
  Salt and ground black pepper

BRING the cauliflower and 4" salted water to a boil in a large pot over high heat. Reduce the heat to medium and cook for 12 to 15 minutes, or until tender. Drain; spread on a rimmed baking sheet and refrigerate for about 30 minutes.

STIR together the mayonnaise, half-and-half, Splenda, vinegar, and mustard in a large bowl. Add the cauliflower, scallions, carrot, eggs, and egg whites and gently toss to coat well. Season with salt and pepper to taste. Cover and refrigerate for 4 to 5 hours.

Makes 8 servings

Per serving: 162 calories, 9 g protein, 25 g carbohydrate, 4 g fat, 1 g saturated fat, 86 mg cholesterol, 717 mg sodium,* 7 g fiber

*Limit saturated fat to 10 percent of total calories—about 17 grams per day for most women—and sodium intake to less than 2,300 milligrams.

Spinach and Tomato Salad

—Elizabeth Clevenger, Oxnard, California

For a different flavor combination, use turkey bacon in place of the shrimp in this crunchy salad. Look for jícama, a South American root vegetable similar to a potato, in the ethnic section of the produce department.

188 Calories

Total time: 15 minutes

- 2 pounds spinach
- 2 large tomatoes, sliced
- 1 red bell pepper, thinly sliced
- 1 green bell pepper, thinly sliced
- 1 cup shredded jícama
- 4 ounces cooked peeled shrimp, coarsely chopped
- ½ cup low-calorie salad dressing, such as French, Italian, or ranch

COOK the spinach in a steamer basket placed over 1" boiling water for 5 minutes, or until wilted. Plunge into a bowl of ice water. Drain the spinach and squeeze any excess water from the spinach.

STIR together the tomatoes, peppers, jícama, shrimp, dressing, and spinach in a large bowl, tossing to coat well.

Makes 4 servings

Per serving: 188 calories, 14 g protein, 26 g carbohydrate, 6 g fat, 1 g saturated fat, 55 mg cholesterol, 571 mg sodium, 9 g fiber

NUTRITION NEWS TO USE

A recent study from the University of Queensland in Australia found that people who ate the most veggies, particularly leafy green ones, had a reduced risk of squamous cell carcinoma—a common type of skin cancer typically found on the face, ears, neck, and hands. The folate found in leafy greens also helps make new skin cells, which keeps your complexion looking fresh. For a skin-saving seasonal salad, pick up some spinach, mustard greens, or kale. Chop and toss with winter fruits like roasted pink grapefruit, blood oranges, sliced apples, or pomegranate seeds. Add beans or nuts for a plant-based protein boost. And top with avocado for healthy fats that help skin glow.

Gazpacho Salad

We turned a favorite chilled summer soup into a salad—with lots more fresh vegetables and spicy flavor. Loaded with juicy tomatoes, this dish requires just a hint of dressing.

Total time: 20 minutes + 1 hour chilling time

2½ cups chopped tomatoes

1 cup chopped red or yellow bell peppers

1 cup chopped green bell peppers

1 cup peeled, seeded, and chopped cucumbers

½ cup chopped onion

2 scallions, chopped

⅓ cup chopped fresh parsley

¼ cup chopped fresh basil

1 tablespoon lime juice or lemon juice

2 tablespoons balsamic vinegar

1 tablespoon honey

3 cloves garlic, minced

¼ teaspoon dried tarragon

3 cups torn leaf lettuce

¼ teaspoon salt

¼ teaspoon ground black pepper

MIX the tomatoes, bell peppers, cucumbers, onion, scallions, parsley, and basil in a large bowl.

MIX the lime juice, vinegar, honey, garlic, and tarragon in a small bowl. Pour over the vegetables. Cover and refrigerate for 1 hour.

ADD the lettuce, salt, and pepper just before serving. Toss well.

Makes 4 servings

Per serving: 88 calories, 3 g protein, 20 g carbohydrate, 1 g fat, 0 g saturated fat, 0 mg cholesterol, 169 mg sodium, 4 g fiber

Broccoli-Tomato Salad

241
Calories

—Donna Groden, West Melbourne, Florida

"My husband and I love this recipe—it's so easy to make and uses all-natural ingredients. Delicious, too!"

Total time: 20 minutes

- 1 **cup whole wheat penne pasta**
- 3 **tablespoons extra-virgin olive oil, divided**
- 1 **head broccoli, cut into bite-size pieces**
- 1 **onion, chopped**
- 2 **cloves garlic, minced**
- 1 **teaspoon red wine vinegar**
- ½ **teaspoon dried oregano**
    Pinch of red pepper flakes
- ½ **pint cherry tomatoes, halved**
- ¼ **cup shredded Parmesan cheese**

PREPARE the pasta according to the package directions. Drain, rinse under cold water, and drain again.

MEANWHILE, heat 2 tablespoons of the oil in a large skillet over medium-low heat. Cook the broccoli, onion, and garlic, stirring, for 3 minutes. Cover and cook 4 minutes longer, or until the broccoli is crisp-tender.

WHISK together the remaining 1 tablespoon oil, vinegar, oregano, and pepper flakes in a large bowl. Add the tomatoes, pasta, and broccoli mixture, tossing to coat well. Sprinkle with the cheese.

Makes 4 servings

Per serving: 241 calories, 9 g protein, 26 g carbohydrate, 13 g fat, 2.5 g saturated fat, 4 mg cholesterol, 141 mg sodium, 6 g fiber

Ruby Grapefruit and Crab Summer Salad

85 Calories

—Melinda Singer, Malibu, California

"The frisée and arugula give this salad a nice bite in contrast to the sweet crab."

Total time: 10 minutes

- 2 cups arugula
- 1 cup frisée lettuce, chopped
- ¼ cup fat-free or low-fat zesty Italian dressing
- 1 cup cooked crab or lump crab
- 20 grape tomatoes
- 1 red grapefruit, halved and sectioned
  Ground black pepper

TOSS together the arugula, lettuce, and dressing in a bowl. Divide among 4 salad plates. Top with the crab. Arrange the tomatoes and grapefruit around the crab. Season with pepper to taste.

Makes 4 servings

Per serving: 85 calories, 9 g protein, 11 g carbohydrate, 1 g fat, 0 g saturated fat, 21 mg cholesterol, 368 mg sodium, 2 g fiber

KITCHEN TIP

If desired, warm the crab slightly before placing on the lettuce.

Mediterranean Tuna Salad

293 Calories

—Hilda Andrade, Etobicoke, Ontario, Canada

"I am a 48-year-old grandmother who's recently lost 38 pounds (and it's still coming off). With the help of prevention.com and *Prevention* magazine, I've found that losing the weight is not that hard if you put your mind and soul into it!"

Total time: 10 minutes

- 3 tablespoons lemon juice
- 2 tablespoons extra-virgin olive oil
- 1 teaspoon Italian seasoning
- 1 can (15 ounces) mixed bean salad
- 2 cans (6 ounces each) light tuna packed in water, drained
- 5 cherry tomatoes, quartered
- 3 scallions, sliced
- 2 hard-cooked eggs, chopped
  Ground black pepper

WHISK together the lemon juice, oil, and Italian seasoning in a medium bowl. Add the mixed bean salad, tuna, tomatoes, and scallions, tossing to coat. Gently stir in the eggs. Season with pepper to taste.

Makes 4 servings

Per serving: 293 calories, 31 g protein, 19 g carbohydrate, 11 g fat, 2 g saturated fat, 132 mg cholesterol, 444 mg sodium, 5 g fiber

NUTRITION NEWS TO USE

Adding just $\frac{1}{2}$ tablespoon of lemon juice to each of your 8 daily cups of water provides nearly 20 percent of the daily value for vitamin C. This major antioxidant not only fights heart disease and boosts immunity but also helps form the collagen we need to heal tendons, ligaments, bones, and blood vessels. Squeeze two whole lemons in your tea, seltzer, or other beverages to get your daily vitamin C quota; fresh juice offers almost twice the C of bottled varieties.

Turbocharged Tuna Salad

326
Calories

—Linda J. Bottjer, Myrtle Beach, South Carolina

"I am 110 pounds lighter than I was 15 months ago, with another 80 pounds to go. Tuna has always been a favorite, especially when it's dripping with mayo and hard-boiled eggs and sandwiched between two pieces of hot buttered toast. Since that's no longer an option, reading *Prevention* has helped me figure out what I could add to make it healthier and still delicious."

Total time: 10 minutes

- 1½ tablespoons olive oil mayonnaise
- 1 teaspoon garlic and herb salt-free seasoning blend
- 2 cans (6 ounces each) solid white albacore tuna packed in water, drained
- 1 can (15.5 ounces) kidney beans or chickpeas, rinsed and drained
- 1½ cups fresh spinach, torn into bite-size pieces
- 1 tomato, chopped
- ½ cup chopped pecans

STIR together the mayonnaise and seasoning blend in a large bowl. Add the tuna, beans, spinach, tomato, and pecans, tossing to coat well.

Makes 4 servings

Per serving: 326 calories, 28 g protein, 16 g carbohydrate, 16 g fat, 1 g saturated fat, 54 mg cholesterol, 486 mg sodium, 6 g fiber

Grilled Sunburst Salmon Salad with Green Goddess Dressing

521 Calories

—Jennifer DePalma, Brooklyn, New York

Full of omega-3 fatty acids, this dish is an awesome way to sneak in a quick healthy meal, even on a weeknight. If you like, serve fillets in individual pieces; cut first before broiling.

Total time: 25 minutes

DRESSING

- ½ cup low-fat mayonnaise
- ½ bunch fresh cilantro
- ¼ cup lime juice
  Salt and ground black pepper

SALAD

- 1 lemon
- 1 lime
- ¼ cup extra-virgin olive oil
  Salt and ground black pepper
- 1¼ pounds salmon fillets
- 4 cups baby spinach leaves
- 1 can (10 ounces) mandarin oranges, drained
- 1 avocado, pitted, peeled, and sliced
- ½ cup grape tomatoes
- ¼ cup slivered almonds

TO MAKE THE DRESSING:

PLACE the mayonnaise, cilantro, and lime juice in a blender. Pulse until smooth. Season with salt and pepper to taste. Transfer to a small bowl, cover, and refrigerate until ready to serve.

TO MAKE THE SALAD:

ZEST the lemon and lime into an 8" x 8" glass baking dish. Squeeze the juice into the dish and add the oil. Season with salt and pepper to taste. Add the salmon, turning to coat. Set aside.

PREHEAT the grill or broiler. Grill or broil the salmon for 8 to 10 minutes, or until the fish flakes easily when tested with a fork.

DIVIDE the spinach, oranges, avocado, tomatoes, and almonds among 4 plates. Top each with salmon and drizzle with the dressing.

Makes 4 servings

Per serving: 521 calories, 32 g protein, 16 g carbohydrate, 37 g fat, 6 g saturated fat,* 94 mg cholesterol, 443 mg sodium, 5 g fiber

*Limit saturated fat to 10 percent of total calories—about 17 grams per day for most women—and sodium intake to less than 2,300 milligrams.

Spicy Cracked Wheat and Scallops Salad

478 Calories

—D.M. Ryan, Topsfield, Massachusetts

"Scallops are a wonderful seafood! With this nutritious salad, a few go a long way. The wheat and spice combination makes a great summertime salad that's unusual and welcoming."

Total time: 35 minutes

- 3 cups water
- 1½ cups medium-grind bulgur
- 4 slices bacon, diced
- ½ cup chopped onion
- 2 cloves garlic, minced
- ¼ cup dried cranberries
- ¼ cup dried apricots, coarsely chopped
- ¼ teaspoon ground cinnamon
- ¼ teaspoon ground cumin
- ¼ teaspoon red pepper flakes
- ½ teaspoon salt
- ¼ teaspoon ground black pepper
- ½ cup sunflower seeds, toasted
- ½ cup walnuts, toasted and coarsely chopped
- ⅓ cup walnut oil
- 2-3 tablespoons cider vinegar
- 2 tablespoons chopped fresh oregano
- 1 bag (10 ounces) mixed field greens
- 10 large sea scallops, halved lengthwise
- 4 lemon slices

BRING the water to a boil in a medium saucepan over high heat. Stir in the wheat. Reduce the heat to low, cover, and simmer for 10 minutes, or until the liquid is absorbed.

MEANWHILE, cook the bacon in a large skillet over medium heat for 3 minutes, or until crisp and browned. Use a slotted spoon to transfer the bacon to paper towels to drain. Place in a large serving bowl.

ADD the onion and garlic to the drippings remaining in the skillet and cook for 4 minutes, or until tender. Add the cranberries, apricots, cinnamon, cumin, pepper flakes, salt, and pepper; cook, stirring, for 3 minutes. Add to the bowl with the bacon. Stir in the sunflower seeds, walnuts, and the cooked wheat.

WHISK together the walnut oil, vinegar, and oregano in a small bowl. Pour over the wheat mixture, tossing to coat well.

LINE a serving plate with the greens. Top with the wheat mixture.

WIPE the skillet clean. Heat the skillet coated with cooking spray over medium-high heat. Cook the scallops in batches for 2 minutes, turning once, until opaque. Place on the wheat salad. Garnish with the lemon slices.

Makes 6 servings

Per serving: 478 calories, 15 g protein, 39 g carbohydrate, 31 g fat, 5 g saturated fat,* 19 mg cholesterol, 383 mg sodium, 10 g fiber

*Limit saturated fat to 10 percent of total calories—about 17 grams per day for most women—and sodium intake to less than 2,300 milligrams.

Greek Chicken and Chickpea Salad with Tomato Vinaigrette

270 Calories

—Sally Sibthorpe, Shelby Township, Michigan

The flavors of the Mediterranean shine in this easy main dish salad. Use lemon pepper seasoning instead of Greek seasoning, if you like.

Total time: 25 minutes

VINAIGRETTE

- ¼ cup lemon juice
- 2 tablespoons white balsamic vinegar
- 1 clove garlic, crushed
- ¾ teaspoon Greek seasoning
- ¼ cup tomato juice
- ¼ teaspoon salt (optional)
- ¼ cup olive oil

SALAD

- 1 cup canned chickpeas, rinsed and drained
- 2 cups chopped cooked chicken breast
- ½ cup chopped fresh flat-leaf parsley
- ½ cup shredded carrot
- ⅓ cup sliced radishes
- ⅓ cup thinly sliced scallions
- ⅓ cup grape or cherry tomatoes, halved
- ¼ cup pitted kalamata (or other) olives
- ¼ cup crumbled feta cheese
- 3 tablespoons chopped pistachios
- 3 cups spring mix

TO MAKE THE VINAIGRETTE:

WHISK together the lemon juice, vinegar, garlic, Greek seasoning, tomato juice, and salt, if using, until well blended. Whisk in the oil until emulsified. Set aside.

TO MAKE THE SALAD:

LIGHTLY mash the chickpeas in a medium bowl with a fork.

ADD the chicken, parsley, carrot, radishes, scallions, tomatoes, olives, cheese, and pistachios. Drizzle with half of the vinaigrette and toss to coat well.

PLACE the spring mix on a serving plate. Top with the chickpea mixture. Pass the remaining dressing for diners to use as desired.

Makes 6 servings

Per serving: 270 calories, 20 g protein, 13 g carbohydrate, 16 g fat, 3 g saturated fat, 47 mg cholesterol, 326 mg sodium, 3 g fiber

NUTRITION NEWS TO USE

Sprinkle pistachios on your salad— Pistachios are one of the best sources of plant sterols, compounds we know reduce absorption of cholesterol. Just remember, 1 ounce contains about 160 calories. So pour a little less dressing on your salad as you add some pistachios, or go easy on butter or oil on your veggies when you sprinkle them on top.

Shredded Chicken Salad

—Theresa Larsen, Redlands, California

"This is one of my favorite salads. I sometimes substitute dried cherries for the peas for an interesting change of pace."

Total time: 10 minutes

- ½ **pound macaroni salad**
- 1 **can (4.5 ounces) chunk chicken, drained**
- 1 **rib celery, chopped**
- ½ **cup cooked frozen peas**
- ½ **cup reduced-fat mayonnaise**
- ½ **teaspoon salt**
- ½ **teaspoon ground pepper**

STIR together the salad, chicken, celery, peas, mayonnaise, salt, and pepper in a large bowl. Chill at least 1 hour before serving.

Makes 2 servings

Per serving: 281 calories, 14 g protein, 29 g carbohydrate, 13 g fat, 3.5 g saturated fat,* 46 mg cholesterol, 826 mg sodium,* 3 g fiber

*Limit saturated fat to 10 percent of total calories—about 17 grams per day for most women—and sodium intake to less than 2,300 milligrams.

SHOPPING SAVVY

Making the Most of Marinades

Grilling's great for cooking with little or no added fat, and marinating adds layers of flavor and moisture to your favorite meats and even vegetables—and those made with good-for-you ingredients can raise the nutritional value of your grilled dish. A few of our favorite bottled sauces boost health and flavor.

For chicken: Drew's Sesame Orange Dressing and 10 Minute Marinade (140 calories, 14 grams fat per 2 tablespoons). This Asia-inspired sauce's oil base (canola and toasted sesame) hikes the fat and calories, so compensate by using less oil in salad dressings or sautéed dishes. For more information, visit chefdrew.com.

For pork: Stonewall Kitchen's Vidalia Onion Fig Sauce (60 calories, 2 grams fat). The rich flavor makes a great dipping sauce, too. For more information, visit stonewallkitchen.com.

For beef: Annie's Naturals Organic Mango Cilantro Marinade (40 calories, 1 gram fat). Sweet, mellow mango zipped up with cilantro and lime gives a tropical punch to grilled goods. For more information, visit consorzio.com.

Joanne Giannini

VITAL STATS
WEIGHT LOST:
55 pounds
HEIGHT: 5′4″
WEIGHT NOW:
129 pounds
HEALTH BONUS:
She has an
unbelievable
amount of
energy!

When Joanne Giannini met the man who would become her husband, she was fit and healthy. The ambitious pair decided to run a real estate business—and within 10 years owned 26 rental units! "My life became a constant stream of renovations; there was no time for healthy food or exercise."

After years of late-night pizzas and long workdays, Joanne had topped out at 184 pounds. "I could tell my husband wasn't crazy about the way I looked, which made me depressed," she recalls.

Finally, they took a rare break in New York. "I was relieved to focus on each other for a change," she says. "But the next day he said, 'I'm moving out.'" He told Joanne that, because of the weight she'd put on, he was no longer attracted to her. "I was devastated," she says.

About a month later, Joanne ran across some old exercise videos and decided to dust one off and give it a try again. "My mind was so cluttered with anger and pain, and exercising washed it away," she says. "It felt unbelievably good to stomp my feet and clear my head. I did the workouts daily—twice when I felt furious."

Before long, Joanne was shedding about 2 pounds each week—just the motivation she needed to take another look at her eating habits. Instead of chowing down on three heavy fast-food meals a day, she ate more often but lighter, with six healthful minimeals. Her mainstays: lean protein sources such as eggs and fish. She also experimented with veggie burgers and soy and started using more healthy fats, including olive oil and nuts. Fiber-rich breads, cereals, and oatmeal filled her up and kept her satisfied. "Over the months, my body changed dramatically," says Joanne. "I even bought bikinis, when before I hated being seen in a bathing suit—period. It was amazing to feel in control of my body and my life.

"I'm making time for things I love. I also own seven rental units of my own, and I work part-time. There may be less of me than before, but I'm capable of so much more!"

SOUPS
AND
STEWS

Chilled Beet Soup with Orange

270
Calories

Beat the heat during the dog days of summer with this easy puree of root vegetables sweetened with orange. If you can wait that long, let it stand overnight in the refrigerator. It gets even more flavorful as the seasonings blend.

Total time: 1 hour + chilling time

- ⅓ cup apple juice
- 1 teaspoon olive oil
- 4 cups chopped beets
- 2 cups chopped onions
- 1 cup chopped carrots
- 2 cloves garlic, minced
- 4 cups low-sodium chicken broth
- 2 tablespoons honey
- 1 teaspoon cider vinegar
- 4 large oranges
- ½ teaspoon ground black pepper
- ⅛ teaspoon salt
- ½ cup nonfat plain yogurt

BRING the apple juice and oil to a boil in a large pot over medium-high heat. Add the beets, onions, carrots, and garlic. Cook, stirring occasionally, for 5 minutes or until the onions are soft, but not browned. Add the broth, honey, and vinegar. When the mixture begins to boil, lower heat to medium and cook for 30 minutes or until the beets are very soft when pierced with a sharp knife.

MEANWHILE, grate 1 tablespoon of orange zest and set aside. Squeeze the juice from the oranges and set aside.

LET the soup cool slightly. Whirl in a blender or food processor, adding the reserved juice to combine. Cover and refrigerate for 3 hours, or until cold. Add the pepper and salt. Stir 2 tablespoons of yogurt into each serving, swirling slightly. Sprinkle each serving with orange rind.

Makes 4 servings

Per serving: 270 calories, 10 g protein, 5 g carbohydrate, 3 g fat, 0.5 g saturated fat, 0 mg cholesterol, 490 mg sodium, 8 g fiber

Minted Pea Soup

128 Calories

You can make this cool, pale green soup anytime with frozen peas. It's at its very best, though, prepared with locally grown fresh peas in June and July.

Total time: 25 minutes + chilling time

- 1 cup chopped onions
- 1/3 cup apple juice
- 1 teaspoon olive oil
- 2 cloves garlic, minced
- 3 cups fat-free reduced-sodium chicken broth
- 1 cup frozen diced potatoes
- 2 cups frozen peas
- 1/4 cup chopped fresh mint
- 1/2 teaspoon ground black pepper
- 1/4 teaspoon salt
- 1/4 cup fat-free plain yogurt

COOK the onions, apple juice, and oil in a Dutch oven over medium-high heat for 5 minutes, or until the onions are tender, stirring occasionally.

ADD the garlic and cook, stirring, for 1 minute. Add the broth and potatoes. Bring to a boil. Reduce the heat to low, cover, and simmer for 10 minutes. Stir in the peas and mint. Cook for 3 minutes, or until the peas are bright green.

PROCESS in a blender or food processor until very smooth. Pour into a large bowl. Stir in the pepper and salt. Cover and refrigerate for 2 hours, or until the soup is very cold. Top each serving with a dollop of the yogurt.

Makes 4 servings

Per serving: 128 calories, 6 g protein, 23 g carbohydrate, 2 g fat, 0.5 g saturated fat, 0 mg cholesterol, 579 mg sodium, 4 g fiber

Feel-Full Black Bean Soup

—Lizz McManus, Watertown, Massachusetts

168 Calories

"This is my absolute go-to recipe! It is quick, I usually have these ingredients on hand, it fills me up, and I have enough so I can eat it all week. Plus, it is great cold and great as a dip for vegetables!"

Total time: 50 minutes

- 2 tablespoons olive oil
- 2 ribs celery, chopped
- 2 carrots, chopped
- 1 small onion, chopped
- 2 cloves garlic, chopped
- 1 tablespoon grated fresh ginger
- 1 jalapeño pepper, finely chopped (wear plastic gloves when handling)
- $\frac{1}{8}$ teaspoon ground cinnamon
- $\frac{1}{8}$ teaspoon ground nutmeg
- $\frac{1}{8}$ teaspoon ground allspice
- $4\frac{1}{4}$ cups reduced-sodium vegetable or chicken broth
- 2 cans (15.5 ounces each) black beans, rinsed and drained
- 1 cup frozen corn
- 1 tablespoon chopped fresh cilantro
- 1 lime, sliced (optional)
- 1 avocado, pitted, peeled, and chopped (optional)

HEAT the oil in a large saucepan over medium-high heat. Add the celery, carrots, and onion; cook for 6 minutes, or until the onions are tender. Add the garlic, ginger, jalapeño, cinnamon, nutmeg, and allspice; cook, stirring, for 2 minutes, adding some broth if spices stick to bottom.

STIR in the broth and beans and bring to a simmer. Simmer for 20 minutes, or until the carrots are tender. Reserve 2 cups of the soup. Puree the remaining soup in a food processor or blender. Return to the saucepan with the reserved soup and corn. Cook over medium heat for 4 minutes, or until the corn is heated through. Stir in the cilantro.

GARNISH with lime and avocado, if using.

Makes 6 servings

Per serving: 168 calories, 7 g protein, 27 g carbohydrate, 5 g fat, 1 g saturated fat, 0 mg cholesterol, 474 mg sodium, 8 g fiber

Skinny Minny Minestrone Soup

259 Calories

—Jennifer DePalma, Brooklyn, New York

"A few years back, I lost 25 pounds, and it's healthy recipes like this soup—loaded with fiber and important vitamins and minerals—that help me keep the weight off."

Total time: 45 minutes

- 2 tablespoons extra-virgin olive oil
- 1 small onion, chopped
- 2 cloves garlic, minced
- 2 carrots, chopped
- 2 ribs celery, chopped
- 2 zucchini, chopped
- 2 yellow squash, chopped
- 8 ounces button mushrooms, sliced
- 1 can (28 ounces) crushed tomatoes
- 1 can (15 ounces) no-salt-added red kidney beans, rinsed and drained
- 1 bunch fresh flat-leaf parsley, chopped
  Salt and ground black pepper

HEAT the oil in a large pot over medium-high heat. Add the onion and garlic; cook for 2 minutes, or until the onions begin to soften. Stir in the carrots, celery, zucchini, squash, and mushrooms and cook for 3 minutes, until the vegetables begin to soften.

STIR in the tomatoes and beans, reduce the heat to low, and simmer for 30 minutes, or until the vegetables are very soft. Add the parsley and season with salt and pepper to taste.

Makes 4 servings

Per serving: 259 calories, 13 g protein, 40 g carbohydrate, 8 g fat, 1 g saturated fat, 0 mg cholesterol, 398 mg sodium, 14 g fiber

Italian Sausage, Bacon, and Bean Soup

262 Calories

—Charlene Chambers, Ormond Beach, Florida

Don't let the Italian sausage fool you. The lime juice, cilantro, and cumin lend a South-of-the-Border frame to this rib-sticking soup.

Total time: 45 minutes

- 1 can (15 ounces) no-salt-added black beans, rinsed and drained
- 1 can (15 ounces) no-salt-added red kidney beans, rinsed and drained
- 2 links hot Italian turkey sausage, skinned and broken up
- ½ cup chopped onion
- ¼ cup chopped carrot
- ¼ cup chopped celery
- 2 cloves garlic, minced
- 2 slices bacon, cooked and crumbled
- 1 can (14.5 ounces) reduced-sodium chicken broth
- 1 can (14.5 ounces) diced tomatoes
- 2 tablespoons chopped fresh cilantro
- 1 tablespoon tomato paste
- 1 tablespoon lime juice
- 1 teaspoon ground cumin
- ⅛ teaspoon ground red pepper
- ½ cup reduced-fat sour cream (optional)
  Cilantro leaves (optional)

MASH ¼ cup each of the black and kidney beans in a small bowl with a potato masher. Set aside.

COOK the sausage in a Dutch oven coated with cooking spray over medium heat for 5 minutes, or until no longer pink. Transfer to a plate.

RECOAT the Dutch oven with cooking spray. Add the onion, carrot, celery, and garlic and cook over medium-high heat for 3 minutes, or until tender. Stir in the bacon, broth, tomatoes, cilantro, tomato paste, lime juice, cumin, red pepper, mashed beans, and the remaining beans. Bring to a boil; reduce the heat to low. Stir in the sausage and simmer for 10 minutes, or until thickened.

SERVE topped with the sour cream and cilantro leaves, if using.

Makes 4 servings

Per serving: 262 calories, 20 g protein, 31 g carbohydrate, 6 g fat, 1 g saturated fat, 29 mg cholesterol, 863 mg sodium,* 12 g fiber

*Limit saturated fat to 10 percent of total calories—about 17 grams per day for most women—and sodium intake to less than 2,300 milligrams.

Spicy Lentil Soup

—Cristen Dutcher, Marietta, Georgia

Quick and fiber-rich, this soup is a perfect last-minute supper. And leftovers taste even better the next day. Round it out with a salad and thick slices of whole-grain bread.

219
Calories

Total time: 30 minutes

- 1 tablespoon olive oil
- ½ onion, finely chopped
- ⅓ cup chopped carrot
- ¼ cup chopped celery
- 2 cloves garlic, minced
- 3 cups reduced-sodium vegetable broth
- 1 cup dried green or red lentils, picked over and rinsed
- 1 can (4 ounces) green chiles, drained
- 1 tablespoon ground cumin
  Salt and ground black pepper

HEAT the oil in a large saucepan over medium-high heat. Add the onion, carrot, and celery and cook, stirring, for 5 minutes, or until tender. Add the garlic and cook, stirring, for 1 minute. Stir in the broth, lentils, chiles, and cumin. Bring to a boil.

REDUCE the heat to low, cover, and simmer for 10 to 15 minutes, or until the lentils are tender. Season with salt and pepper to taste.

Makes 4 servings

Per serving: 219 calories, 11 g protein, 34 g carbohydrate, 5 g fat,1 g saturated fat, 0 mg cholesterol, 312 mg sodium, 10 g fiber

Deanne's Hearty Slow-Cooked Lentil Soup

—Deanne O'Donnell, Greensburg, Pennsylvania

This soup is the perfect dish to have waiting for you when you get home. Just break out some crusty multigrain rolls for a satisfying meal—perfect for cold nights.

Total time: 8 hours

- 1 pound dried lentils, picked over and rinsed
- 4 potatoes, peeled and chopped
- 1 onion, coarsely chopped
- 2 carrots, coarsely chopped
- 2 ribs celery, coarsely chopped
- 6 cups water
- 4 reduced-sodium vegetable bouillon cubes
- 2 cloves garlic, minced
- 1½ teaspoons chopped fresh thyme or ½ teaspoon dried
- 1 teaspoon soy sauce
- 2 teaspoons nutritional yeast
- 4 teaspoons white rice vinegar
- 2 bay leaves
- ½ cup chopped fresh parsley
- 1 large bunch kale, stemmed and chopped

PLACE the lentils, potatoes, onion, carrots, celery, water, bouillon, garlic, thyme, soy sauce, yeast, vinegar, bay leaves, and parsley in a 5- to 7-quart slow cooker. Top with the kale. Cover and cook on high for 8 hours, or until the lentils and potatoes are tender. Stir to blend, discarding the bay leaves.

Makes 10 servings

Per serving: 233 calories, 15 g protein, 45 g carbohydrate, 1 g fat, 0 g saturated fat, 0 mg cholesterol, 455 mg sodium, 8 g fiber

South-of-the-Border Black Bean Chowder

199 Calories

—Mary Shivers, Ada, Oklahoma

"My family loves chowder, and this recipe adds delicious Mexican flavors that give it extra zip. It's completely meatless yet robust and hearty enough to be a meal in itself."

Total time: 50 minutes

- 2 tablespoons olive oil
- 2 cups chopped onions
- ½ cup chopped celery
- 1 clove garlic, minced
- 8 cups reduced-sodium chicken broth
- 3 medium potatoes, peeled and diced
- 2 teaspoons ground cumin
- ½ teaspoon ground black pepper
- ⅛ teaspoon ground red pepper
- 3 cans (15.5 ounces each) low-sodium black beans, rinsed and drained
- 1 can (4 ounces) diced green chiles
- ¼ cup jarred roasted red bell pepper, rinsed and diced
- ¼ cup chopped fresh cilantro
- ¼ cup chopped fresh parsley
- 1 cup low-fat sour cream (optional)
  Cilantro sprigs (optional)

HEAT the oil in a Dutch oven over medium-high heat. Add the onions and cook, stirring, for 5 minutes, or until tender. Stir in the celery and garlic; cook, stirring, for 3 minutes.

ADD the broth, potatoes, cumin, black pepper, and ground red pepper. Bring to a boil. Reduce the heat to medium and simmer for 30 minutes, or until the potatoes are very soft. Stir until the potatoes are small pieces and begin to thicken the soup.

STIR in the beans, chiles, bell pepper, cilantro, and parsley. Cook until the mixture just begins to boil. Remove from the heat. Ladle into bowls. Garnish each bowl with a dollop of sour cream and a cilantro sprig, if using.

Makes 8 servings

Per serving: 199 calories, 10 g protein, 33 g carbohydrate, 4 g fat, 0.5 g saturated fat, 0 mg cholesterol, 510 mg sodium, 8 g fiber

Wisconsin Cheese Chowder

111 Calories

Cheese lovers give four stars to this creamy chowder, which is thick with extra-sharp Cheddar and Swiss. Pureeing a small amount of the soup gives it a creamier texture.

Total time: 40 minutes

- 1 small red or green bell pepper, minced
- 1 small onion, minced
- 1 cup sliced celery
- ¼ cup apple juice
- 1 teaspoon minced garlic
- ⅓ cup all-purpose flour
- 2 cups reduced-sodium chicken broth
- 4 cups chopped potatoes
- 1 cup fat-free milk
- ¾ cup shredded extra-sharp low-fat Cheddar cheese
- ¼ cup shredded fat-free Swiss cheese

HEAT a Dutch oven coated with cooking spray over medium heat. Add the pepper, onion, celery, apple juice, and garlic. Cook, stirring, for 5 minutes. Add the flour and ½ cup of the broth. Cook, stirring, for 2 minutes.

STIR in the potatoes and the remaining 1½ cups broth. Bring to a boil. Cover and cook for 20 minutes, or until the potatoes are tender.

TRANSFER 1 cup of the soup to a blender or food processor. Process until smooth. Return to the pot. Stir in the milk and cheeses. Cook, stirring, for 3 minutes, or until the cheese melts.

Makes 8 servings

Per serving: 111 calories, 6 g protein, 19 g carbohydrate, 1 g fat, 0.5 g saturated fat, 4 mg cholesterol, 191 mg sodium, 2 g fiber

Roasted Garlic Soup with Turkey

105 Calories

Roasted garlic adds velvety texture and a sweet garlic flavor to soup. When garlic is in season in late spring and early summer, roast extra and freeze the puree for up to 1 year.

Total time: 1 hour 45 minutes

- 4 whole heads garlic
- 1 teaspoon olive oil
- 4 cups reduced-sodium chicken broth
- 2 carrots, sliced
- 1 small onion, sliced
- 1 cup corn
- 4 ounces turkey cutlets, chopped
- ½ cup chopped fresh parsley
- ¼ teaspoon salt
- ¼ teaspoon ground black pepper

PREHEAT the oven to 350°F. Slice the top ¼" off each head of garlic with a sharp knife; discard the tops. Lightly brush the heads with the oil. Place in a shallow baking dish. Bake, covered with foil, for 55 to 60 minutes. Remove the foil and bake for 10 minutes, or until the garlic skin is browned and the interior is very soft. Set aside until cool enough to handle. Squeeze the cloves to release the roasted garlic; discard the skin.

PROCESS the garlic and 1 cup of the broth in a blender or food processor until smooth. Cook the carrots, onion, corn, and 1 cup of the broth in a Dutch oven, stirring, over medium-high heat for 10 minutes, or until the onions are tender. Add the turkey, garlic mixture, and the remaining 2 cups broth. Bring to a boil. Reduce the heat to medium and simmer, stirring occasionally, for 20 minutes, or until the turkey is cooked through. Stir in the parsley, salt, and pepper.

Makes 6 servings

Per serving: 105 calories, 8 g protein, 15 g carbohydrate, 1 g fat, 0 g saturated fat, 8 mg cholesterol, 548 mg sodium, 2 g fiber

Asian Stone Soup

—Charlotte E. Halliday, Hermosa Beach, California

"I came up with this recipe (my version of egg drop soup) when I was on the Atkins diet and wanted something different to eat. I needed something new to do with eggs! I love this recipe because it is simple and fast and can be made with whatever vegetables are on hand."

43 Calories

Total time: 25 minutes

  4 cups reduced-sodium chicken broth
 ¼ head cabbage, shredded
  1 carrot, shredded
  1 rib celery, chopped
 ¼ teaspoon Thai chili paste or chili garlic paste
  2 large eggs, lightly beaten

BRING the broth to a simmer in a medium saucepan over medium-low heat. Add the cabbage, carrot, and celery. Cover and cook for 15 to 20 minutes, or until the cabbage is tender. Stir in the chili paste.

REMOVE the saucepan from the heat. Stir the soup and slowly add the eggs in a thin stream (it will cook as soon as it hits the broth).

Makes 6 servings

Per serving: 43 calories, 3 g protein, 4 g carbohydrate, 2 g fat, 0.5 g saturated fat, 71 mg cholesterol, 344 mg sodium, 1 g fiber

Festive Vegetable Stew

175 Calories

—Charlene Chambers, Ormond Beach, Florida

This flavorful dish uses the oil from oil-packed sun-dried tomatoes to add rich flavor. If you don't have the oil-packed type, use olive oil instead.

Total time: 55 minutes + standing time

- 1 large eggplant, coarsely chopped
- 3 large zucchini, coarsely chopped
- 1 teaspoon salt
- 2 ounces julienned sun-dried tomatoes in oil, drained, with 3 tablespoons oil reserved
- 1 onion, sliced
- 2 cloves garlic, chopped
- 1 large red bell pepper, coarsely chopped
- 1 large yellow bell pepper, coarsely chopped
- 1 can (14.5 ounces) diced fire-roasted tomatoes
- 1 teaspoon coriander seeds, crushed
- 1 fresh rosemary sprig
- 1 fresh thyme sprig
  Salt and ground black pepper
- ¼ cup fresh basil leaves, chopped
  Fresh Italian parsley sprigs (optional)

SPRINKLE the eggplant and zucchini with the salt in a large colander. Top them with a heavy skillet to extract bitter juices. Let stand for about 20 minutes. Rinse and pat dry.

HEAT the reserved tomato oil in a large saucepan over medium-high heat. Add the onion and cook for 5 minutes, or until tender. Add the garlic and cook, stirring, for 2 minutes. Stir in the peppers, eggplant, and zucchini. Cook, stirring, for 5 minutes, or until lightly browned. Stir in the diced tomatoes, coriander seeds, rosemary, and thyme. Reduce the heat to medium-low and simmer for 30 minutes.

STIR in the sun-dried tomatoes and salt and pepper to taste. Simmer for 10 minutes. Stir in the basil. Garnish with parsley, if using.

Makes 6 servings

Per serving: 175 calories, 5 g protein, 22 g carbohydrate, 9 g fat, 1.5 g saturated fat, 0 mg cholesterol, 567 mg sodium, 8 g fiber

Three-Bean Chili

—Cristen Dutcher, Marietta, Georgia

215
Calories

"This recipe is my healthy alternative to meat-based chili and is full of fiber to satisfy even a manly hunger."

Total time: 30 minutes

- 2 **tablespoons olive oil**
- 1 **onion, chopped**
- 2 **tablespoons chili powder**
- 1 **tablespoon ground cumin**
- 1 **teaspoon ground cinnamon**
- 1 **can (4 ounces) chopped green chiles**
- 1 **can (15.5 ounces) black beans, rinsed and drained**
- 1 **can (15.5 ounces) dark kidney beans, rinsed and drained**
- 1 **can (15.5 ounces) pinto beans, rinsed and drained**
- 1 **can (14.5 ounces) no-salt-added diced tomatoes**
- 1 **can (15.5 ounces) no-salt-added tomato sauce**
  - **Salt and ground black pepper**
- 1 **cup shredded low-fat Monterey Jack cheese**
  - **Baked tortilla chips (optional)**

HEAT the oil in a Dutch oven over medium heat. Add the onion and cook, stirring, for 5 minutes, or until tender. Stir in the chili powder, cumin, and cinnamon and cook, stirring, for 1 minute. Stir in the chiles, beans, tomatoes, and tomato sauce and bring to a simmer. Cook for 15 minutes, or until flavors blend. Season with salt and pepper to taste.

PREHEAT the broiler.

DIVIDE the chili among 4 ovenproof ramekins or bowls. Place on a baking sheet and sprinkle each with ¼ cup cheese. Broil for 2 minutes, or until the cheese melts. Serve with the tortilla chips, if using.

Makes 4 servings

Per serving: 215 calories, 11 g protein, 27 g carbohydrate, 7 g fat, 2 g saturated fat, 10 mg cholesterol, 564 mg sodium, 9 g fiber

White Chicken Chili

308 Calories

—Judith Mueller, Alliance, Ohio

"I recently began the South Beach Diet eating plan and came up with this recipe on Phase I. It tastes great, is very flavorful, and has made following the diet a bit easier for me. My family loves it, too!"

Total time: 50 minutes

- 1 tablespoon olive oil
- ½ cup chopped celery
- ½ cup chopped onion
- ½ cup chopped red or green bell pepper
- 1 can (14.5 ounces) diced tomatoes
- 1 can (14.5 ounces) reduced-sodium chicken broth
- 1 cup fat-free refried beans
- 12 ounces cooked boneless skinless chicken breasts, shredded
- 1 cup canned no-salt-added black beans, rinsed and drained
- 2 teaspoons chili powder
- 1 teaspoon garlic powder
- 1 teaspoon chopped fresh cilantro
- 1 teaspoon ground cumin
- 1 teaspoon lime juice
  Ground black pepper
- ¼ cup reduced-fat sour cream
- ¼ cup reduced-fat Cheddar cheese

HEAT the oil in a Dutch oven over medium-high heat. Add the celery, onion, and bell pepper and cook for 5 minutes, or until tender.

STIR in the tomatoes and broth; bring to a simmer. Slowly stir in the refried beans until incorporated into the soup. Add the chicken, beans, chili powder, garlic powder, cilantro, cumin, and lime juice. Cover and simmer for 30 minutes, stirring occasionally. Season with pepper to taste.

GARNISH each serving with 1 tablespoon sour cream and 1 tablespoon cheese.

Makes 4 servings

Per serving: 308 calories, 31 g protein, 26 g carbohydrate, 8 g fat, 3 g saturated fat, 60 mg cholesterol, 895 mg sodium,* 8 g fiber

*Limit saturated fat to 10 percent of total calories—about 17 grams per day for most women—and sodium intake to less than 2,300 milligrams.

Sweet Potato Chili with Pork and Black Beans

325 Calories

—Linda Croley, Hoover, Alabama

Try ground turkey in place of the pork in this hearty chili—either way it's delicious topped with shredded low-fat Cheddar cheese or your favorite chili fixings.

Total time: 50 minutes

- 1 pound ground pork or turkey
- 2 tablespoons olive oil
- 1 onion, chopped
- 1½ cups peeled and cubed sweet potato
- 2 tablespoons mild chili powder
- 1 teaspoon salt
- 1 teaspoon garlic powder
- ¼ teaspoon hot chili powder or cayenne pepper
- ⅛ teaspoon ground cloves
- ⅛ teaspoon ground cinnamon
- ½ teaspoon ground cumin
- ½ teaspoon ground black pepper
- 2 cups water
- 1 can (15.5 ounces) black beans, rinsed and drained
- 1 can (14.5 ounces) reduced-sodium chicken broth
- 2 chipotle chiles in adobo sauce, chopped

COOK the pork in a large nonstick skillet over medium heat, breaking up the pieces, for 5 minutes, or until no longer pink. Drain and place in a bowl; set aside.

HEAT the oil in the same skillet over medium heat. Add the onion and cook for 5 minutes, or until tender. Add the sweet potato and cook, stirring, for 5 minutes. Stir in the mild chili powder, salt, garlic powder, hot chili powder, cloves, cinnamon, cumin, black pepper, and the pork. Cook for 5 minutes.

STIR in the water, beans, broth, and chiles. Bring to a boil. Reduce the heat to low, cover, and simmer for 20 minutes.

Makes 6 servings

Per serving: 325 calories, 17g protein, 17 g carbohydrate, 21 g fat, 7 g saturated fat,* 54 mg cholesterol, 244 mg sodium, 4 g fiber

*Limit saturated fat to 10 percent of total calories—about 17 grams per day for most women—and sodium intake to less than 2,300 milligrams.

Turkey Sausage Stew

235
Calories

There are so many flavors of turkey or chicken sausage available today. You could go the traditional route with sweet Italian turkey sausage or try something more unusual like turkey-Cheddar or chicken-spinach-feta.

Total time: 55 minutes

- 12 ounces turkey or chicken sausage, chopped
- 4 cups reduced-sodium chicken broth
- 1 cup chopped onions
- 1 cup sliced carrots
- 1 cup cauliflower florets
- 1 can (16 ounces) whole tomatoes, chopped
- 1 can (15.5 ounces) navy beans, rinsed and drained
- 1 small eggplant, coarsely chopped
- 1 clove garlic, minced
- 2 teaspoons Italian herb seasoning
- ½ teaspoon ground cumin
- ¼ cup grated Parmesan cheese

COOK the sausage in a Dutch oven coated with cooking spray over medium-high heat, stirring, for 5 to 8 minutes, or until the sausage is browned. Add ½ cup of the broth. Bring to a boil, scraping to loosen any browned bits from the bottom.

ADD the onions, carrots, and cauliflower. Cook, stirring, for 5 minutes, or until the onions are tender. Add the tomatoes, beans, eggplant, garlic, seasoning, cumin, and the remaining 3½ cups broth. Bring to a boil. Reduce the heat to medium. Cook, stirring occasionally, for 30 to 40 minutes, or until thick. Serve sprinkled with the cheese.

Makes 6 servings

Per serving: 235 calories, 19 g protein, 26 g carbohydrate, 6 g fat, 2 g saturated fat, 45 mg cholesterol, 1106 mg sodium,* 8 g fiber

*Limit saturated fat to 10 percent of total calories—about 17 grams per day for most women—and sodium intake to less than 2,300 milligrams.

Mexican Beef Stew with Garlic Spanish Rice

360 Calories

—Susan Riley, Allen, Texas

"I love very flavorful foods because they make me feel more satisfied. The bold flavors of Mexico are highlighted in this dish. If you can't find Mexican oregano, any other oregano will do."

Total time: 2 hours

STEW

2 teaspoons olive oil

1½ pounds chuck steak, trimmed of fat and cut into ¾" cubes

2 cloves garlic, minced

½ small onion, chopped

1 can (14.5 ounces) crushed tomatoes

1 cup water

1 tablespoon dried Mexican oregano

1 teaspoon salt

1 teaspoon ground black pepper

RICE

2 cups water

1 cup rice

2 cloves garlic, pressed

¼ cup prepared salsa

½ teaspoon salt

TO MAKE THE STEW:

HEAT the oil in a Dutch oven over medium-high heat. Add the steak and cook for 5 minutes, or until well browned on all sides. Add the garlic and onion and cook, stirring, for 2 minutes. Stir in the tomatoes and water. Reduce the heat to low, cover, and simmer for 1½ hours. (Add a little water if the stew becomes too dry.) Stir in the oregano, salt, and pepper and simmer, covered, for 20 minutes.

TO MAKE THE RICE:

BRING the water to a boil in a medium saucepan. Stir in the rice, garlic, salsa, and salt. Reduce the heat to low, cover, and simmer for 20 minutes, or until all the liquid is absorbed. Serve the stew over the rice.

Makes 6 servings

Per serving: 360 calories, 25 g protein, 32 g carbohydrate, 14 g fat, 5 g saturated fat,* 75 mg cholesterol, 797 mg sodium,* 2 g fiber

*Limit saturated fat to 10 percent of total calories—about 17 grams per day for most women—and sodium intake to less than 2,300 milligrams.

Irish Beef Stew

375
Calories

Potatoes and carrots are the hearty foundation of this warming stew. To cut fat but not flavor, lean beef is used instead of the traditional lamb.

Total time: 1 hour

- 3 **pounds lean boneless beef chuck roast, trimmed of fat and cut into 1" pieces**
- 3 **tablespoons all-purpose flour**
- 2 **tablespoons olive oil**
- 1 **cup reduced-sodium beef broth**
- 3 **cups chopped onions**
- 1 **clove garlic, minced**
- 1 **can (28 ounces) whole tomatoes, chopped**
- 3 **cups cubed red potatoes**
- ½ **cup chopped carrot**
- ½ **teaspoon salt**
- ½ **teaspoon ground black pepper**
- ¼ **teaspoon ground red pepper**

DREDGE the beef in the flour in a resealable bag, coating all sides. Shake off the excess. Heat the oil in a Dutch oven over medium-high heat. Add the beef and cook, stirring, for 5 minutes, or until browned. Transfer to a plate.

STIR the broth into the pot. Bring to a boil, scraping to loosen any browned bits from the bottom. Add the onions and garlic; cook, stirring, for 5 minutes, or until the onions are tender. Add the tomatoes, potatoes, carrot, and beef. Bring to a boil. Reduce the heat to medium-low, cover, and simmer for 35 minutes, or until the beef is tender. Stir in the salt, black pepper, and red pepper.

Makes 8 servings

Per serving: 375 calories, 41 g protein, 23 g carbohydrate, 12 g fat, 4 g saturated fat,* 92 mg cholesterol, 535 mg sodium, 3 g fiber

*Limit saturated fat to 10 percent of total calories—about 17 grams per day for most women—and sodium intake to less than 2,300 milligrams.

SNACKS
SANDWICHES
PIZZAS
AND SIDES

Strawberry Popcorn

37 Calories

—Kristina Hendershot, Marietta, Ohio

"I've lost 45 pounds but had lost my momentum until entering this contest. It's reminded me that there were plenty of healthy recipes I made in the past and I can start all over again!"

Total time: 5 minutes

- 6 cups air-popped popcorn
- 1 box (0.3 ounce) sugar-free strawberry gelatin

  Salt

PLACE the popcorn in a resealable plastic bag. Spray with butter-flavored cooking spray and sprinkle with the gelatin. Sprinkle with salt to taste. Seal and shake to coat.

Makes 6 servings

Per serving: 37 calories, 2 g protein, 6 g carbohydrate, 0.5 g fat, 0 g saturated fat, 0 mg cholesterol, 130 mg sodium, 1 g fiber

Barbecued Popcorn

Forget potato chips. Here's another way to turn plain air-popped corn into a zesty treat with a mixture of sweet and spicy sauces.

55 Calories

Total time: 55 minutes

- 2 tablespoons molasses
- 2 tablespoons reduced-sodium barbecue sauce
- 1 tablespoon reduced-sodium ketchup
- ½ teaspoon paprika
- ½ teaspoon garlic powder
- 8 cups air-popped popcorn

PREHEAT the oven to 200°F. Line a large baking sheet with foil and coat with cooking spray.

STIR together the molasses, barbecue sauce, ketchup, paprika, and garlic powder in a large bowl. Add the popcorn and toss to coat. Spread the popcorn mixture on the prepared sheet. Bake for 20 minutes. Turn off the oven and let the popcorn cool in the oven for 30 minutes, or until crisp.

Makes 8 servings

Per serving: 55 calories, 1 g protein, 12 g carbohydrate, 0 g fat, 0 g saturated fat, 0 mg cholesterol, 72 mg sodium, 1 g fiber

Healthy Spinach Artichoke Dip

136
Calories

—Katherine J. Bright, Austin, Texas

"I first made this recipe for a tailgating football party. I received so many compliments that I have continued to make it for social occasions, and people can't even tell it's a reduced-fat recipe!"

Total time: 2 hours 5 minutes

- 2 cups shredded reduced-fat mozzarella
- 1 container (8 ounces) reduced-fat onion and chive cream cheese
- ¼ cup grated Parmesan cheese
- ¼ large onion, chopped
- 1 bag (10 ounces) frozen spinach, thawed
- 1 can (13.75 ounces) artichoke hearts, drained and chopped
- ¼ teaspoon garlic powder
- ¼ teaspoon ground red pepper
  Salt and ground black pepper
  Baked tortilla chips (optional)
  Celery and carrot sticks (optional)

STIR together the mozzarella, cream cheese, Parmesan, onion, spinach, artichokes, garlic powder, and red pepper in a 3- to 5-quart slow cooker. Season with salt and pepper to taste. Cover and cook on high for 2 hours, stirring occasionally, until heated through. Serve warm with tortilla chips or celery and carrot sticks.

Makes 12 servings

Per serving: 136 calories, 11 g protein, 7 g carbohydrate, 8 g fat, 5 g saturated fat,* 30 mg cholesterol, 527 mg sodium, 2 g fiber

*Limit saturated fat to 10 percent of total calories—about 17 grams per day for most women—and sodium intake to less than 2,300 milligrams.

Black Bean Fruit Salsa Dip

143 Calories

—Cristen Dutcher, Marietta, Georgia

"I love Mexican flavors and wanted a healthier dip for parties and entertaining. This one is spicy, fresh, and delicious—no one will miss the cheese or chips!"

Total time: 10 minutes

- 1 tablespoon olive oil
- ¼ cup yellow onion, chopped
- 2 cloves garlic, minced
- ½ teaspoon ground cumin
- 1 can (15.5 ounces) black beans, rinsed and drained
- ¼ teaspoon ground red pepper
  Vegetable broth or water (2–3 tablespoons)
- 1 mango, peeled, seeded, and chopped
- ½ red onion, finely chopped
- 1 jalapeño pepper, finely chopped (wear plastic gloves when handling)
- ¼ cup chopped fresh cilantro
  Salt and ground black pepper
  Sliced bell pepper, celery, fennel, and baby carrots (optional)
  Whole-grain crackers (optional)

HEAT the oil in a medium skillet over medium-high heat. Add the yellow onion, garlic, and cumin and cook for 5 minutes, or until the onion is tender.

PUREE the beans, red pepper, and onion mixture in a food processor or blender until smooth. Add 1 tablespoon broth at a time to thin the mixture if too thick. Place in a medium bowl.

STIR together the mango, red onion, jalapeño, and cilantro in a small bowl. Season with salt and pepper to taste. Spread over the bean mixture. Serve with vegetables and crackers, if using.

Makes 4 servings

Per serving: 143 calories, 5 g protein, 25 g carbohydrate, 4 g fat, 0.5 g saturated fat, 0 mg cholesterol, 379 mg sodium, 6 g fiber

Smokin' Saltines

145
Calories

—Jillian Bartlett, Trion, Georgia

"The reason I like this recipe is that the pepper really makes me feel full. I can munch on a couple between meals and it will satisfy me. The ingredients are healthy, and they really taste great. You can't beat that combination!"

Total time: 10 minutes + standing time

- 1 box saltine crackers, unsalted tops
- 1⅓ cups canola oil
- 1 package ranch dressing mix
- 2 tablespoons crushed red pepper
- 2 tablespoons ground red pepper

PLACE the saltines in a large container with a lid, such as an empty gallon ice cream container. Stir together the oil, ranch dressing mix, and red peppers in a medium bowl. Pour the mixture over the saltines. Cover with the lid and roll the container gently back and forth to coat crackers as evenly as possible. Let the crackers stand for a few hours until the liquid is absorbed.

Makes 30 servings (4 per serving)

Per serving: 145 calories, 1 g protein, 9 g carbohydrate, 11 g fat, 1 g saturated fat, 0 mg cholesterol, 139 mg sodium, 1 g fiber

Shrimp Toasts

A favorite appetizer at Chinese restaurants, shrimp toasts are inexpensive and simple to make with frozen shrimp.

51 Calories

Total time: 10 minutes

8 slices whole wheat bread
8 ounces frozen peeled and cooked medium shrimp, thawed
1 egg white
1 teaspoon minced fresh ginger
½ teaspoon minced garlic
¼ teaspoon salt
¼ teaspoon ground black pepper
2 tablespoons minced scallion

PREHEAT the broiler. Cut the bread slices in half diagonally and arrange on a large baking sheet. Process the shrimp, egg white, ginger, garlic, salt, and pepper in a blender or food processor until smooth. Transfer to a medium bowl. Stir in the scallion. Spread on the bread. Broil 4" from the heat for 3 minutes, or until golden brown.

Makes 8 servings

Per serving: 51 calories, 5 g protein, 6 g carbohydrate, 1 g fat, 0 g saturated fat, 22 mg cholesterol, 127 mg sodium, 1 g fiber

Low-Carb Baked Teriyaki Hot Wings

188 Calories

—Christine Fontanin, Viera, Florida

"I love buffalo-style chicken wings; however, restaurant teriyaki wings are full of sugar and often fried. After a few trials, I came up with these no-sugar, low-carb ones."

Total time: 35 minutes

- 1 **pound chicken drummettes**
- 4 **tablespoons butter or margarine, melted**
- ½ **cup hot sauce**
- ⅓ **cup light soy sauce**
- 15 **drops liquid artificial sweetener**
  Tabasco sauce (optional)

PREHEAT the oven to 400°F. Place the drummettes on a large rimmed baking sheet. Bake for 30 minutes, turning once, until cooked through.

STIR together the butter, hot sauce, soy sauce, sweetener, and Tabasco, if using, in a large glass or metal bowl. Add the hot wings and toss to coat.

Makes 8 servings

Per serving: 188 calories, 11 g protein, 1 g carbohydrate, 15 g fat, 6 g saturated fat,* 58 mg cholesterol, 957 mg sodium,* 0 g fiber

*Limit saturated fat to 10 percent of total calories—about 17 grams per day for most women—and sodium intake to less than 2,300 milligrams.

Freshly Minted Turkey Lettuce Wraps with Asian Pear

95 Calories

—Janice Elder, Charlotte, North Carolina

"After a 30-pound weight loss a few years ago, I'm vigilant about not gaining the weight back, and this is one of my favorite treats—filling, fun, and delicious. It can also be used as a light entrée, serving about four generously."

Total time: 20 minutes

- 1 **pound deli turkey, sliced into 4 thick pieces and chopped**
- 1 **onion, finely chopped**
- 1 **tablespoon grated fresh ginger**
- 1 **clove garlic, minced**
- ¼ **cup hoisin sauce**
- ⅓ **cup barbecue sauce**
- 1 **large Asian pear, peeled and finely chopped**
- 1 **tablespoon lime juice**
- ¾ **cup peeled, seeded, and chopped cucumber**
- ¼ **cup torn fresh mint leaves**
- ¼ **cup slivered almonds, lightly toasted**
- 12 **large Boston, butter, or iceberg lettuce leaves, well chilled**

HEAT a large nonstick skillet coated with cooking spray over medium heat. Add the turkey and onion and cook, stirring, for 5 minutes, or until the onion is tender. Stir in the ginger, garlic, hoisin, and barbecue sauce. Reduce the heat to low. Simmer for 5 minutes (add a spoonful of water if the mixture begins to look dry).

MEANWHILE, stir together the Asian pear and lime juice; place in a small serving bowl and set aside.

REMOVE the turkey mixture from the heat. Stir in the cucumber, mint, and almonds.

TO serve, spoon the warm turkey mixture into the lettuce leaves and top with the pear mixture.

Makes 12 servings

Per serving: 95 calories, 8 g protein, 13 g carbohydrate, 2 g fat, 0 g saturated fat, 15 mg cholesterol, 631 mg sodium,* 2 g fiber

*Limit saturated fat to 10 percent of total calories—about 17 grams per day for most women—and sodium intake to less than 2,300 milligrams.

French Roasted Vegetable Sandwiches

219 Calories

This easy sandwich, inspired by those served in the south of France, makes a great brown-bag lunch because it keeps for several hours without getting soggy. Cut into smaller portions, it's an out-of-the-ordinary party appetizer.

Total time: 55 minutes + chilling time

- 1 small eggplant, peeled and cut into thick slices
- 1 red bell pepper, quartered
- 1 tomato, halved
- 1 small onion, cut into thick slices
- 2 tablespoons olive oil
- 2 teaspoons minced garlic
- ½ teaspoon dried rosemary, crushed
- 1 round loaf Italian bread (8" diameter)
- 2 tablespoons fat-free plain yogurt
- 3 tablespoons balsamic vinegar
- 2 teaspoons grated Parmesan cheese
- ½ cup tightly packed spinach leaves

PREHEAT the oven to 400°F. Coat a large baking sheet with cooking spray.

ARRANGE the eggplant, pepper, tomato, and onion on the sheet. Brush with the oil. Sprinkle with the garlic and rosemary. Bake for 45 minutes, or until browned and tender.

SPLIT the bread horizontally and scoop out the interior, leaving a 1" shell. (Reserve the interior for another use.) Spread the yogurt over the bottom of the shell. Sprinkle with the vinegar. Arrange the vegetables in the bottom of the shell. Sprinkle with the cheese. Top with the spinach. Place the top of the bread over the filling. Wrap tightly in plastic wrap and refrigerate for 30 minutes, or until chilled. Cut into 8 wedges.

Makes 8 servings

Per serving: 219 calories, 6 g protein, 36 g carbohydrate, 6 g fat, 1 g saturated fat, 1 mg cholesterol, 346 mg sodium, 4 g fiber

Skillet Antipasto in Whole-Grain Sandwich Pockets

269 Calories

—Barbara Estabrook, Rhinelander, Wisconsin

"I love this sandwich because it's full of fiber and extremely low in fat and calories. It'll fill you up and leave you feeling satisfied for hours."

Total time: 40 minutes + standing and chilling time

- 2 cups cubed eggplant
- ½ teaspoon salt
- 1 tablespoon olive oil
- ¾ cup thinly sliced red onion
- ½ cup chopped yellow squash
- ¼ cup thinly sliced green bell pepper
- ¼ cup thinly sliced red bell pepper
- ¾ cup thinly sliced baby portobello mushrooms
- 1 clove garlic, minced
- 1 cup diced canned tomatoes, well drained
- 2 tablespoons extra-dry vermouth (optional)
- ½ cup canned chickpeas, rinsed and drained
- ¼ cup sliced black olives
- 1 tablespoon chopped fresh basil
- 1 tablespoon chopped fresh oregano
- ½ teaspoon ground black pepper
- ¼ cup crumbled feta cheese
- 6 whole-grain pitas (6" diameter)
- 6 red lettuce leaves

PLACE the eggplant in a colander and sprinkle with the salt, tossing to coat. Place the colander on a plate to catch the liquid. Let stand for 30 minutes to draw out moisture. Pat the cubes with paper towels.

HEAT the oil in a large nonstick skillet over medium-high heat. Add the onion, squash, and bell peppers. Cook, stirring, for 5 minutes. Stir in the mushrooms, garlic, and eggplant. Cook, stirring, for 5 minutes, or until the eggplant begins to soften.

ADD the tomatoes, vermouth, and chickpeas. Reduce the heat to medium-low, cover, and simmer for 25 minutes, stirring occasionally. Stir in the olives, basil, oregano, and pepper. Cook for 5 minutes to blend flavors. Transfer to a medium bowl. Cool, cover, and refrigerate for 3 hours. Stir in the cheese.

CUT ½" off the top of each pita. Open the pitas carefully. Slide a lettuce leaf into each pocket and fill with a scant ½ cup antipasto.

Makes 6 servings

Per serving: 269 calories, 10 g protein, 47 g carbohydrate, 6.5 g fat, 2 g saturated fat, 6 mg cholesterol, 765 mg sodium,* 8 g fiber

*Limit saturated fat to 10 percent of total calories—about 17 grams per day for most women—and sodium intake to less than 2,300 milligrams.

Buffalo and Blue Chicken Wraps

376 Calories

—Jenny L. Miller, Columbia, Missouri

"I am a personal trainer who loves to eat! The recipe for the chicken was inspired by my craving for hot wings combined with my desire to eat healthy. I couldn't eat fried hot wings and face my clients to whom I am constantly preaching the benefits of healthy eating."

Total time: 20 minutes

- 2 tablespoons butter or margarine
- ⅓ cup hot sauce
- 2 boneless, skinless chicken breast halves, cut into 1" pieces
- 3 cups mixed greens or spinach
- 1 tomato, sliced
- 1 avocado, pitted, peeled, and sliced
- 3 whole-grain tortillas (8" diameter)
- 3 tablespoons low-fat blue cheese dressing

MELT the butter in a large nonstick skillet over medium-high heat.

WHISK in the hot sauce. Add the chicken. Reduce the heat to low, cover, and simmer, stirring occasionally, for 15 minutes, or until the chicken is no longer pink.

DIVIDE the greens, tomato, avocado, and chicken among the tortillas. Drizzle each with 1 tablespoon of the dressing and roll up.

Makes 3 servings

Per serving: 376 calories, 31 g protein, 39 g carbohydrate, 18 g fat, 6.5 g saturated fat,* 86 mg cholesterol, 611 mg sodium,* 7 g fiber

*Limit saturated fat to 10 percent of total calories—about 17 grams per day for most women—and sodium intake to less than 2,300 milligrams.

Cold Ceviche Wraps

—Elaine Fry, St. Charles, Missouri

Ceviche is a Latin American dish made by marinating fish in citrus juice, usually lime. The acid in the juice "cooks" the fish, making it firm and opaque.

Total time: 15 minutes + chilling time

- 4 **limes**
- 1 **pound frozen tilapia, thawed and cut into 1" cubes**
- 1 **cup seeded and finely chopped tomato**
- ½ **cup finely chopped red onion**
- ½ **green bell pepper, finely chopped**
- ½ **cup chopped fresh cilantro**
- ¼ **cup olive oil**
- 1 **jalapeño pepper, seeded and finely chopped (wear plastic gloves when handling)**
- 4 **whole-grain tortillas (8" diameter)**

ZEST the limes and place in a plastic storage bag. Squeeze the juice and add to the zest. Add the tilapia, tomato, onion, bell pepper, cilantro, oil, and jalapeño. Refrigerate for at least 2 hours, or until the tilapia is opaque.

DIVIDE the fish mixture among the tortillas and roll up.

Makes 4 servings

Per serving: 348 calories, 27 g protein, 33 g carbohydrate, 16 g fat, 3 g saturated fat, 57 mg cholesterol, 334 mg sodium, 5 g fiber

---

SHOPPING SAVVY

A Fiber-Full Sandwich

Now you can boost your sandwich's fiber content beyond its bookend bread slices— just replace your regular lunchmeat with a faux variety. Pile on five pieces of Tofurky Peppered Deli Slices for 13 grams of protein along with 3 grams of fiber (you won't get that from regular turkey!). From Turtle Island Foods, these extra-thin slices are made of (you guessed it) tofu, also known as soybean curd. Certified 100 percent vegan and sliced extra thin,

Tofurky meatless deli slices include oven-roasted, hickory-smoked, cranberry and stuffing, and Philly-style flavors—all just 100 calories and 3 grams of fat per serving. For more information and to find a store that carries these and other Tofurky products, such as hot dogs, sausages, and burgers, visit tofurky.com.

Herbed Honey-Mustard Turkey Pitas

338 Calories

—Mary Shivers, Ada, Oklahoma

"When on the go, I still want a healthy lunch or dinner for my family. This colorful and delicious hand-held meal is the perfect solution."

Total time: 15 minutes

- 1 tablespoon canola oil
- 1¼ pounds extra-lean ground turkey
- ½ teaspoon garlic powder
- ½ teaspoon onion powder
- ½ teaspoon salt
- ½ teaspoon ground black pepper
- 2 tablespoons chopped fresh basil
- 2 tablespoons chopped fresh parsley
- 2 teaspoons chopped fresh rosemary
- 6 whole wheat pitas (6" diameter), halved
- ¾ cup light honey-mustard dressing
- 2 cups chopped fresh spinach
- 2 tomatoes, diced
- ⅓ cup diced red onion

PREHEAT the oven to 350°F.

HEAT the oil in a medium skillet over medium-high heat. Add the turkey, garlic powder, onion powder, salt, and pepper. Cook, stirring, for 8 to 10 minutes, or until the turkey is no longer pink. Stir in the basil, parsley, and rosemary. Remove from the heat.

MEANWHILE, wrap the pitas in foil and heat for 5 minutes. Spread a thin layer of dressing inside each pita half. Spoon turkey into each. Top the pitas with the spinach, tomatoes, and onion. Drizzle with the remaining dressing.

Makes 6 servings

Per serving: 338 calories, 31 g protein, 39 g carbohydrate, 8 g fat, 0.5 g saturated fat, 38 mg cholesterol, 805 mg sodium,* 5 g fiber

*Limit saturated fat to 10 percent of total calories—about 17 grams per day for most women—and sodium intake to less than 2,300 milligrams.

Thai Shrimp Lettuce Roll-Ups with Ginger-Melon Compote

352 Calories

—Wolfgang Hanau, West Palm Beach, Florida

Forget the carbs—these wraps use lettuce instead of bread to encase the shrimp mixture. Use whatever melon you like, such as honeydew, cantaloupe, or watermelon.

Total time: 25 minutes + marinating time

COMPOTE

1½ cups sugar

½ cup water

¼ cup lime juice

1" piece fresh ginger, peeled and grated

1½ teaspoons ground cardamom

    Ground red pepper

8 cups melon cut into 3" × ¼" × ¼" sticks

SHRIMP

⅓ cup peanut oil

2 tablespoons mirin (rice wine)

1 scallion, finely chopped

1 teaspoon minced garlic

1 teaspoon mint

½ teaspoon salt

1 pound large shrimp, peeled and deveined

ROLL-UPS

3 tablespoons lime juice

2 tablespoons chopped scallion

1 tablespoon chopped fresh cilantro

1 tablespoon fish sauce (nam pla)

8 Boston or red lettuce leaves

TO MAKE THE COMPOTE:

BRING the sugar and water to a boil in a small saucepan. Reduce the heat to low and simmer for 3 minutes. Cool slightly. Stir in the lime juice, ginger, cardamom, and red pepper to taste. Place in a large bowl. Add the melon and toss to coat. Cover and refrigerate until ready to serve.

TO MAKE THE SHRIMP:

WHISK together the oil, mirin, scallion, garlic, mint, and salt in a medium bowl. Add the shrimp and marinate in the refrigerator for up to 2 hours.

PREHEAT the grill. Coat a grill basket with cooking spray. Transfer the shrimp from the marinade to the basket; discard the marinade. Grill the shrimp, turning once, for 4 minutes, or until opaque.

TO MAKE THE ROLL-UPS:

STIR together the lime juice, scallion, cilantro, and fish sauce in a small bowl. Spoon onto the lettuce leaves. Divide the shrimp among the lettuce leaves and roll up. Serve with the melon compote.

Makes 8 servings

Per serving: 352 calories, 12 g protein, 55 g carbohydrate, 10.5 g fat, 2 g saturated fat, 75 mg cholesterol, 421 mg sodium, 2 g fiber

Curried Chicken and Peach Wraps

266 Calories

—Maryalice Wood, Langley, British Columbia, Canada

"This is a meal in one, and you don't even need dessert afterward—it's included! Our six kids enjoyed these in their teen years, and now our grandkids request them as well."

Total time: 20 minutes

- 1 tablespoon canola oil
- 1 pound boneless, skinless chicken breasts, cut into ½" pieces
- ¼ cup sliced almonds
- 2 scallions, chopped
- 2 teaspoons curry powder
- ½ teaspoon hot sauce
- 4 peaches, peeled, pitted, and sliced
- 2 tablespoons apple cider vinegar
- 4 romaine lettuce leaves, torn into bite-size pieces
- 4 whole wheat tortillas (8" diameter)

HEAT the oil in a large skillet over medium heat. Add the chicken, almonds, scallions, curry powder, and hot sauce. Cook, stirring, for 5 minutes, or until the chicken is cooked through. Remove with a slotted spoon to a large bowl. Cover to keep warm.

ADD the peaches and vinegar to the same skillet. Cook, stirring, for 3 minutes, or until the peaches are just heated through. Stir the peaches and lettuce into the chicken mixture. Divide among the tortillas and roll up.

Makes 4 servings

Per serving: 266 calories, 22 g protein, 27 g carbohydrate, 8 g fat, 1 g saturated fat, 44 mg cholesterol, 174 mg sodium, 4 g fiber

Spicy Beef Wraps

406 Calories

Thaw the meat in the fridge until it's partially frozen, and then cut the flank steak into strips. Let it thaw right in the lime marinade. The thinner the beef strips, the more flavor they can hold.

Total time: 25 minutes + marinating time

- ¼ cup lime juice
- 2 teaspoons olive oil
- 4 cloves garlic, minced
- 1½ teaspoons ground cumin, divided
- 1½ pounds frozen flank steak, trimmed of fat
- 2 cups chopped red bell peppers
- 1 cup chopped green bell peppers
- 2 cups chopped onions
- 1 cup fat-free plain yogurt
- ½ cucumber, peeled and grated
- ¼ teaspoon salt
- 6 pitas (6" diameter)

STIR together lime juice, oil, garlic, and 1 teaspoon of the cumin in a shallow glass dish. Slice the steak across the grain into thin strips with a serrated knife.

STIR the steak into the lime mixture. Cover and refrigerate for 1 hour, stirring occasionally.

HEAT a large nonstick skillet coated with cooking spray over medium-high heat. Add the bell peppers and onions. Cook, stirring, for 5 minutes, or until tender. Add the steak and marinade. Cook, stirring, for 8 minutes, or until the steak is lightly browned.

STIR together the yogurt, cucumber, salt, and the remaining ½ teaspoon cumin in a small bowl. Warm the pitas in the microwave on high power for 1 to 2 minutes. Spoon the steak mixture onto the top of the whole pitas. Top with the yogurt sauce and roll up.

Makes 6 servings

Per serving: 406 calories, 33 g protein, 48 g carbohydrate, 9 g fat, 3 g saturated fat, 38 mg cholesterol, 510 mg sodium, 4 g fiber

Open-Faced Peppered Steak Sandwiches

196 Calories

Lean flank steak is the healthiest choice for these marinated steak sandwiches. Cut into eight pieces for a hearty appetizer.

Total time: 15 minutes + marinating time

- 1 **pound flank steak, trimmed of fat**
- ½ **cup balsamic vinegar**
- 1 **teaspoon ground black pepper**
- ¼ **cup fat-free reduced-sodium beef broth**
- 2 **cups chopped onions**
- 1 **loaf French bread (about 8 ounces)**
- 1 **teaspoon olive oil**
- 1 **tablespoon low-fat blue cheese, crumbled**
- 2 **teaspoons minced garlic**

PLACE the steak in a large shallow glass dish and drizzle with the vinegar. Cover and refrigerate for 8 hours or overnight, turning occasionally.

REMOVE the steak from the vinegar and pat dry; discard the vinegar. Rub the steak with the pepper.

BRING the broth to a boil in a large nonstick skillet over medium-high heat. Add the onions. Cook, stirring, for 5 minutes, or until tender. Increase the heat to high. Cook, stirring, for 3 minutes, or until golden brown. Transfer to a plate.

ADD the steak to the skillet. Cook for 15 minutes, turning once, or until browned on both sides and a thermometer inserted in the center registers 145°F for medium-rare. Transfer to a cutting board. Let stand for 5 minutes. Cut into thin crosswise slices.

PREHEAT the oven to 400°F. Split the bread in half lengthwise. Brush the cut sides with the oil. Place the bread, cut side up, on a baking sheet. Bake for 5 minutes, or until golden brown. Top with the blue cheese, garlic, onions, and steak. Cut into 4 pieces.

Makes 4 servings

Per serving: 196 calories, 15 g protein, 21 g carbohydrate, 5 g fat, 1.5 g saturated fat, 20 mg cholesterol, 245 mg sodium, 2 g fiber

Italian Meatball Sandwiches

Stuffed with flavor, these subs will satisfy even hungry teens. Plus, it's cheaper when you make the subs at home rather than buying them from a take-out restaurant.

293 Calories

Total time: 40 minutes

- 1 **pound extra-lean ground beef**
- ¼ **cup dry bread crumbs**
- 1 **cup chopped onions**
- 4 **cloves garlic, minced**
- 1 **can (14 ounces) no-salt-added tomatoes (with juice), chopped**
- 2 **tablespoons tomato paste**
- 1 **tablespoon sugar**
- 1 **teaspoon dried basil**
- ½ **teaspoon dried oregano**
- 1 **long loaf (16 ounces) Italian or French bread, halved horizontally**
- ½ **cup shredded low-fat mozzarella cheese**

MIX the beef, bread crumbs, and ¼ cup of the onions in a medium bowl. Form into 1" meatballs.

COAT a large nonstick skillet with cooking spray and place over medium-high heat. When the skillet is hot, add the garlic and the remaining ¾ cup onions. Cook, stirring occasionally, for 5 minutes, or until the onions are golden brown. Add the meatballs and cook for 5 minutes, or until the meatballs are browned on the bottom. Turn the meatballs; add the tomatoes (with juice), tomato paste, sugar, basil, and oregano. Cover and cook for 10 minutes, or until the meatballs are no longer pink in the center (check by inserting the tip of a sharp knife into the center of 1 meatball).

SCOOP out the bread from the bottom half of the loaf (reserve the bread crumbs for another use). Spoon the meatballs and sauce into the bread shell. Top with the cheese and the remaining half of the bread. Cut into 8 sandwiches.

Makes 8 servings

Per serving: 293 calories, 20 g protein, 38 g carbohydrate, 6 g fat, 2.5 g saturated fat, 39 mg cholesterol, 466 mg sodium, 3 g fiber

Ann's Veggie and Chicken Asiago Pizza

205 Calories

—Ann Elizardo-Shaw, Round Rock, Texas

If you can't find spinach, chicken, and asiago sausage, look for any fully cooked chicken-cheese sausage.

Total time: 20 minutes

- 1 whole wheat pita (6" diameter)
- 1 link spinach-chicken-asiago sausage, chopped
- ¼ cup chopped onion
- ¼ cup sliced mushrooms
- 3 large green olives stuffed with garlic, sliced
- 2 teaspoons olive juice
- ½ cup baby spinach leaves
- 1 tablespoon marinara sauce (optional)
- ¼ cup shredded part-skim mozzarella cheese

PREHEAT the oven to 400°F. Place the pita on the oven rack. Bake for 5 minutes. Remove to a baking sheet.

BROWN the sausage in a large skillet over medium heat for 3 minutes. Stir in the onion, mushrooms, and olives. Cook for 5 minutes, or until the onion is tender. Add the olive juice and spinach and cook for 3 minutes, or until the spinach wilts.

SPREAD the sauce, if using, over the pita. Top with the sausage mixture and sprinkle with the cheese. Bake for 4 minutes, or until the cheese melts. Cut into 4 pieces.

Makes 2 servings

Per serving: 205 calories, 15 g protein, 22 g carbohydrate, 6 g fat, 2.5 g saturated fat, 42 mg cholesterol, 810 mg sodium,* 3 g fiber

*Limit saturated fat to 10 percent of total calories—about 17 grams per day for most women—and sodium intake to less than 2,300 milligrams.

Pizza Primavera

Make these easy springtime pizzas with pita bread rounds—your preparation
will take just minutes. Feel free to use whatever frozen vegetables you have on hand.

219 Calories

Total time: 25 minutes

- 2 whole wheat pitas (6" diameter)
- 1 teaspoon canola oil
- 1 cup pizza sauce
- ¼ cup chopped onion
- ¼ cup chopped red bell pepper
- ¼ cup frozen broccoli florets, thawed
- ¼ cup frozen artichoke hearts, thawed and chopped
- 1 teaspoon dried Italian herb seasoning
- 1 cup shredded low-fat mozzarella cheese

PREHEAT the oven to 400°F. Split the pitas
into 2 thin disks each. Place, rough side up, on a
large baking sheet. Brush the tops with the oil.
Top with the pizza sauce. Top with the onion,
pepper, broccoli, and artichoke hearts. Sprinkle
with the seasoning and mozzarella. Bake for
15 minutes, or until the cheese is bubbling.

Makes 4 servings

Per serving: 219 calories, 13 g protein, 27 g
carbohydrate, 7 g fat, 3 g saturated fat, 15 mg
cholesterol, 618 mg sodium, 5 g fiber

*Limit saturated fat to 10 percent of total
calories—about 17 grams per day for most
women—and sodium intake to less than
2,300 milligrams.

SHOPPING SAVVY

Build a Better Pizza

Pizza's a family favorite, but most parlor-
style and frozen versions are way too
heavy on the calories and fat. Create
slimmed-down slices with these fixings.

Start with Boboli 100% Whole Wheat
Thin Crust, which provides 3 grams of
fiber—more than 10 percent of your daily
recommendation (in supermarkets; for
more information, visit boboli.com).

Spread it with 365 Everyday Value All
Natural Pesto & Sundried Tomato Pasta
Sauce; it's low in sugar, with less than
1 gram per ½ cup (at Whole Foods;
wholefoodsmarket.com).

Next, sprinkle on Trader Joe's
Shredded Mozzarella Cheese Low-Moisture
Part-Skim—a quarter cup offers 20 percent
of your daily calcium recommendation (at
Trader Joe's; traderjoes.com).

Top it off with a skinnier version of your
favorite meat topping. Try Lightlife Smart
Deli Pepperoni Style—you can
eat 13 peppery, chewy slices
for just 50 calories and no
grease (just 1 gram of fat).
One serving of the spicy, soy-
based circles packs 9 grams
of protein.

Tangy and Nutty Thai Chicken Pizza

350 Calories

—Susan Riley, Allen, Texas

Don't be fooled by this recipe becasue it calls for refrigerated pizza dough. The flavors of Thai cuisines—soy, ginger, sesame oil, red-pepper flakes—turn ordinary pizza into a gourmet treat!

Total time: 20 minutes

- ¼ cup reduced-fat creamy peanut butter
- ¼ cup apricot preserves, large chunks chopped up
- 1 tablespoon rice wine vinegar
- 1 tablespoon soy sauce
- 2 teaspoons minced fresh ginger
- 2 cloves garlic, minced
- 2 teaspoons toasted sesame oil
- 1 can (13.8 ounces) refrigerated pizza dough
- 1½ cups chopped cooked chicken
- 1 small red bell pepper, chopped
- ½ teaspoon red pepper flakes
- 6 ounces shredded part-skim mozzarella cheese
- 6 scallions, sliced
- 1 large carrot, shredded
- ¼ cup chopped dry-roasted peanuts

PREHEAT the oven to 400°F. Coat a 16" × 11" rimmed baking sheet with cooking spray.

WHISK together the peanut butter, preserves, vinegar, soy sauce, ginger, garlic, and sesame oil in a medium glass bowl. Microwave on high power for 1 minute; stir well.

SPREAD the dough on the prepared pan. Bake for 8 minutes. Spread the peanut sauce over the crust and top with the chicken, bell pepper, pepper flakes, and cheese. Bake for 10 to 12 minutes, or until the cheese melts. Remove from the oven and sprinkle with the scallions, carrot, and peanuts.

Makes 8 servings

Per serving: 350 calories, 21 g protein, 38 g carbohydrate, 13 g fat, 4 g saturated fat,* 36 mg cholesterol, 657 mg sodium,* 3 g fiber

*Limit saturated fat to 10 percent of total calories—about 17 grams per day for most women—and sodium intake to less than 2,300 milligrams.

Pesto-Tomato Pizza

270
Calories

Earmark this recipe for late summer when you're faced with a bumper crop of tomatoes and basil. Nothing could be more simple or delicious.

Total time: 45 minutes + rising time

DOUGH

- 1 cup warm water (about 110°F)
- 1 tablespoon active dry yeast
- 1 tablespoon sugar
- ½ cup yellow cornmeal
- ¼ teaspoon salt
- 2 tablespoons olive oil, divided
- 2½ cups all-purpose flour

TOPPING

- 1 cup chopped fresh basil
- ½ cup soft bread crumbs
- 2 cloves garlic, halved
- 4 tomatoes, sliced
- 1 cup shredded low-fat mozzarella cheese

TO MAKE THE DOUGH:

STIR together the water, yeast, and sugar in a large bowl. Let stand in a warm place for 5 minutes, or until foamy. Stir in the cornmeal, salt, and 1 tablespoon of the oil. Stir in up to 2¼ cups of the flour to make a kneadable dough. Turn the dough out onto a lightly floured surface. Knead, adding more of the remaining ¼ cup flour as necessary, for 10 minutes, or until smooth and elastic.

COAT another large bowl with cooking spray. Add the dough and turn to coat all sides. Cover loosely with a kitchen towel and set in a warm place for 15 minutes.

PREHEAT the oven to 450°F. Coat two 12" round pizza pans with cooking spray. Divide the dough in half. Roll each half into a 12" circle. Place the circles on the pizza pans. Brush the surface of each pizza with the remaining 1 tablespoon oil.

TO MAKE THE TOPPING:

PUREE the basil, bread crumbs, and garlic in a blender or food processor until smooth. Spread over the dough. Top with the tomatoes and cheese. Bake for 20 minutes, or until the crusts are golden brown and the cheese is bubbling.

Makes 8 servings

Per serving: 270 calories, 10 g protein, 43 g carbohydrate, 7 g fat, 1.6 g saturated fat, 8 mg cholesterol, 201 mg sodium, 3 g fiber

Italian Pizza Bread

109
Calories

Try this loaf version of traditional pizza. Savory herb-scented bread is formed into a long strip, filled with pizza ingredients, then rolled into a baguette.

Total time: 1 hour 20 minutes + rising and cooling time

FILLING

- 1 teaspoon olive oil
- ½ cup chopped onion
- ½ cup chopped red bell pepper
- ½ cup chopped mushrooms
- 1 cup pizza sauce
- ½ teaspoon Italian herb seasoning

DOUGH

- 1 cup warm water (about 110°F)
- 1 tablespoon active dry yeast
- 1 tablespoon sugar
- 2½ cups all-purpose flour
- ¼ teaspoon salt
- 1 cup shredded low-fat mozzarella cheese

TO MAKE THE FILLING:

HEAT the oil in a large nonstick skillet over medium-high heat. Add the onion, pepper, and mushrooms. Cook, stirring, for 5 minutes, or until the onions are tender. Add the pizza sauce and seasoning. Bring to a simmer. Remove from the heat and let cool.

TO MAKE THE DOUGH:

STIR together the water, yeast, and sugar in a large bowl. Let stand in a warm place for 5 minutes, or until foamy. Stir in 1 cup of the flour. Cover and set in a warm place for 30 minutes, or until doubled in size.

STIR in the salt and about 1 cup of the remaining flour to make a kneadable dough. Turn the dough out onto a lightly floured surface. Knead, adding up to ½ cup more flour, for 10 minutes, or until smooth and elastic.

COAT another large bowl with cooking spray. Add the dough and turn to coat all sides. Cover and set in a warm place for 1 hour, or until doubled in size.

COAT a large baking sheet with cooking spray. On a lightly floured surface, roll the dough into a 14" × 10" rectangle. Spread with the filling, then sprinkle with the cheese. Roll up, starting from a long side, pinching the ends and edges together to seal. Place, seam side down, on the prepared baking sheet. Let stand for 15 minutes.

PREHEAT the oven to 350°F. Bake for 45 to 60 minutes, or until golden brown. Let cool before slicing.

Makes 12 servings

Per serving: 109 calories, 5 g protein, 18 g carbohydrate, 2 g fat, 1 g saturated fat, 4 mg cholesterol, 145 mg sodium, 1 g fiber

Beets in Balsamic Vinegar Sauce

138 Calories

The ruby red hues of this salad are especially dramatic served over a bed of chopped greens, such as curly endive or spinach.

Total time: 15 minutes + chilling time

- 2 tablespoons olive oil
- 2 tablespoons balsamic vinegar
- 1 tablespoon honey or sugar
- 3 cloves garlic, minced
- 1 teaspoon Dijon mustard
- ¼ teaspoon salt
- ¼ teaspoon ground black pepper
- 1 jar (16 ounces) sliced beets, drained
- 1 cup chopped red bell peppers
- ⅓ cup chopped fresh parsley
- ¼ cup chopped red onion

WHISK together the oil, vinegar, honey, garlic, mustard, salt, and black pepper in a large bowl. Stir in the beets, red peppers, parsley, and onion. Cover and refrigerate for 1 hour, stirring frequently.

Makes 4 servings

Per serving: 138 calories, 2 g protein, 18 g carbohydrate, 7 g fat, 1 g saturated fat, 0 mg cholesterol, 239 mg sodium, 3 g fiber

Broccoli Puff

99
Calories

—Joan L. Grube, Alexandria, Ohio

"Since losing several pounds, I have made a hobby out of trying to reduce the calorie content of my old favorite recipes without losing the flavor and hopefully without my family being any the wiser."

Total time: 55 minutes

- 1 package (10 ounces) frozen chopped broccoli, thawed
- 1 can (10.75 ounces) 98% fat-free cream of celery soup
- ½ cup shredded 2% Cheddar cheese
- 1 teaspoon seasoned salt
- ¼ cup fat-free milk
- ¼ cup fat-free mayonnaise
- ⅓ cup egg substitute
- ½ cup panko bread crumbs

PREHEAT the oven to 350°F. Coat an 11" × 7" baking dish with cooking spray.

PLACE the broccoli in the prepared dish. Stir together the soup, cheese, and seasoned salt in a medium bowl. Gradually stir in the milk, mayonnaise, and egg substitute until well blended. Pour over the broccoli in the baking dish. Top with the bread crumbs and coat with butter-flavored cooking spray. Bake for 45 minutes, or until bubbly and the top is lightly browned.

Makes 6 servings

Per serving: 99 calories, 6 g protein, 11 g carbohydrate, 4 g fat, 2 g saturated fat, 10 mg cholesterol, 921 mg sodium,* 2 g fiber

*Limit saturated fat to 10 percent of total calories—about 17 grams per day for most women—and sodium intake to less than 2,300 milligrams.

Sesame-Curry Cauliflower

43 Calories

Curry powder and toasted sesame oil are an extraordinary combination in this winter vegetable side dish. To make a vegetarian version, substitute reduced-sodium vegetable broth for the chicken broth.

Total time: 20 minutes

- 4 cups cauliflower florets
- 1/3 cup reduced-sodium chicken broth
- 3 cloves garlic, minced
- 1 teaspoon toasted sesame oil
- 1 teaspoon curry powder
- 1/2 teaspoon sugar
- 2 tablespoons minced fresh cilantro or parsley
- 1/8 teaspoon red-pepper flakes
- 1/8 teaspoon salt
- 1/8 teaspoon ground black pepper

COMBINE the cauliflower, broth, garlic, sesame oil, curry powder, and sugar in a large nonstick skillet. Bring to a boil over medium-high heat. Reduce the heat to medium-low, cover, and simmer for 10 minutes, or until the cauliflower is crisp-tender.

STIR in the cilantro, pepper flakes, salt, and black pepper; toss to blend well.

Makes 4 servings

Per serving: 43 calories, 2 g protein, 6 g carbohydrate, 1 g fat, 0 g saturated fat, 0 mg cholesterol, 135 mg sodium, 2 g fiber

Corn Custard

Cold weather comfort foods like this creamy custard are staples of Midwestern harvest dinners. Baking the custard in a hot water bath keeps it from browning too much.

255
Calories

Total time: 1 hour 20 minutes

- 1 cup evaporated fat-free milk
- 3 eggs
- 1 egg white
- 2 tablespoons chopped onion
- ½ teaspoon salt
- ½ teaspoon ground black pepper
- 4 cups frozen corn

PREHEAT the oven to 325°F. Coat an 8" × 8" baking dish with cooking spray.

PUREE the milk, eggs, egg white, onion, salt, pepper, and 2 cups of the corn in a blender or food processor until smooth. Transfer to a large bowl. Stir in the remaining 2 cups corn.

POUR into the prepared baking dish. Place the baking dish in a larger ovenproof pan. Add hot water to the larger pan to a depth of 1".

BAKE for 1 hour 15 minutes, or until a knife inserted in the center of the custard comes out clean.

Makes 4 servings

Per serving: 255 calories, 16 g protein, 42 g carbohydrate, 5 g fat, 1.5 g saturated fat, 161 mg cholesterol, 436 mg sodium, 4 g fiber

Simple Succotash

90 Calories

This recipe combines old-fashioned flavor with up-to-the-minute speed. In season, fresh corn and lima beans are the obvious choice.

Total time: 5 minutes

- 1 teaspoon olive oil
- 1 cup frozen lima beans, thawed
- 1 cup frozen corn, thawed
- 1 tablespoon chopped onion
- 2 cloves garlic, minced
- 2 tablespoons chopped fresh chives or scallion
- ¼ teaspoon salt
- ⅛ teaspoon paprika

HEAT the oil in a large nonstick skillet coated with cooking spray over medium-high heat. Add the lima beans, corn, onion, and garlic. Cook, stirring, for 5 minutes, or until the onion is tender. Stir in the chives, salt, and paprika.

Makes 4 servings

Per serving: 90 calories, 3 g protein, 17 g carbohydrate, 2 g fat, 0 g saturated fat, 0 mg cholesterol, 212 mg sodium, 3 g fiber

---

SHOPPING SAVVY

Soup's On

When you want food fast but want to avoid fast food, pop the top on a can of one of Pacific Natural Foods' artisan-inspired soups, featuring organic ingredients such as chicken andouille sausage, champignon mushrooms, and hardwood-smoked bacon. Each pull-tab can contains about 1½ servings; the dieter-friendliest versions include Savory Chicken and Wild Rice (per serving: 90 calories, 0.5 gram fat, 1 gram fiber, and 5 grams protein), Chicken and Penne Pasta (100 calories, 1 gram fat, 1 gram fiber, 6 grams protein), Minestrone with Beef Steak (100 calories, 3 grams fat, 2 grams fiber, 5 grams protein), and Spicy Chicken Fajita (150 calories, 2.5 grams fat, 5 grams fiber, 8 grams protein).

If you're among the 74 percent of office workers who eat lunch at their desks, tote a can to work and pair it with a whole grain (a 100-calorie portion of microwave popcorn, perhaps) for a quick and healthy midday meal. If you're hankering for something comforting, try the latest offerings from Pacific Natural Foods: low-sodium creamy soups in butternut squash, tomato, and roasted red pepper flavors, at 90, 100, and 110 calories, respectively, and 2 grams of fat per serving. Each pourable 32-ounce box contains four servings. The soups are sold nationwide in mainstream grocery and natural food stores. For more information, visit pacificfoods.com.

Fennel Bake with Parmesan

96 Calories

Fennel has a sweet, anise flavor. Select firm, compact bulbs with crisp stalks and healthy bright green fronds. Reserve the fronds for garnish, if desired.

Total time: 45 minutes

- ½ cup reduced-sodium chicken broth
- 2 fennel bulbs (1 pound each), trimmed and thinly sliced
- 2 tablespoons chopped onion
- ¼ teaspoon dry mustard
- ¼ teaspoon ground black pepper
- ⅛ teaspoon salt
- ¼ cup grated Parmesan cheese

PREHEAT the oven to 400°F.

BRING the broth to a boil in a Dutch oven over medium-high heat. Add the fennel. Cook, stirring, for 10 minutes, or until the liquid has evaporated and the fennel is tender.

IN a small bowl, combine the onion, mustard, pepper, and salt. Sprinkle over the fennel. Top with the cheese. Cover and bake for 25 minutes, or until golden brown.

Makes 4 servings

Per serving: 96 calories, 5 g protein, 17 g carbohydrate, 2 g fat, 1 g saturated fat, 4 mg cholesterol, 324 mg sodium, 7 g fiber

Stuffed Baked Onions

Depending on the time of year, you may use different onions for a variety of flavor. Go for sweet Vidalias in the spring, farmers' market yellow onions in August, or red onions in the fall.

163 Calories

Total time: 1 hour 15 minutes

- 4 **large onions**
- 1 **cup soft bread crumbs**
- ½ **cup chopped tomato**
- ¼ **cup chopped red bell pepper**
- ¼ **cup chopped celery**
- ¼ **cup raisins**
- 2 **tablespoons balsamic vinegar**
- ½ **teaspoon dried oregano**
- ⅓ **cup reduced-sodium chicken broth**
- 1 **tablespoon olive oil**

PREHEAT the oven to 375°F. Bring a large pot of water to a boil over high heat. Peel the onions and slice ½" off the top of each. Place in the pot. Cover and cook for 3 minutes, or until slightly softened. Drain in a colander. Let stand until cool enough to handle.

WITH a sharp spoon or melon baller, scoop the interior from each onion, leaving a 1" shell. Reserve the center portions for another use.

STIR together the bread crumbs, tomato, pepper, celery, raisins, vinegar, and oregano in a medium bowl. Stuff into the onion cavities. Place the onions in an 8" × 8" baking dish. Pour the broth around the onions. Drizzle with the oil. Cover and bake for 1 hour, or until the onions are soft.

Makes 4 servings

Per serving: 163 calories, 3 g protein, 30 g carbohydrate, 4 g fat, 1 g saturated fat, 0 mg cholesterol, 130 mg sodium, 4 g fiber

Zesty Zucchini

—Elena Dodge, Erie, Pennsylvania

So simple yet so satisfying! You can vary the zest in this dish by using different salsas, such as chipotle (very smoky), extra hot (super spicy), or peach mango (cool and refreshing).

Total time: 10 minutes

- 1 **tablespoon olive oil**
- 1 **large zucchini, sliced**
- 1 **cup salsa**
   Salt and ground black pepper

HEAT oil in a large nonstick skillet coated with cooking spray over medium-high heat. Add the zucchini. Cook, stirring, for 6 minutes, or until tender. Add the salsa and cook for 4 minutes, or until the flavors blend. Sprinkle with salt and pepper to taste.

Makes 4 servings

Per serving: 76 calories, 2 g protein, 9 g carbohydrate, 4 g fat, 1 g saturated fat, 0 mg cholesterol, 568 mg sodium, 3 g fiber

Spinach with Olives and Feta Cheese

—Lesley Pew, Lynn, Massachusetts

"This lively dish makes a great light lunch or vegetable course for supper."

Total time: 25 minutes

- 1 **package (8 ounces) refrigerated tortellini or ravioli pasta**
- 2 **tablespoons olive oil**
- ¼ **cup chopped scallions**
- 2 **cloves garlic, minced**
- ½ **cup coarsely chopped pistachios**
- 1 **bag (1 pound) fresh spinach, trimmed and torn into bite-size pieces**
  Juice of 1 lemon
- ¼ **cup sliced olives**
- 2 **ounces reduced-fat feta cheese, crumbled**
- 1 **teaspoon grainy mustard**
  Pinch of ground black pepper
  Grated Parmesan cheese (optional)

PREPARE the pasta according to the package directions. Drain and place in a large bowl.

HEAT the oil in a large skillet over medium-high heat. Add the scallions, garlic, and pistachios. Cook, stirring, for 3 minutes. Add the spinach and lemon juice and cook for 2 minutes, or until the spinach is wilted. Remove from the heat. Stir in the olives, feta, mustard, and black pepper. Pour over the pasta, tossing to coat. Sprinkle with the Parmesan, if using.

Makes 4 servings

Per serving: 348 calories, 16 g protein, 37 g carbohydrate, 17 g fat, 4.5 g saturated fat,* 26 mg cholesterol, 638 mg sodium,* 6 g fiber

*Limit saturated fat to 10 percent of total calories—about 17 grams per day for most women—and sodium intake to less than 2,300 milligrams.

NUTRITION NEWS TO USE

Quick tip—Pair leafy greens with a healthy fat. Add olive oil, nuts, or avocado to veggie-packed salads. This increases your absorption of disease-fighting compounds called carotenoids—including lutein and zeaxanthin, which protect against cataracts and macular degeneration.

Orange-Scented Mint Couscous with Dried Cranberries

227 Calories

—Laurie Lufkin, Essex, Massachusetts

Here's a delicious way to get your whole grains. Opting for whole wheat couscous increases the nutritional value of your dishes, and it's ready in just 10 minutes!

Total time: 15 minutes

- 2 tablespoons olive oil
- 2 tablespoons chopped shallot
- 1½ teaspoons grated fresh ginger
- 1¼ cups reduced-sodium vegetable or chicken broth
- ½ cup dried cranberries
- 1 tablespoon grated orange zest
- 2 tablespoons orange juice
- ¼ cup chopped mint leaves
- ½ teaspoon ground cinnamon
- 1 cup whole wheat couscous
  Salt and ground black pepper

HEAT the oil in a large saucepan over medium heat. Add the shallot and ginger. Cook, stirring, for 2 minutes, or until the shallot is tender. Stir in the broth, cranberries, orange zest, orange juice, mint, and cinnamon. Bring to a simmer. Stir in the couscous. Remove from the heat. Cover and let stand for 10 minutes, or until the liquid is absorbed. Fluff with a fork and season with salt and pepper to taste.

Makes 4 servings

Per serving: 227 calories, 4 g protein, 39 g carbohydrate, 7.5 g fat, 1 g saturated fat, 0 mg cholesterol, 106 mg sodium, 5 g fiber

Couscous with Currants

Couscous, a tiny grainlike pasta, is a favorite in Middle Eastern cooking.
You can use whole wheat couscous in this dish for a healthy change of pace.

221
Calories

Total time: 10 minutes

2 **cups reduced-sodium chicken broth**
½ **cup currants**
½ **cup chopped scallions**
¼ **teaspoon salt**
¼ **teaspoon ground black pepper**
1 **cup couscous**
2 **tablespoons minced fresh parsley**

BRING the broth, currants, scallions, salt, and pepper to a boil in a medium saucepan over medium-high heat. Stir in the couscous. Remove from the heat. Cover and let stand for 10 minutes, or until the liquid is absorbed. Stir in the parsley and fluff with a fork.

Makes 4 servings

Per serving: 221 calories, 7 g protein, 48 g carbohydrate, 0.5 g fat, 0 g saturated fat, 0 mg cholesterol, 379 mg sodium, 4 g fiber

SHOPPING SAVVY

Go Green

Talk about a super brew: Research suggests that antioxidant-rich green tea protects against heart disease, cancer, Alzheimer's, and osteoporosis and shifts your fat-fighting metabolism into high gear—assuming you down at least 4 cups a day. If you haven't yet tossed your cup of joe for green tea, now it's easier than ever:

Crystal Light Green Tea On The Go packets fit in your pocket or handbag—add one to a bottle of water anytime, anywhere. You get 40 milligrams of antioxidants per packet for a paltry 5 calories. For more information, visit kraftfoods.com/crystallight.

Asian-Style Wild Rice Sauté

Wild rice and white rice mix in this easy stove-top side dish. Wild rice, which is really a wild grass, is harvested from lakes in Canada and the northern United States.

179 Calories

Total time: 55 minutes

½ cup chopped onion

⅓ cup chopped celery

⅓ cup chopped red bell pepper

⅓ cup frozen corn, thawed

1 cup wild rice

¼ cup apple juice

5 cups reduced-sodium chicken broth

1 cup white rice

2 tablespoons chopped fresh parsley

1 teaspoon reduced-sodium soy sauce

½ teaspoon toasted sesame oil

¼ teaspoon crushed red pepper flakes

HEAT a Dutch oven coated with cooking spray over medium-high heat. Add the onion, celery, bell pepper, and corn. Cook, stirring, for 5 minutes, or until the onions are tender. Add the wild rice and apple juice. Cook, stirring, for 5 minutes, or until the liquid is absorbed.

STIR in the broth. Bring to a boil. Reduce the heat to medium, cover, and cook for 10 minutes. Stir in the white rice. Cover and cook for 30 minutes, or until the wild rice is tender. Stir in the parsley, soy sauce, sesame oil, and pepper flakes.

Makes 8 servings

Per serving: 179 calories, 6 g protein, 37 g carbohydrate, 1 g fat, 0.5 g saturated fat, 0 mg cholesterol, 314 mg sodium, 2 g fiber

NUTRITION NEWS TO USE

Have 2 cups of green tea daily. Studies have shown that green tea helps keep cholesterol in check and may lower cancer risk. Now researchers say the drink may also work to maintain cognitive function. A Japanese study of 1,000 people over age 70 found that those who drank 2 cups of green tea daily did better on a variety of tests of mental abilities (including memory)—and the more green tea they drank, the better they performed. It's possible that something else is responsible for the mental clarity, such as the socializing the Japanese tend to do over a cup. But the results might partially explain why rates of dementia, including Alzheimer's disease, are lower in Japan (where green tea is commonly consumed) than in the United States.

Rice and Carrot Slaw

275 Calories

A tart ginger dressing adds zest to this side salad. Consider making it the next time you have extra Chinese takeout.

Total time: 20 minutes

- 2 cups reduced-sodium chicken broth
- 1 cup white rice
- 1 tablespoon balsamic vinegar
- 1 teaspoon toasted sesame oil
- 2 cloves garlic, minced
- ½ teaspoon minced fresh ginger
- ¼ cup chopped fresh cilantro
- 2 cups shredded carrots
- 2 cups frozen peas, thawed
- ½ cup broccoli florets
- ½ cup chopped red bell pepper
- 1 tablespoon lemon juice

BRING the broth and rice to a boil in a medium saucepan over medium-high heat. Reduce the heat to low, cover, and simmer for 20 minutes, or until the rice is tender.

MEANWHILE, whisk together the vinegar, sesame oil, garlic, ginger, and cilantro in a large bowl. Set aside.

HEAT a large nonstick skillet coated with cooking spray over medium heat. Add the carrots, peas, broccoli, pepper, and lemon juice. Cover and cook over medium-high heat for 3 minutes, or until the broccoli is crisp-tender. Place in the bowl with the vinaigrette. Stir in the rice, tossing to coat well.

Makes 4 servings

Per serving: 275 calories, 9 g protein, 55 g carbohydrate, 2 g fat, 0.5 g saturated fat, 0 mg cholesterol, 359 mg sodium, 6 g fiber

Millet and Sweet Potato Cakes

63
Calories

Millet is a grain prized in Europe for its chewy texture. In this country, it's a frequent component of birdseed mixtures. But don't let the birds get all its fiber and nutty flavor. Use it in recipes like this, where millet blends with grated sweet potatoes in savory pancakes that are an inspired match to pork or beef.

Total time: 45 minutes

- 1 **cup reduced-sodium chicken broth**
- ⅓ **cup millet**
- 1 **small sweet potato, peeled and shredded**
- ¼ **cup minced onion**
- 2 **eggs, lightly beaten**
- 1 **tablespoon all-purpose flour**
- ½ **teaspoon dried thyme**
- ⅛ **teaspoon crushed red pepper flakes**
- ⅛ **teaspoon salt**
- ⅛ **teaspoon ground black pepper**

BRING the broth and millet to a boil in a small saucepan over medium-high heat. Reduce the heat to low, cover, and simmer for 25 minutes, or until the millet is tender.

STIR together the sweet potato, onion, eggs, flour, thyme, pepper flakes, salt, and black pepper in a medium bowl. Stir in the cooked millet, tossing until well blended.

HEAT a large nonstick skillet coated with cooking spray over medium-high heat. Drop spoonfuls of the batter into the skillet. Cook for 6 to 7 minutes, or until golden brown, turning once. Transfer to a plate and cover to keep warm. Repeat with the remaining batter.

Makes 4 servings

Per serving: 63 calories, 3 g protein, 9 g carbohydrate, 2 g fat, 0.5 g saturated fat, 53 mg cholesterol, 113 mg sodium, 1 g fiber

Pasta and Navy Beans with Sage

276 Calories

Here's an easy side dish for your next potluck. Alternately add some slivered cooked chicken, pork, or beef to this side dish for a fast, light supper.

Total time: 50 minutes

- 1 tablespoon olive oil
- 1 cup chopped onions
- 1 cup sliced carrots
- 4 cloves garlic, minced
- 2 cups chopped tomatoes
- 1 cup canned no-salt-added navy beans, rinsed and drained
- ½ cup orzo pasta
- 1 cup reduced-sodium chicken broth
- 1 teaspoon dried sage
- ½ teaspoon dried thyme
- ¼ teaspoon ground black pepper
- ¼ teaspoon salt
- ¼ cup dry bread crumbs
- 2 tablespoons grated Parmesan cheese

PREHEAT the oven to 425°F. Heat the oil in a Dutch oven coated with cooking spray. Add the onions, carrots, and garlic; cook over medium-high heat, stirring, for 5 minutes, or until the onions are tender. Add the tomatoes, beans, and pasta. Cook, stirring, for 3 minutes, or until the tomatoes soften. Add the broth, sage, thyme, pepper, and salt. Bring to a boil.

COVER and bake for 20 to 25 minutes, or until the pasta is tender and most of the liquid is absorbed. Sprinkle the bread crumbs and cheese on top. Bake for 5 minutes, or until the topping is golden brown.

Makes 4 servings

Per serving: 276 calories, 11 g protein, 47 g carbohydrate, 5.5 g fat, 1 g saturated fat, 2 mg cholesterol, 384 mg sodium, 8 g fiber

Creamy Spinach Parmesan Orzo

174 Calories

A creamy low-fat sauce coats the tiny rice-shaped pasta called orzo in this comforting side dish. Serve with lemony roasted chicken breasts and steamed carrots.

Total time: 15 minutes

- 1 cup orzo pasta
- 1 tablespoon olive oil
- 2 cloves garlic, chopped
- 2 cups baby spinach leaves
- ½ cup chopped red bell pepper
- ½ cup low-fat ricotta cheese
- ¼ cup grated Parmesan cheese
- ½ teaspoon ground black pepper

PREPARE the pasta according to the package directions. Drain and place in a medium bowl.

MEANWHILE, heat the oil in a large nonstick skillet coated with cooking spray over medium-high heat. Add the garlic and cook, stirring, for 2 minutes. Add the spinach and bell pepper. Cook, stirring, for 6 minutes, or until the liquid from the spinach has evaporated. Place in the bowl with the pasta.

PUREE the ricotta, Parmesan, and black pepper in a blender or food processor until smooth. Pour over the pasta, tossing to coat well.

Makes 6 servings

Per serving: 174 calories, 8 g protein, 24 g carbohydrate, 5 g fat, 2 g saturated fat, 9 mg cholesterol, 92 mg sodium, 2 g fiber

Buttermilk Dinner Rolls

157 Calories

Most yeast breads can be formed into a variety of shapes—including these dinner rolls. They freeze well, and leftover rolls are great for brown-bag sandwiches.

Total time: 40 minutes + rising time

1¼ cups low-fat buttermilk
 3 tablespoons sugar
 1 tablespoon active dry yeast
 4 cups all-purpose flour
 ¾ cup yellow cornmeal
 3 tablespoons canola oil
 1 egg white, lightly beaten

WARM the buttermilk in a small saucepan over medium heat (about 110°F). Pour into a large bowl. Stir in the sugar and yeast. Let stand in a warm place for 5 minutes, or until foamy. Stir in 2 cups of the flour. Cover and set in a warm place for 30 minutes, or until doubled in size. Stir in the cornmeal, oil, and about 1½ cups of the remaining flour to make a kneadable dough. Turn the dough out onto a lightly floured surface. Knead, adding up to ½ cup more flour, for 10 minutes, or until smooth and elastic.

COAT another large bowl with cooking spray. Add the dough and turn to coat all sides. Cover and set in a warm place for 1 hour, or until doubled in size. Coat 2 large baking sheets with cooking spray. Divide the dough into 18 pieces. Roll each into a ball and place on the prepared baking sheets, leaving about 2" between rolls. Cover and set in a warm place for 10 minutes.

PREHEAT the oven to 375°F. Brush the rolls with the egg white. Bake for 15 to 20 minutes, or until the rolls are golden brown.

Makes 18 servings

Per serving: 157 calories, 4 g protein, 28 g carbohydrate, 3 g fat, 0.5 g saturated fat, 1 mg cholesterol, 23 mg sodium, 1 g fiber

Onion-Cheese Focaccia

153 Calories

This Italian flatbread is a delightful addition to a company meal. Focaccia freezes well and tastes freshly baked even after thawing and reheating.

Total time: 35 minutes + rising time

- 1 cup warm water (about 110°F)
- ¼ cup sugar
- 1 tablespoon active dry yeast
- 2 tablespoons chopped onion
- 2 teaspoons olive oil, divided
- 3 cups all-purpose flour
- ¼ cup grated Parmesan cheese
- 2 tablespoons minced garlic
- ½ teaspoon ground red pepper
- 2 tablespoons yellow cornmeal
- 1 teaspoon dried thyme

STIR together the water, sugar, and yeast in a large bowl. Let stand in a warm place for 5 minutes, or until foamy.

HEAT a large nonstick skillet coated with cooking spray over medium-high heat. Add the onion and 1 teaspoon of the oil. Cook, stirring, for 3 minutes, or until slightly tender. Stir into the yeast mixture. Stir in 1½ cups of the flour. Cover and set in a warm place for 30 minutes, or until doubled in size. Stir in the cheese, garlic, red pepper, and about 1 cup of the remaining flour to make a kneadable dough. Turn out onto a lightly floured work surface.

KNEAD, adding up to ½ cup more flour, for 10 minutes, or until smooth and elastic. Coat a large baking sheet with cooking spray and sprinkle with the cornmeal. Roll the dough into a 12" × 9" rectangle. Place on the prepared baking sheet. Cover and set in a warm place for 30 minutes, or until doubled in size.

PREHEAT the oven to 425°F. With your fingertips, press ¼"-deep indentations over the surface of the dough. Brush with the remaining 1 teaspoon oil and sprinkle with the thyme. Bake for 20 minutes, or until golden brown.

Makes 12 servings

Per serving: 153 calories, 4 g protein, 30 g carbohydrate, 2 g fat, 0.5 g saturated fat, 1 mg cholesterol, 28 mg sodium, 1 g fiber

Hearty Health Bread

—Yolande Lippe, Joliette, Quebec, Canada

128 Calories

This dense bread, studded with sunflower, poppy, sesame, and flaxseeds, makes a wonderful sandwich. Delicious toasted and spread with honey, too.

Total time: 10 minutes + baking time

1¼ cups water, at room temperature

 2 tablespoons honey

 2 tablespoons canola oil

 2 cups all-purpose flour

 1 cup whole wheat flour

1½ teaspoons salt

 ¼ cup flax seeds

 2 tablespoons sesame seeds

 1 tablespoon poppy seeds

 2 tablespoons unsalted sunflower seeds

 1 tablespoon bulgur

 2 teaspoons active dry yeast

PLACE the water, honey, oil, flours, salt, flaxseeds, bulgur, and yeast in a bread machine pan in the order recommended by the manufacturer. Follow manufacturer's directions for baking. Remove the baked bread from the pan and cool on a wire rack. Every bread maker will be different as far as baking directions.

Makes 16 servings

Per serving: 128 calories, 4 g protein, 20 g carbohydrate, 4 g fat, 0.5 g saturated fat, 0 mg cholesterol, 223 mg sodium, 2 g fiber

VEGETARIAN
SEAFOOD
AND PASTA

Butternut Squash Risotto

320 Calories

When choosing butternut squash, look for the darkest skin, which indicates a higher concentration of beta-carotene. Store in a cool, well-ventilated place for up to 1 month.

Total time: 45 minutes

- 1 large butternut squash
- 5 cups reduced-sodium vegetable broth
- 1 tablespoon olive oil
- 3 cloves garlic, minced
- 2 cups Arborio rice
- 1 cup spinach
- ¼ cup chopped fresh parsley
- ¼ cup grated Parmesan cheese
- ¼ teaspoon salt
- ¼ teaspoon ground black pepper

PIERCE the squash several times with a sharp knife. Place on a paper towel in the microwave. Microwave on high power for 5 minutes. Halve the squash lengthwise. Remove and discard the seeds. Place the halves back on the paper towel and microwave on high power for 5 minutes, or until tender. Let cool slightly, then scoop the flesh into a bowl; discard the shells.

PLACE the broth in a medium saucepan and bring to a simmer over medium-high heat. Reduce the heat to low; keep the broth warm.

HEAT the oil in a Dutch oven coated with cooking spray over medium-high heat. Cook the garlic, stirring, for 1 minute. Add the rice and cook, stirring, for 5 minutes. Add the squash and ½ cup of the broth. Cook, stirring continuously, until the liquid is absorbed. Add ½ cup of the broth. Cook, stirring, until the liquid is absorbed. Continue to add stock, ½ cup at a time. After each addition, stir until the liquid is absorbed. Cook for a total of 25 minutes, or until the rice is creamy and tender. Stir in the spinach, parsley, cheese, salt, and pepper.

Makes 6 servings

Per serving: 320 calories, 8 g protein, 65 g carbohydrate, 4 g fat, 1 g saturated fat, 3 mg cholesterol, 270 mg sodium, 6 g fiber

Winter Kasha with Potatoes and Carrots

209 Calories

Kasha is a common name for hulled, crushed buckwheat kernels. Look for toasted buckwheat, which has a wonderful nutty flavor, in supermarkets and natural food stores.

Total time: 35 minutes

- 1 teaspoon olive oil
- 1 cup chopped onions
- 1 cup sliced carrots
- 2 small red potatoes, chopped
- 1 cup kasha
- 2 cups reduced-sodium vegetable broth
- ¼ cup minced fresh parsley
- ½ teaspoon ground black pepper
- ¼ teaspoon salt

HEAT the oil in a medium saucepan coated with cooking spray over medium-high heat until hot. Add the onions and carrots; cook, stirring, for 5 minutes, or until the onions are tender. Add the potatoes and kasha. Cook, stirring, for 3 minutes. Add the broth. Bring to a boil. Reduce the heat to medium, cover, and simmer for 15 minutes, or until the potatoes are soft and the kasha is tender. Stir in the parsley, pepper, and salt.

Makes 4 servings

Per serving: 209 calories, 6 g protein, 44 g carbohydrate, 2 g fat, 0.5 g saturated fat, 0 mg cholesterol, 246 mg sodium, 7 g fiber

Crepes with Creamy Vegetable Filling

117 calories

Crepes are an especially light, thin pancake that make an excellent wrapper for sweet and savory fillings—in this case, a delicious blend of veggies and cheese.

Total time: 50 minutes

CREPES

- 1 cup fat-free milk
- ½ cup all-purpose flour
- 2 eggs
- 1 teaspoon oil
- ¼ teaspoon ground nutmeg

FILLING

- 1 small clove garlic, minced
- 1 teaspoon olive oil
- 2 cups broccoli florets
- 1 cup sliced mushrooms
- ½ cup shredded carrots
- 2 tablespoons reduced-sodium chicken broth
- 1 teaspoon chopped chives
- ⅛ teaspoon ground black pepper
- ⅓ cup fat-free cottage cheese
- 2 tablespoons fat-free plain yogurt
- 2 teaspoons grated Parmesan cheese

TO MAKE THE CREPES:

COMBINE the milk, flour, eggs, oil, and nutmeg in a blender or food processor. Blend for 2 minutes. Pour into a bowl and refrigerate for 10 minutes.

COAT a medium nonstick skillet with cooking spray. Place the skillet over medium-high heat until a drop of water sizzles when sprinkled on its surface. Pour 2 tablespoons of the batter into the center of the skillet; swirl to form a very thin circle about 7" across. Immediately pour any excess batter back into the bowl. Cook the crepe for 1 minute, or until bubbles appear around the edges. Turn and cook the other side for 30 seconds. Continue cooking the crepes until all the batter is used. You should have 12 crepes. Stack the cooked crepes on a plate until ready to fill.

TO MAKE THE FILLING:

HEAT a large nonstick skillet over medium-high heat and add the garlic and oil. Cook for 1 minute, or until fragrant. Add the broccoli, mushrooms, carrots, and broth. Cover and cook for 3 minutes. Remove from the heat; add the chives and pepper.

PREHEAT the broiler. Coat a 13" × 9" baking dish with cooking spray.

COMBINE the cottage cheese and yogurt in a blender or food processor and pulse until very smooth. Transfer to a large bowl. Stir in the vegetable mixture. Spoon about 1 tablespoon into each crepe; roll tightly. Place the crepes, seam side down, in the baking dish. Sprinkle with the Parmesan; broil for 1 minute, or until the cheese melts.

Makes 6 servings

Per serving: 117 calories, 8 g protein, 14 g carbohydrate, 4 g fat, 1 g saturated fat, 72 mg cholesterol, 125 mg sodium, 2 g fiber

Chile-Cheese Quiche

This lively Southwestern treatment of the French classic is a wonderful brunch or light supper dish. It's made far healthier by leaving out the crust.

174 Calories

Total time: 50 minutes

- 1 cup chopped onions
- 2 cloves garlic, minced
- 2 teaspoons olive oil
- 1 cup sliced carrots
- 1 cup sliced mushrooms
- 1 cup chopped tomatoes
- 1 cup chopped scallions
- ½ teaspoon ground cumin
- ¼ teaspoon ground coriander
- 1 cup shredded low-fat extra-sharp Cheddar cheese
- 4 eggs
- ½ cup fat-free sour cream
- 1 tablespoon all-purpose flour
- 1 can (12 ounces) whole mild green chile peppers
- ¼ cup grated Parmesan cheese

PREHEAT the oven to 375°F. Coat a 9" pie plate with cooking spray.

COOK the onions and garlic in the oil in a large nonstick skillet over medium-high heat for 2 minutes. Add the carrots, mushrooms, tomatoes, scallions, cumin, and coriander. Cook, stirring, for 10 minutes, or until the vegetables are very soft.

PUREE the Cheddar, eggs, sour cream, and flour in a blender or food processor until smooth. Slit the chile peppers lengthwise and arrange on the bottom and up the sides of the prepared pie plate, overlapping slightly. Spoon the vegetable mixture over the peppers. Pour the egg mixture over the vegetables. Sprinkle with the Parmesan.

BAKE for 30 minutes, or until the quiche is golden brown and firm.

Makes 6 servings

Per serving: 174 calories, 13 g protein, 15 g carbohydrate, 8 g fat, 3 g saturated fat, 150 mg cholesterol, 486 mg sodium, 3 g fiber

Garden Frittata

223
Calories

A frittata is an Italian omelet where the ingredients are stirred into the egg mixture instead of placed on top. Frittatas are typically cooked for a few minutes on the stove and then finished in the oven.

Total time: 30 minutes

- 1 teaspoon olive oil
- 2 cups chopped onions
- 1 cup sliced carrots
- 3 cloves garlic, minced
- 2 cups frozen broccoli florets, thawed
- 1 package (10 ounces) frozen artichoke hearts, thawed and chopped
- 1 cup shredded low-fat extra-sharp Cheddar cheese
- ½ cup fat-free milk
- 4 egg whites, lightly beaten
- 2 eggs, lightly beaten
- ⅛ teaspoon crushed red pepper flakes
- 2 tablespoons grated Parmesan cheese

PREHEAT the oven to 325°F. Heat the oil in a large nonstick ovenproof skillet over medium-high heat. Add the onions, carrots, and garlic. Cook, stirring, for 5 minutes, or until the onions are tender. Add the broccoli and artichoke hearts. Cook, stirring, for 3 minutes.

STIR together the Cheddar, milk, egg whites, eggs, and pepper flakes in a medium bowl. Add to the skillet and stir once. Cook for 3 minutes, or until the eggs begin to set on the bottom.

BAKE for 15 to 20 minutes, or until the frittata is firm and golden brown. Sprinkle with the Parmesan.

Makes 4 servings

Per serving: 223 calories, 19 g protein, 21 g carbohydrate, 8 g fat, 3 g saturated fat, 115 mg cholesterol, 425 mg sodium, 7 g fiber

NUTRITION NEWS TO USE

Crushing garlic cloves—and letting them stand for up to 30 minutes before heating them—activates and preserves the garlic's heart-protecting compounds, according to a 2007 study from Argentina. Cooking uncrushed garlic for as little as 6 minutes can completely suppress its protective strength.

Vegetable Patties

141 Calories

Hearty mushrooms boost the flavor of these tasty vegetable burgers. Allow three or four patties per serving. This recipe makes a nice large batch to freeze for quick future meals.

Total time: 50 minutes

 3 cups chopped mushrooms
1/4 cup chopped onion
1/4 cup reduced-sodium vegetable broth
 2 teaspoons minced garlic
 2 cups shredded potatoes
 2 cups chopped broccoli florets
 1 cup shredded low-fat Swiss cheese
1/4 cup grated Parmesan cheese
 2 eggs, lightly beaten
 1 teaspoon dried thyme
1/2 teaspoon salt
3/4 cup dry bread crumbs

COOK the mushrooms, onion, broth, and garlic, stirring, in a large nonstick skillet coated with cooking spray over medium-high heat for 10 minutes, or until the mushrooms release liquid. Add the potatoes and broccoli. Cook, stirring, for 5 minutes, or until the broccoli is soft. Transfer to a medium bowl. Stir the Swiss, Parmesan, eggs, thyme, and salt into the bowl.

SHAPE the mixture into 24 small patties. Place the bread crumbs on a plate. Dip the patties in the bread crumbs, patting to make sure the crumbs adhere.

COOK the patties in batches in a large non-stick skillet coated with cooking spray for 10 minutes, turning once, until golden brown.

Makes 8 servings

Per serving: 141 calories, 10 g protein, 18 g carbohydrate, 3 g fat, 1.5 g saturated fat, 60 mg cholesterol, 323 mg sodium, 2 g fiber

Sweet Potatoes Stuffed with Chili

467
Calories

Black bean chili looks stunning spooned over bright orange sweet potatoes. If you have fresh cilantro on hand, mince some for a pretty garnish. The amount of fiber in this dish—18 grams—is sure to leave you feeling satisfied for hours!

Total time: 1 hour 5 minutes

- 4 large sweet potatoes (about 2 pounds total)
- ¼ cup dry sherry or apple juice
- 1 teaspoon olive oil
- ½ cup chopped onion
- ½ cup sliced carrots
- 2 teaspoons minced garlic
- ¼ cup salsa
- 2 cans (15 ounces each) no-salt-added black beans, rinsed and drained
- 1 can (14.5 ounces) whole tomatoes, chopped
- ½ cup frozen peas
- 1 tablespoon chili powder
- 1 teaspoon ground cumin
- ¼ teaspoon salt
- ¼ cup fat-free plain yogurt

PREHEAT the oven to 400°F. Pierce the sweet potatoes several times with a fork. Place on a large baking sheet. Bake for 1 hour, or until very tender.

MEANWHILE, bring the sherry and oil to a boil in a large skillet over medium-high heat. Add the onion, carrots, and garlic. Cook, stirring, for 3 minutes. Stir in the salsa. Cook for 5 minutes, or until the vegetables soften.

STIR in the beans, tomatoes, peas, chili powder, cumin, and salt. Reduce the heat to low. Cover and simmer, stirring frequently, for 20 minutes, or until the chili is thick. Split the sweet potatoes and mash the pulp lightly with a fork. Top with the chili and yogurt.

Makes 4 servings

Per serving: 467 calories, 16 g protein, 93 g carbohydrate, 2 g fat, 0.5 g saturated fat, 1 mg cholesterol, 593 mg sodium, 18 g fiber

Spicy Tofu and Vegetable Stir-Fry

89 calories

This easy stir-fry is easily adaptable. Prefer a little more heat? Add another dash of red pepper. Likewise, feel free to substitute bell peppers, summer squash, or bok choy for the other veggies—enjoy whatever is in season!

Total time: 1 hour 15 minutes

- 8 ounces extra-firm reduced-fat tofu, cut into ½" cubes
- 6 scallions, minced
- ¼ cup reduced-sodium soy sauce
- ¼ cup dry sherry or apple juice
- 5 cloves garlic, minced
- 1 teaspoon grated fresh ginger
- ½ teaspoon ground red pepper
- ⅓ cup reduced-sodium chicken broth
- ½ onion, thinly sliced
- 1 large carrot, julienned
- 1 cup broccoli florets
- ½ teaspoon chili oil

COMBINE the tofu, scallions, soy sauce, sherry, garlic, ginger, and red pepper in a shallow glass dish. Cover and refrigerate for 1 hour, stirring occasionally.

BRING the broth to a boil in a large nonstick skillet over medium-high heat. Add the onion and cook for 2 minutes. Add the carrot, cover, and cook for 2 minutes longer. Add the broccoli and cook for 2 minutes, or until the vegetables are tender.

STRAIN the tofu mixture, reserving 2 tablespoons of the marinade. Add the tofu mixture to the skillet; cook and stir gently for 1 minute, or until heated through. Add the reserved marinade and chili oil. Toss well.

Makes 4 servings

Per serving: 89 calories, 7 g protein, 9 g carbohydrate, 2 g fat, 0 g saturated fat, 1 mg cholesterol, 701 mg sodium,* 2 g fiber

*Limit saturated fat to 10 percent of total calories—about 17 grams per day for most women—and sodium intake to less than 2,300 milligrams.

Spicy Bean Pancakes with Tomato-Pepper Puree

286 Calories

Canned beans make moist, hearty pancakes that taste great with a Southwestern sea-soned tomato sauce. If you're pressed for time, serve with your favorite salsa instead.

Total time: 50 minutes

PANCAKES

- ½ cup canned navy or pinto beans, rinsed and drained
- 2 eggs, lightly beaten
- ⅓ cup all-purpose flour
- ⅓ cup yellow cornmeal
- 1 teaspoon baking powder
- ½ cup low-fat buttermilk
- ½ cup shredded low-fat extra-sharp Cheddar cheese
- ½ small jalapeño pepper, seeded and minced (wear plastic gloves when handling)
- 1 teaspoon olive oil

PUREE

- 1½ cups tomato puree
- 1 red bell pepper, chopped
- 2 tablespoons lime juice
- 1 tablespoon finely chopped garlic
- 1 tablespoon chopped fresh cilantro or parsley
- 1 teaspoon honey
- ½ teaspoon dried thyme
- ½ teaspoon ground black pepper

TO MAKE THE PANCAKES:

PLACE the beans in a medium bowl and mash well with a fork. Stir in the eggs until well blended. Stir in the flour, cornmeal, and baking powder. Add the buttermilk, cheese, jalapeño, and oil. Stir until the mixture resembles a thick sauce.

HEAT a large nonstick skillet coated with cooking spray over medium-high heat until hot. Add 2 tablespoons of the batter per pancake, leaving room between. Cook for 1 to 2 minutes, or until bubbles appear on the surface of the pancakes. Turn and cook for 2 minutes, or until golden brown. Place on a plate; cover to keep warm. Repeat with the remaining batter to make a total of 12 pancakes.

TO MAKE THE PUREE:

PROCESS the tomato puree, bell pepper, lime juice, and garlic in a blender or food processor until smooth. Transfer to a medium saucepan. Stir in the cilantro, honey, thyme, and black pepper. Cook, stirring occasionally, over medium heat for 10 minutes. Serve with the pancakes.

Makes 4 servings

Per serving: 286 calories, 17 g protein, 38 g carbohydrate, 8 g fat, 3 g saturated fat, 216 mg cholesterol, 837 mg sodium,* 5 g fiber

*Limit saturated fat to 10 percent of total calories—about 17 grams per day for most women—and sodium intake to less than 2,300 milligrams.

Eggplant Rolls

197 Calories

If desired, serve marinara sauce with these easy eggplant rolls—a modern twist on traditional pasta dishes. Eggplant tends to absorb oil easily, so this version makes smart use of vegetable broth for noticeably lighter results.

Total time: 1 hour

- 2 large eggplants
- 1 cup chopped onions
- 1 cup chopped red bell peppers
- 1 teaspoon olive oil
- 1 cup reduced-sodium vegetable broth
- ½ cup chopped fresh parsley
- ½ cup shredded fat-free mozzarella cheese
- ½ cup fat-free ricotta cheese
- ½ cup grated Parmesan cheese

PREHEAT the broiler. Coat 2 large baking sheets with cooking spray. With a serrated knife, cut the eggplants lengthwise into ¼" slices. Place on the prepared baking sheets. Coat with cooking spray. Broil 4" from the heat for 8 minutes, or until golden brown, turning once. Let cool.

TURN the oven temperature to 350°F. Coat a 13" × 9" baking dish with cooking spray.

COOK the onions, peppers, and oil, stirring, in a large skillet over medium-high heat for 3 minutes, or until the onions are golden brown. Add ¼ cup of the broth. Cook for 5 minutes, or until the vegetables are very soft. Place in a medium bowl. Stir in the parsley, mozzarella, ricotta, and Parmesan.

SPREAD the cheese mixture on the eggplant slices. Roll tightly to enclose the filling. Arrange, seam side down, in a single layer in the prepared baking dish. Pour the remaining broth around the rolls. Bake for 40 minutes, or until hot.

Makes 4 servings

Per serving: 197 calories, 15 g protein, 26 g carbohydrate, 5 g fat, 2 g saturated fat, 16 mg cholesterol, 338 mg sodium, 11 g fiber

Cheesy Cornmeal Cakes with Salsa

76 Calories

Inspired by Italian polenta, or cooked cornmeal, these economical cornmeal cakes are as easy to make as they are to enjoy. It's also a great way to use some leftover polenta.

Total time: 40 minutes

SALSA

- 1 small onion, minced
- 1 cup chopped tomatoes
- 2 cloves garlic, minced
- 1 tablespoon chopped fresh basil
- 1 teaspoon crushed red pepper flakes

CORNMEAL CAKES

- 1¼ cups yellow cornmeal
- 1 cup cold water
- 2 tablespoons grated Parmesan cheese
- ½ cup shredded low-fat mozzarella cheese
- ½ cup shredded low-fat extra-sharp Cheddar cheese

TO MAKE THE SALSA:

STIR together the onion, tomatoes, garlic, basil, and pepper flakes in a small bowl. Let stand for 30 minutes, stirring occasionally.

TO MAKE THE CORNMEAL CAKES:

BRING the cornmeal and water to a boil in a medium saucepan over medium-high heat. Cook, stirring frequently, for 12 to 15 minutes, or until the mixture is thick. Remove from the heat; stir in the Parmesan. Line a 9" × 3" baking pan with wax paper; spoon the cornmeal mixture onto the pan and spread an even thickness. Cover with plastic wrap and refrigerate for 20 minutes, or until firm.

PREHEAT the broiler. Cut the cornmeal mixture into 12 pieces; place on a large baking sheet. Coat with cooking spray. Broil 4" from the heat for 2 minutes, or until golden brown. Turn and coat the other side with the spray. Top with the mozzarella and Cheddar. Broil for 2 minutes, or until the cheese melts. Serve with the salsa.

Makes 6 servings

Per serving: 76 calories, 4 g protein, 11 g carbohydrate, 2 g fat, 1 g saturated fat, 4 mg cholesterol, 81 mg sodium, 1 g fiber

Pad Thai Rice Bowls with Shrimp and Peanuts

414 Calories

—Susan Riley, Allen, Texas

"I love the combination of sweet and savory as well as the many textures in this low-fat dish."

Total time: 20 minutes

- 2 teaspoons canola oil, divided
- 1 pound medium shrimp, peeled and deveined
- 2 eggs, lightly beaten
- ⅓ cup reduced-sodium Thai fish sauce
- ⅓ cup sugar
- 1½ teaspoon rice wine vinegar
- 5 cloves garlic, minced
- 2 tablespoons minced shallot
- 5 cups cold cooked jasmine rice
- ½ cup chopped scallions
- 2 cups fresh bean sprouts
- ¾ cup roasted salted peanuts, chopped
  Quartered limes, chopped cucumbers, shredded carrots (optional)

HEAT 1 teaspoon of the oil in a large nonstick skillet over medium-high heat. Add the shrimp and cook, stirring, for 7 minutes, or until opaque. Transfer to a plate and keep warm.

ADD the eggs to the skillet. Cook for 1 to 2 minutes until set (do not stir). Remove to a plate, chop, and set aside.

IN a small bowl, combine the fish sauce, sugar, and vinegar. Heat the remaining 1 teaspoon oil in the skillet over medium heat. Add the garlic and shallot. Cook for 1 minute, or until softened. Add the rice and cook for 1 minute. Stir in the shrimp, eggs, and vinegar mixture. Cook for 2 minutes, or until heated through.

REMOVE from the heat. Stir in the scallions, bean sprouts, and peanuts. Garnish with limes, cucumber, and carrots, if using.

Makes 4 servings

Per serving: 414 calories, 24 g protein, 51 g carbohydrate, 14 g fat, 2 g saturated fat, 171 mg cholesterol, 918 mg sodium,* 3 g fiber

*Limit saturated fat to 10 percent of total calories—about 17 grams per day for most women—and sodium intake to less than 2,300 milligrams.

Seared Sea Scallops with Quinoa Pilaf

468
Calories

Shannon Abdollmohammadi, USA

"Eating healthy works best for me when the food explodes with flavor and unique textures like this delicious dish."

Total time: 1 hour

SAUCE

- 2 cups pomegranate juice
- 1½ teaspoons reduced-sodium soy sauce
- 1½ teaspoons Chinese five-spice powder
- ¼ cup minced shallot
- 2 teaspoons minced fresh ginger
- 1 teaspoon cornstarch
- 1 tablespoon water

PILAF

- 1 teaspoon olive oil
- 1 small onion, chopped
- 2 cups quinoa, rinsed very well
- 2 cups reduced-sodium chicken broth
- ¼ teaspoon ground cinnamon
- ⅛ teaspoon saffron threads, crushed
- ⅛ teaspoon ground red pepper
- ½ cup raisins
- ½ cup dried cranberries
- ¼ cup toasted sliced almonds
- 2 teaspoons lemon juice

SCALLOPS

- 2 pounds large sea scallops, patted dry
  Salt and ground black pepper
- 2 tablespoons olive oil, divided
- ½ teaspoon sesame oil, divided
- 2 teaspoons black sesame seeds (optional)

TO MAKE THE SAUCE:

BRING first five ingredients to a simmer over medium-low heat. Simmer for 45 minutes, or until the sauce reduces to about ½ cup. Mix the cornstarch and water until smooth and add to sauce. Stir until thickened. Keep warm.

MEANWHILE, TO MAKE THE PILAF:

HEAT the oil in a large pan over medium-high heat. Add the onion and cook, stirring, for 5 minutes. Stir in the quinoa and cook for 5 minutes. Stir in the broth, cinnamon, saffron, and pepper. Bring to a boil. Reduce the heat to low, cover, and simmer 20 to 25 minutes, or until tender. Remove from the heat. Stir in remaining ingredients. Cover and set aside.

TO MAKE THE SCALLOPS:

SPRINKLE the scallops with salt and pepper to taste. Heat half of the olive oil and half of the sesame oil in a large nonstick skillet over high heat. Cook half of the scallops for 4 minutes, turning once, until opaque. Transfer to a plate and keep warm. Repeat with remaining oil and scallops. Drizzle with the sauce and garnish with sesame seeds, if using. Serve with the pilaf.

Makes 6 servings

Per serving: 468 calories, 20 g protein, 72 g carbohydrate, 12 g fat, 1.5 g saturated fat, 20 mg cholesterol, 362 mg sodium, 6 g fiber

Spicy Shrimp and Black Bean Enchiladas

441 Calories

—Debbie Reid, Clearwater, Florida

"I recently lost 89 pounds on a low-fat, high-fiber diet. (I should actually say a change in lifestyle, not diet!) One of the many things I did was to use fat-free or reduced-fat products when they were available."

Total time: 55 minutes

- 1 can (10 ounces) enchilada sauce
- 12 ounces peeled and deveined large shrimp, coarsely chopped
- 1 teaspoon lime juice
- 4 ounces fat-free cream cheese, softened
- 1 canned chipotle pepper, seeds removed, minced (wear plastic gloves when handling)
- ¼ teaspoon adobo sauce
- 4 flour tortillas (8" diameter)
- 1 cup canned no-salt-added black beans, rinsed and drained
- 1 cup shredded reduced-fat sharp Cheddar cheese
- ⅓ cup reduced-fat sour cream
- ½ teaspoon ground cumin
- ¼ teaspoon smoked paprika
- ¼ teaspoon ground coriander

PREHEAT the oven to 375°F. Spray a 9" × 9" baking dish with cooking spray. Spread 2 tablespoons of the enchilada sauce over the bottom of the baking dish.

STIR together the shrimp, lime juice, and ⅓ cup of the remaining enchilada sauce in a medium bowl.

STIR together the cream cheese, chipotle, and adobo sauce in a small bowl. Spread over the tortillas. Top with the shrimp, black beans, and cheese. Roll the tortillas up tightly into a cigar shape and place, seam side down, in the prepared baking dish.

STIR together the remaining enchilada sauce, sour cream, cumin, paprika, and coriander in a medium bowl. Spread over the tortillas to cover completely.

COVER and bake for 30 minutes, or until hot and bubbly.

Makes 4 servings

Per serving: 441 calories, 37 g protein, 40 g carbohydrate, 15 g fat, 6.5 g saturated fat,* 196 mg cholesterol, 1,226 mg sodium,* 5 g fiber

*Limit saturated fat to 10 percent of total calories—about 17 grams per day for most women—and sodium intake to less than 2,300 milligrams.

Lemon-Herb Shrimp and Cannellini Beans over Tuscan Toast

329 Calories

—Janice Elder, Charlotte, North Carolina

What a refreshing combination! Lemon and herbs are fresh and delicious tossed with tomatoes, beans, and shrimp. This easy dish is sure to become a weeknight lifesaver.

Total time: 15 minutes

- 2 tablespoons extra-virgin olive oil, divided
- 16 large shrimp, peeled and deveined
- 4 tablespoons sliced almonds
  Salt and ground black pepper
- ½ cup dry-packed sun-dried tomatoes, julienned
- 1 can (15.5 ounces) no-salt-added cannellini beans, rinsed and drained
- 2 cloves garlic, minced
- ½ cup reduced-sodium chicken broth
  Juice of 1 lemon
- 2 tablespoons chopped fresh sage
- 2 tablespoons chopped fresh basil
- 4 slices whole wheat bread, lightly toasted and quartered
- 1 small tomato, seeded and diced

HEAT 1 tablespoon of the oil in a large skillet over medium-high heat. Add the shrimp and almonds. Cook, stirring, for 3 minutes, or until the shrimp are opaque. Season with salt and pepper to taste. Transfer to a bowl with a slotted spoon. Keep warm.

ADD the sun-dried tomatoes, beans, garlic, broth, and lemon juice to the skillet. Bring to a boil over medium-high heat. Cook, stirring, for 5 minutes, or until the liquid is reduced. Stir in the sage and basil.

ARRANGE the toast quarters on 4 plates. Spoon the bean mixture and shrimp over the toasts. Top with the diced tomato and drizzle with the remaining 1 tablespoon oil.

Makes 4 servings

Per serving: 329 calories, 16 g protein, 43 g carbohydrate, 12 g fat, 1.5 g saturated fat, 43 mg cholesterol, 659 mg sodium,* 8 g fiber

*Limit saturated fat to 10 percent of total calories—about 17 grams per day for most women—and sodium intake to less than 2,300 milligrams.

Shrimp and Orzo Salad

387 calories

Orzo is an inexpensive rice-shaped pasta that is easily found in supermarkets. If using less expensive bulk orzo, measure 3 cups (uncooked) for this recipe. If you can find fiber-rich whole wheat orzo, by all means buy it to use in this dish.

Total time: 20 minutes

- 1 package (16 ounces) orzo pasta
- 8 ounces peeled and deveined medium shrimp
- 1 cup diced, no-salt-added canned tomatoes, drained
- 1 cup shredded carrots
- 1 cup peeled, seeded, and sliced cucumbers
- ½ cup chopped scallions
- 1 teaspoon grated lemon rind
- ¼ cup lemon juice
- 2 tablespoons olive oil
- 2 tablespoons fat-free plain yogurt
- 1 tablespoon grated Parmesan cheese
- 1 teaspoon minced garlic
- ½ teaspoon salt
- ½ teaspoon ground black pepper

BRING a large pot of water to a boil over medium-high heat. Add the orzo and cook for 6 minutes. Add the shrimp and cook for 2 minutes longer, or until the shrimp turn pink and the orzo is al dente. Drain well and allow to cool slightly.

TRANSFER the orzo and shrimp to a large salad bowl and add the tomatoes, carrots, cucumbers, scallions, lemon rind and juice, oil, yogurt, cheese, garlic, salt, and pepper. Toss to combine.

Makes 4 servings

Per serving: 387 calories, 19 g protein, 62 g carbohydrate, 7 g fat, 1.5 g saturated fat, 58 mg cholesterol, 299 mg sodium, 4 g fiber

Fish with Jerk Seasoning

183 Calories

Hailing from the Caribbean, spicy jerk seasoning adds bold flavor to mild fish. In this recipe, jalapeño serves as a stand-in for the traditional—and much hotter—Scotch bonnet chile.

Total time: 15 minutes + chilling time

⅓ cup finely chopped red bell pepper
¼ cup finely chopped onion
 1 jalapeño pepper, finely chopped (wear plastic gloves when handling)
 1 tablespoon minced garlic
 1 tablespoon minced fresh ginger
 1 tablespoon reduced-sodium soy sauce
 2 teaspoons canola oil
½ teaspoon dried thyme
¼ teaspoon ground allspice
¼ teaspoon ground black pepper
 2 pounds firm white fish fillets, such as red snapper, grouper, or halibut

STIR together the bell pepper, onion, jalapeño, garlic, ginger, soy sauce, oil, thyme, allspice, and black pepper in a glass baking dish. Add the fish, turning to coat. Cover and refrigerate for 1 hour, turning once.

PREHEAT the broiler. Coat the rack of a broiler pan with cooking spray. Place the fish on the rack. Broil 4" from the heat, turning once, for 5 to 9 minutes, or until the fish flakes easily with a fork.

Makes 6 servings

Per serving: 183 calories, 32 g protein, 3 g carbohydrate, 4 g fat, 1 g saturated fat, 56 mg cholesterol, 199 mg sodium, 1 g fiber

Cod with Mustard Sauce

234 Calories

Peaches, mustard, and brown sugar blend to make a sweet-tangy marinade for tender fish. Scrod or flounder works equally well as a substitute for the cod. By all means, feel free to use fresh peaches when in season.

Total time: 15 minutes

- ⅓ cup packed brown sugar
- ¼ cup chopped onion
- ¼ cup frozen sliced peaches, thawed
- 2 tablespoons Dijon mustard
- 2 tablespoons reduced-sodium soy sauce
- 1 teaspoon minced garlic
- ¼ teaspoon ground red pepper
- 1½ pounds cod fillets

PREHEAT the oven to 400°F. Coat a 13" × 9" baking dish with cooking spray.

PUREE the brown sugar, onion, peaches, mustard, soy sauce, garlic, and pepper in a blender or food processor until smooth. Place the fish in the prepared pan. Top with the peach puree. Bake for 7 to 10 minutes, or until the fish flakes easily with a fork.

Makes 4 servings

Per serving: 234 calories, 31 g protein, 22 g carbohydrate, 1 g fat, 0.5 g saturated fat, 73 mg cholesterol, 580 mg sodium, 0 g fiber

Spicy Fish with Peppers

128 calories

This island-style recipe calls for a colorful medley of sweet and hot peppers. Serve with brown rice or roasted sweet potatoes for an authentic—and flavorful—combination.

Total time: 30 minutes

- 1 green bell pepper, chopped
- 1 red bell pepper, chopped
- ¼ cup chopped fresh parsley
- 1 small jalapeño pepper, seeded and chopped (wear plastic gloves when handling)

    Juice of 1 lime
- 2 tablespoons cider vinegar
- 4 cloves garlic, minced
- 2 teaspoons packed brown sugar
- 4 cod fillets (4 ounces each)

MIX the bell peppers, parsley, jalapeño, lime juice, vinegar, garlic, and brown sugar in a small bowl. Let stand at room temperature for 15 minutes.

PREHEAT the oven to 400°F. Coat a 13" × 9" glass baking dish with cooking spray; arrange the fish in the baking dish. Top with the sauce.

BAKE for 15 minutes, or until the fish flakes easily with a fork.

Makes 4 servings

Per serving: 128 calories, 21 g protein, 8 g carbohydrate, 1 g fat, 0 g saturated fat, 49 mg cholesterol, 67 mg sodium, 2 g fiber

Catfish with Sweet-and-Sour Onions and Pineapple

417 Calories

One rule of thumb when buying fresh fish—it should never smell fishy. Here in this particular dish, onions become an intriguing Asian-style relish that's delicious over catfish.

Total time: 25 minutes

- 1 tablespoon olive oil
- 4 onions, sliced
- 2 cloves garlic, minced
- 1 can (20 ounces) pineapple chunks packed in juice
- ¼ cup cider vinegar
- 1 tablespoon reduced-sodium soy sauce
- 2 tablespoons cornstarch
- 3 tablespoons apple juice
- 1½ pounds catfish fillets

HEAT the oil in a large nonstick skillet coated with cooking spray over medium heat. Add the onions and garlic. Cook, stirring, for 5 minutes, or until the onions are tender. Add the pineapple with juice, vinegar, and soy sauce. Bring to a boil.

PLACE the cornstarch in a cup. Add the apple juice and stir until smooth. Add to the skillet. Cook, stirring, for 5 minutes, or until the sauce thickens. Place the fish over the sauce. Cover and cook for 8 minutes, or until the fish flakes easily with a fork.

Makes 4 servings

Per serving: 417 calories, 29 g protein, 38 g carbohydrate, 17 g fat, 3.5 g saturated fat,* 80 mg cholesterol, 249 mg sodium, 3 g fiber

*Limit saturated fat to 10 percent of total calories—about 17 grams per day for most women—and sodium intake to less than 2,300 milligrams.

Cod with Salsa Verde

Baked cod stays moist and flavorful when topped with a sprightly green salsa. Other worthy substitutes include halibut or snapper.

226 Calories

Total time: 20 minutes

- ½ cup chopped scallions
- ½ cup chopped fresh parsley
- ¼ cup minced onion
- ¼ cup lemon juice
- 2 tablespoons capers, rinsed and chopped
- 4 cloves garlic, minced
- 2 teaspoons olive oil
- 2 teaspoons minced jalapeño pepper (wear plastic gloves when handling)
- 4 cod fillets (8 ounces each)

PREHEAT the oven to 400°F. Place an 18" × 24" piece of foil on a baking sheet.

STIR together the scallions, parsley, onion, lemon juice, capers, garlic, oil, and pepper in a small bowl. Arrange the cod on the foil in a single layer. Top with the scallion mixture. Fold the sides of the foil over the fish to create a sealed packet.

BAKE for 10 minutes, or until the fish flakes easily with a fork.

Makes 4 servings

Per serving: 226 calories, 41 g protein, 5 g carbohydrate, 4 g fat, 0.5 g saturated fat, 98 mg cholesterol, 257 mg sodium, 1 g fiber

South-of-France Baked Cod

244 Calories

The fragrance of tomatoes, capers, and olives in this sauce will bring back summer any time of the year. Baking fish on top of a bed of vegetables, as with this dish, is an easy way to prevent them from sticking.

Total time: 35 minutes

- 1½ cups chopped onions
- 1 green bell pepper, chopped
- 1 red bell pepper, chopped
- ¼ cup apple juice
- 4 cups chopped tomatoes
- 2 cups cubed red potatoes
- ¼ cup chopped fresh parsley
- 1 teaspoon minced garlic
- 1 tablespoon capers, rinsed
- 2 teaspoons packed brown sugar
- 1 teaspoon chopped black olives
- 4 cod fillets (4 ounces each)

PREHEAT the oven to 400°F. Heat a large nonstick skillet coated with cooking spray over medium-high heat. Add the onions, peppers, and apple juice. Cook, stirring, for 5 minutes, or until the peppers are soft. Add the tomatoes, potatoes, parsley, and garlic. Cook, stirring occasionally, for 10 minutes, or until the sauce thickens slightly. Add the capers, brown sugar, and olives. Stir well.

SPREAD half of the sauce in the bottom of a 13" × 9" baking dish. Place the cod on top. Cover with the remaining sauce. Cover and bake for 15 minutes, or until the fish flakes easily with a fork.

Makes 4 servings

Per serving: 244 calories, 25 g protein, 34 g carbohydrate, 1.5 g fat, 0.5 g saturated fat, 49 mg cholesterol, 153 mg sodium, 6 g fiber

Cod in Sweet Tomato Sauce

231
Calories

Slow-cooking the tomatoes creates a super-sweet sauce for the cod in this simple one-pot main dish. To mute the taste of frozen fish, if that's what's available at the market, thaw the fish in a shallow dish of milk.

Total time: 30 minutes

- 2 teaspoons olive oil
- 2 cups chopped onions
- 1 cup chopped red bell peppers
- 1 cup chopped celery
- 2 cups chopped tomatoes
- 2 teaspoons minced garlic
- 1 teaspoon sugar
- ¼ cup reduced-sodium chicken broth
- ¼ teaspoon salt
- ¼ teaspoon ground black pepper
- 1½ pounds cod fillets

HEAT the oil in a Dutch oven coated with cooking spray over medium-high heat. Add the onions, bell peppers, and celery. Cook, stirring, for 5 minutes, or until the onions are tender.

ADD the tomatoes, garlic, and sugar. Reduce the heat to medium, cover, and cook, stirring, for 10 minutes, or until the tomatoes soften. Add the broth, salt, and black pepper. Bring to a boil.

PLACE the cod on top of the tomato sauce. Reduce the heat to medium, cover, and simmer for 10 to 12 minutes, or until the fish flakes easily with a fork.

Makes 4 servings

Per serving: 231 calories, 33 g protein, 16 g carbohydrate, 4 g fat, 1 g saturated fat, 73 mg cholesterol, 293 mg sodium, 4 g fiber

Grilled Salmon with Citrus Salsa

510 Calories

—Marie Sheppard, Chicago, Illinois

Fresh and flavorful, this salsa is a lovely blend of orange, olive, onion, and fennel—delicious atop grilled salmon. To save prep time, look for pitted olives; they're often available in the olive bar.

Total time: 20 minutes

- 2 **tablespoons sherry vinegar**
- 3 **tablespoons + 2 teaspoons extra-virgin olive oil, divided**
- 1 **navel orange, peeled and chopped**
- ½ **cup chopped kalamata olives**
- ⅓ **cup minced red onion**
- ⅓ **cup chopped fennel**
- 1 **tablespoon chopped fresh oregano**
- 1 **tablespoon chopped fresh flat-leaf parsley**
- 4 **salmon fillets (4 to 6 ounces each)**

PLACE the vinegar in a large bowl and whisk in 3 tablespoons of the olive oil. Stir in the orange, olives, onion, fennel, oregano, and parsley. Set aside.

HEAT a ridged nonstick grill pan or skillet over medium-high heat. Brush both sides of the salmon with 2 teaspoons of the oil. Cook the salmon, shaking the pan occasionally to prevent sticking and turning once, for 6 to 8 minutes, or until the salmon flakes easily with a fork.

REMOVE the salmon from pan and place on a serving platter. Spoon over the salmon.

Makes 4 servings

Per serving: 510 calories, 24 g protein, 12 g carbohydrate, 40 g fat, 6 g saturated fat,* 67 mg cholesterol, 997 mg sodium,* 2 g fiber

*Limit saturated fat to 10 percent of total calories—about 17 grams per day for most women—and sodium intake to less than 2,300 milligrams.

Pan-Fried Trout

470
Calories

Wedges of fresh lemon, if you have them on hand, can be squeezed over the trout just before serving. Using ground oats instead of bread crumbs is an easy way to sneak more fiber into your diet.

Total time: 15 minutes

- ½ cup all-purpose flour
- ½ teaspoon ground black pepper
- ¼ teaspoon salt
- ¼ cup fat-free milk
- 2 eggs, lightly beaten
- 1½ cups rolled oats
- 2 whole trout (12 ounces each)

STIR together the flour, pepper, and salt in a shallow bowl. Stir together the milk and eggs in another shallow bowl. Grind the oats to a fine powder in a blender or food processor; place in a third bowl. Dredge the trout in the flour mixture. Dip into the egg mixture. Dredge in the oats. Coat with cooking spray.

HEAT a large nonstick skillet coated with cooking spray over medium-high heat. Add the fish. Cook for 10 minutes, turning once, until golden brown and the fish flakes easily with a fork.

TO serve, cut the trout lengthwise down to the backbone. Remove the top 2 fillets to dinner plates. Remove and discard the backbones. Repeat.

Makes 4 servings

Per serving: 470 calories, 46 g protein, 33 g carbohydrate, 16 g fat, 3 g saturated fat, 205 mg cholesterol, 276 mg sodium, 4 g fiber

Field Berry-Drizzled Snapper

—Maryalice Wood, Langley, British Columbia, Canada

293 Calories

"The added color livens up any dinner table, and the tartness of the sauce livens up the tastebuds. For variety, try tilapia fillets."

Total time: 20 minutes

- ½ cup light mayonnaise
- ½ red onion, chopped
- 1 teaspoon lemon pepper
- 1 cup frozen mixed berries, thawed
- 1½ pounds snapper fillets

PREHEAT the oven to 375°F. Coat a baking sheet with cooking spray.

STIR together the mayonnaise, onion, and lemon pepper in a small bowl. Fold in the berries. Place the fish on the baking sheet. Spoon on the mayonnaise mixture. Bake for 15 minutes, or until the fish flakes easily with a fork.

Makes 4 servings

Per serving: 293 calories, 35 g protein, 8 g carbohydrate, 12 g fat, 2 g saturated fat, 73 mg cholesterol, 349 mg sodium, 1 g fiber

Snapper with Orange Sauce

214 Calories

With ingredients that you have right on your pantry shelf, you can whip up this exotic entrée in no time. Serve with quinoa or any small grain dish that will help soak up this delicious sauce.

Total time: 20 minutes

- ½ cup reduced-sodium chicken broth
- ½ cup reduced-calorie orange marmalade
- 1 teaspoon toasted sesame oil
- ½ teaspoon Dijon mustard
- ⅓ cup all-purpose flour
- 1 teaspoon paprika
- ⅛ teaspoon salt
- ⅛ teaspoon ground black pepper
- 4 frozen red snapper fillets (4 ounces each), thawed

BRING the broth, marmalade, sesame oil, and mustard to a boil in a medium saucepan over medium-high heat. Cook, stirring, for 5 minutes, or until the sauce thickens slightly.

STIR together the flour, paprika, salt, and pepper in a shallow dish.

HEAT a large nonstick skillet coated with cooking spray over medium-high heat until hot. Dip the snapper into the flour mixture and place in the skillet. Coat with cooking spray. Cook for 10 minutes, turning once, until golden brown and the fish flakes easily with a fork. Serve with the sauce.

Makes 4 servings

Per serving: 214 calories, 25 g protein, 20 g carbohydrate, 3 g fat, 0.5 g saturated fat, 42 mg cholesterol, 217 mg sodium, 0 g fiber

Spinach and Parmesan Pasta

With a heavy-duty food processor that's always ready to save the day, it actually takes less time to make this pungent pasta topper than it does to cook the pasta.

353 Calories

Total time: 15 minutes

- 1 **pound whole wheat linguine pasta**
- 2 **cups packed baby spinach leaves**
- 2 **cups chopped fresh parsley**
- ¼ **cup grated Parmesan cheese**
- ¼ **cup chopped onion**
- 2 **tablespoons minced garlic**
- 2 **tablespoons chopped walnuts or almonds**
- 2 **tablespoons olive oil**
- 1 **tablespoon dried oregano**
- ⅛ **teaspoon salt**

PREPARE the pasta according to the package directions.

MEANWHILE, process the spinach, parsley, cheese, onion, garlic, walnuts, oil, oregano, and salt in a blender or food processor until smooth. Place in a large bowl and toss with the hot pasta.

Makes 6 servings

Per serving: 353 calories, 14 g protein, 61 g carbohydrate, 8 g fat, 2 g saturated fat, 3 mg cholesterol, 131 mg sodium, 11 g fiber

NUTRITION NEWS TO USE

Spinach is an excellent source of iron, a mineral that helps carry oxygen to your muscles. Getting enough keeps you from feeling tired and sluggish— great for a calorie-burning workout!

Gardener's Pasta

Feel free to use any type of pasta with this versatile recipe. If you like, you can turn it into a hearty main course by adding cooked shrimp, chicken, or sausage.

230 Calories

Total time: 20 minutes

1	teaspoon olive oil
½	cup chopped onion
½	cup chopped red bell pepper
1	tablespoon minced garlic
2½	cups chopped tomatoes
¼	teaspoon dried oregano
2	tablespoons chopped fresh parsley
1	pound rotini pasta

HEAT the oil in a large saucepan over medium-high heat. Add the onion, pepper, and garlic. Cook, stirring, over medium-high heat for 5 minutes, or until the onions are tender. Stir in the tomatoes and oregano. Cook, stirring occasionally, for 10 minutes, or until thick. Stir in the parsley.

MEANWHILE, prepare the pasta according to the package directions. Place in a large bowl. Top with the sauce.

Makes 8 servings

Per serving: 230 calories, 9 g protein, 46 g carbohydrate, 1.5 g fat, 0.5 g saturated fat, 0 mg cholesterol, 0.5 mg sodium, 3 g fiber

---

SHOPPING SAVVY

Pasta Perfect

One of your best diet moves: Swap refined-grain products for whole grain, fiber-rich versions. Large studies have repeatedly shown that eating enough fiber can help reduce your risk of heart disease and diabetes and may even help you avoid weight gain. If it's been a while since you

tried whole grain pasta, it's time to give it another go. Today's offerings have a much more pleasant texture and flavor than the gummy, gritty types of yesteryear. Particularly notable: De Cecco whole wheat pasta, which packs a whopping 7 grams of fiber—plus 8 grams of protein—into a 2-ounce serving that contains just 180 calories and 1.5 grams fat. De Cecco's whole grain offerings include spaghetti, linguine, fusilli, and penne rigate, so you can transform your favorite pasta dish into a super-healthy, super-satisfying dinner. For more information, visit dececcousa.com.

Vegetable Stroganoff over Noodles

470 Calories

When you have a craving for creamy pasta, consider this satisfying stroganoff, made with plenty of vegetables and a low-fat sauce. For even more fiber in the finished dish, use whole-grain, yolk-free egg noodles instead.

Total time: 20 minutes

- 12 ounces yolk-free egg noodles
- ½ cup reduced-sodium chicken broth
- 1 teaspoon olive oil
- 3 cups sliced mushrooms
- 2 cups frozen broccoli florets
- 1 cup sliced carrots
- ¼ cup chopped onion
- 2 cloves garlic, minced
- ¼ teaspoon caraway seeds, crushed
- 2 teaspoons cornstarch
- ¼ cup water
- 1 tablespoon tomato paste
- 1 cup reduced-fat sour cream
- ½ cup fat-free plain yogurt
- 1 tablespoon all-purpose flour
- ¼ teaspoon dried dill
- ¼ teaspoon salt
- ¼ teaspoon pepper

PREPARE the noodles according to the package directions. Place in a large bowl.

BRING the broth and oil to a boil in a large nonstick skillet over medium-high heat. Add the mushrooms, broccoli, carrots, onion, garlic, and caraway seeds. Cook, stirring, for 5 minutes, or until the onions are tender.

WHISK together the cornstarch and water in a cup. Stir in the tomato paste. Add to the skillet. Cook, stirring, for 2 minutes, or until the sauce is thick.

STIR together the sour cream, yogurt, flour, dill, salt, and pepper in a medium bowl. Add to the skillet, stirring well to combine. Cook for 1 minute, or until hot. Toss with the noodles.

Makes 4 servings

Per serving: 470 calories, 18 g protein, 80 g carbohydrate, 10 g fat, 5 g saturated fat,* 24 mg cholesterol, 346 mg sodium, 5 g fiber

*Limit saturated fat to 10 percent of total calories—about 17 grams per day for most women—and sodium intake to less than 2,300 milligrams.

Rotelle with Sweet Pepper Sauce

314 Calories

Colored sweet peppers all seem to ripen at once—as gardeners know. If you're faced with a bumper crop, freeze the extra sauce for up to 4 months.

Total time: 40 minutes

- 1 teaspoon olive oil
- 1 cup chopped onions
- 4 cloves garlic, minced
- ¼ cup reduced-sodium chicken broth
- 4 cups chopped red or yellow bell peppers
- 1 cup chopped tomatoes
- ½ teaspoon dried basil
- ¼ teaspoon salt
- 8 ounces rotelle pasta
- ¼ cup grated Parmesan cheese

HEAT the oil in a large nonstick skillet over medium-high heat. Add the onions and garlic and cook, stirring occasionally, for 5 minutes, or until the onions are golden brown. Add the broth. When the mixture comes to a boil, add the peppers. Cook for 5 minutes, or until the peppers begin to soften. Add the tomatoes, basil, and salt. Cover and cook, stirring occasionally, for 20 minutes, or until the peppers are very soft.

MEANWHILE, cook the rotelle according to the package directions. Drain well and keep warm.

POUR 1 cup of the sauce into a blender or food processor and pulse until smooth. Return the puree to the skillet and mix well. Serve the sauce over the pasta and sprinkle with the cheese.

Makes 4 servings

Per serving: 314 calories, 12 g protein, 58 g carbohydrate, 4 g fat, 1.5 g saturated fat, 4 mg cholesterol, 263 mg sodium, 6 g fiber

Penne with Summer Vegetables

333 Calories

Use the ripest produce from your garden or your local farmers' market for this colorful pasta dish. Just a hint of orange zest and thyme help to make this dish something far from ordinary.

Total time: 30 minutes

- ¼ cup balsamic vinegar
- 2 tablespoons minced garlic
- 1 cup chopped onions
- 1 cup chopped eggplant
- 1 cup chopped yellow summer squash
- 1 red bell pepper, chopped
- 2 cups chopped tomatoes
- ¼ cup chopped fresh parsley
- 1 tablespoon olive oil
- ¼ cup grated Parmesan cheese
- 1 teaspoon sugar
- ½ teaspoon grated orange zest
- ½ teaspoon salt
- ½ teaspoon chopped fresh thyme
- 8 ounces penne pasta

PLACE the vinegar and garlic in a large nonstick skillet over medium-high heat. Cook, stirring, for 3 minutes, or until the garlic softens. Add the onions, eggplant, squash, and pepper. Cook, stirring, for 5 minutes, or until the onions are tender. Add the tomatoes and parsley. Cook, stirring, for 15 minutes, or until the tomatoes are very soft.

ADD the oil, cheese, sugar, orange zest, salt, and thyme to the sauce. Cook for 3 minutes, or until the sauce thickens.

MEANWHILE, prepare the pasta according to the package directions. Place in a large bowl. Top with the sauce and toss to coat.

Makes 4 servings

Per serving: 333 calories, 12 g protein, 59 g carbohydrate, 6 g fat, 2 g saturated fat, 4 mg cholesterol, 385 mg sodium, 5 g fiber

Four-Cheese Macaroni Bake

298 Calories

Who doesn't love creamy mac 'n' cheese? This low-fat version won't disappoint. Plus, you can have it in the oven in about 30 minutes flat.

Total time: 1 hour

- 3 cups elbow macaroni
- 1 cup minced onions
- 2 cloves garlic, minced
- 1 teaspoon olive oil
- 1/3 cup all-purpose flour
- 3 cups fat-free milk
- 3/4 cup fat-free cottage cheese
- 1/2 cup shredded low-fat extra-sharp Cheddar cheese
- 1/2 cup shredded fat-free mozzarella cheese
- 1/2 cup grated Parmesan cheese, divided
- 1/4 teaspoon salt
- 1/4 teaspoon ground black pepper
- 1/2 cup dry bread crumbs

PREHEAT the oven to 375°F. Coat a 13" × 9" baking dish with cooking spray. Prepare the macaroni according to the package directions.

HEAT a large saucepan coated with cooking spray over medium-high heat. Add the onions, garlic, and oil. Cook, stirring, for 5 minutes, or until the onions are tender. Stir in the flour. Cook, stirring, for 2 minutes (the mixture will be dry).

PUREE the milk and cottage cheese in a blender or food processor until smooth. Add to the pan. Cook, stirring constantly, for 5 to 7 minutes, or until the sauce thickens. Add the Cheddar, mozzarella, and 1/4 cup of the Parmesan. Cook for 2 minutes, or until the cheeses melt.

STIR in the macaroni, salt, and pepper. Spoon into the prepared baking dish. Stir together the bread crumbs and the remaining 1/4 cup Parmesan in a small bowl. Sprinkle over the macaroni. Bake for 30 minutes, or until the topping is golden brown.

Makes 8 servings

Per serving: 298 calories, 18 g protein, 47 g carbohydrate, 4 g fat, 1.5 g saturated fat, 11 mg cholesterol, 421 mg sodium, 2 g fiber

Shrimp with Puttanesca Sauce

404 Calories

Shrimp pairs perfectly with this robust sauce, a favorite in Italian cooking. Never rinse pasta unless it will be baked or used in a salad. The starch that's left on the surface will help the sauce cling to the pasta.

Total time: 35 minutes

- 2 teaspoons olive oil
- 2 cups chopped onions
- 2 teaspoons minced garlic
- 1 can (28 ounces) no-salt-added whole tomatoes, chopped
- 1 cup chopped red or green bell peppers
- ¼ cup white wine or apple juice
- 1 teaspoon capers, rinsed
- ½ teaspoon Worcestershire sauce
- ¼ teaspoon crushed dried rosemary
- 1 drop hot sauce
- 12 ounces medium shrimp, peeled and deveined
- 8 ounces spaghetti
- 2 tablespoons chopped fresh parsley

HEAT the oil in a large nonstick skillet coated with cooking spray over medium-high heat. Add the onions and garlic. Cook, stirring, for 5 minutes, or until the onions are tender. Add the tomatoes, peppers, wine, capers, Worcestershire sauce, rosemary, and hot sauce. Cook for 8 minutes, or until the sauce is thick.

ADD the shrimp to the sauce. Cook for 5 minutes, or until the shrimp are opaque.

MEANWHILE, prepare the spaghetti according to the package directions. Place in a large bowl and top with the sauce. Sprinkle with the parsley.

Makes 4 servings

Per serving: 404 calories, 26 g protein, 62 g carbohydrate, 5 g fat, 1 g saturated fat, 119 mg cholesterol, 181 mg sodium, 6 g fiber

Seafood and Pasta Casserole

318 Calories

This rich low-fat sauce is delicious with pasta and fish. If using frozen fish, rest assured it will work well here because the sauce will keep the seafood moist and tender.

Total time: 30 minutes

- ½ cup reduced-sodium vegetable juice
- 1 cup diced onions
- 1 green bell pepper, diced
- 2 cloves garlic, minced
- 1 can (16 ounces) diced tomatoes with basil, garlic, and oregano
- 1 cup reduced-sodium vegetable broth
- 8 ounces spaghetti, broken
- 4 ounces medium shrimp, peeled and deveined
- 4 ounces cod fillets, cut into 1″ cubes
- ½ teaspoon ground black pepper
- ¼ teaspoon salt

COAT a Dutch oven with cooking spray. Add the vegetable juice and bring to a boil over medium-high heat. Add the onions, bell pepper, and garlic. Cook, stirring, for 5 minutes, or until the onions are tender. Add the tomatoes, broth, spaghetti, shrimp, and cod. Bring to a boil. Reduce the heat to medium. Cover and cook for 15 minutes, or until thick. Stir in the black pepper and salt.

Makes 4 servings

Per serving: 318 calories, 19 g protein, 54 g carbohydrate, 2 g fat, 0.5 g saturated fat, 50 mg cholesterol, 525 mg sodium, 4 g fiber

Tuna-Spaghetti Casserole

305
Calories

This twist on a traditional favorite is packed with tasty vegetables. Making your own cream sauce, instead of using canned, helps keep sodium in check.

Total time: 50 minutes

- 1 teaspoon olive oil
- 2 cups sliced mushrooms
- 3 cloves garlic, minced
- 1 tablespoon all-purpose flour
- 2 cups fat-free milk
- ½ cup shredded low-fat extra-sharp Cheddar cheese
- 8 ounces spaghetti
- 2 cups broccoli florets
- 2 cans (6 ounces each) water-packed tuna, drained and flaked
- ½ cup shredded carrots
- ¼ cup chopped fresh parsley
- ¼ cup dry bread crumbs
- ¼ teaspoon salt
- ¼ teaspoon ground black pepper

PREHEAT the oven to 400°F. Coat a 13" × 9" baking dish with cooking spray.

HEAT a large nonstick skillet coated with cooking spray over medium-high heat. Add the oil, mushrooms, and garlic. Cook, stirring, for 5 to 8 minutes, or until the mushrooms are very soft. Reduce the heat to low. Stir in the flour (the mixture will be dry). Cook, stirring, for 2 minutes. Gradually add the milk and cheese. Cook, stirring frequently, for 5 to 8 minutes, or until the sauce thickens. Remove from the heat.

MEANWHILE, prepare the spaghetti according to the package directions. Place in a large bowl. Add the broccoli, tuna, carrots, and mushroom sauce, tossing to coat. Place in the prepared baking dish. Stir together the parsley, bread crumbs, salt, and pepper in a small bowl. Sprinkle over the tuna mixture. Bake for 15 to 20 minutes, or until hot and bubbly.

Makes 6 servings

Per serving: 305 calories, 26 g protein, 40 g carbohydrate, 4 g fat, 1.5 g saturated fat, 27 mg cholesterol, 459 mg sodium, 3 g fiber

Pork and Pasta Tetrazzini

490 Calories

A creamy sauce and a bounty of vegetables make this casserole both comforting and colorful. It's an ideal Sunday supper and a snap to make. You can use fresh green beans and corn if they're in season, but frozen will work well if they're not.

Total time: 45 minutes

- 8 ounces spaghetti
- 8 ounces pork shoulder, trimmed and cut into 1" strips
- ½ cup chopped red bell pepper
- 1 cup frozen pearl onions
- 1 cup sliced mushrooms
- 1 cup corn
- 1 cup sliced green beans
- 2 cloves garlic, minced
- ¼ cup all-purpose flour
- ½ teaspoon dried thyme
- 1½ cups fat-free milk
- ¾ cup shredded fat-free sharp Cheddar cheese
- ¼ cup grated Parmesan cheese
- 1 teaspoon paprika

PREHEAT the oven to 350°F. Coat a 13" × 9" baking dish with cooking spray.

PREPARE the spaghetti according to the package directions. Place in a large bowl.

HEAT a large nonstick skillet coated with cooking spray over medium-high heat. Add the pork, pepper, and onions. Cook, stirring, for 5 minutes, or until the pork is no longer pink. Add the mushrooms, corn, beans, and garlic. Cook, stirring, for 5 minutes, or until the vegetables are tender. Add the flour and thyme. Cook, stirring, for 2 minutes.

GRADUALLY add the milk, stirring constantly. Cook for 2 minutes, or until the sauce thickens. Pour over the spaghetti. Add the Cheddar and Parmesan, tossing to coat.

PLACE in the prepared baking dish. Sprinkle with the paprika. Bake for 20 minutes, or until hot and bubbly.

Makes 4 servings

Per serving: 490 calories, 33 g protein, 40 g carbohydrate, 9 g fat, 3.5 g saturated fat,* 49 mg cholesterol, 298 mg sodium, 6 g fiber

*Limit saturated fat to 10 percent of total calories—about 17 grams per day for most women—and sodium intake to less than 2,300 milligrams.

Vegetarian Lasagna

268 Calories

To save time, consider using no-boil lasagna noodles and skip having to refrigerate the dish overnight before baking. Just be sure to cover the noodles completely with sauce or cheese so they bake evenly.

Total time: 2 hours +
overnight chilling time

- 1 onion, thinly sliced
- 1 cup shredded carrots
- ³⁄₄ cup apple juice
- 4 cups shredded zucchini
- 1 cup chopped broccoli
- 2 cups chopped fresh spinach
- 1 teaspoon dried basil
- ½ teaspoon dried marjoram
- 2 cups fat-free cottage cheese
- ¼ cup grated Parmesan cheese
- 1 cup shredded low-fat mozzarella cheese
- 12 uncooked lasagna noodles
- 2 cups reduced-sodium tomato sauce

HEAT a large nonstick skillet over medium-high heat and add the onion, carrots, and apple juice. Cook, stirring occasionally, for 2 minutes. Add the zucchini and broccoli; cook, stirring occasionally, for 3 minutes, or until the vegetables are soft. Add the spinach, basil, and marjoram. Cover the skillet, remove it from the heat, and let stand for 2 minutes.

IN a blender or food processor, combine the cottage cheese, Parmesan, and ½ cup of the mozzarella. Blend until smooth.

COAT a 13" × 9" baking dish with cooking spray. Place 3 uncooked noodles in the bottom of the baking dish. Top with one-third of the cheese mixture and one-third of the vegetable mixture. Repeat layering 2 more times. Top with the remaining 3 noodles, the tomato sauce, and the remaining ½ cup mozzarella. Cover the dish with plastic wrap; refrigerate overnight to soften the noodles.

REMOVE the baking dish from the refrigerator and let stand for 30 minutes.

PREHEAT the oven to 350°F. Remove the plastic wrap from the baking dish and cover the dish with foil. Bake the lasagna for 40 minutes. Remove the foil and bake for an additional 15 to 20 minutes, or until the noodles are soft and the top is golden brown. Let stand for 5 minutes before serving.

Makes 8 servings

Per serving: 268 calories, 18 g protein, 42 g carbohydrate, 4 g fat, 2 g saturated fat, 15 mg cholesterol, 399 mg sodium, 4 g fiber

Chinese Chicken and Noodles

241 Calories

Instead of ordering takeout at your local Chinese restaurant, whip up this easy, delicious noodle dish. Cooking for yourself is the easiest way to avoid extra calories.

Total time: 20 minutes

- ½ cup reduced-sodium chicken broth
- ¼ cup reduced-sodium soy sauce
- 2 tablespoons packed brown sugar
- 2 tablespoons frozen orange juice concentrate, thawed
- 4 ounces spaghetti or fettuccine
- 3 cloves garlic, minced
- 1 tablespoon grated fresh ginger
- 1 red bell pepper, chopped
- 1 small onion, chopped
- 8 ounces boneless, skinless chicken breasts, cut into strips
- ½ cup snow peas, diagonally cut in thirds
- 2 scallions, thinly sliced

STIR together the broth, soy sauce, brown sugar, and juice in a medium bowl.

PREPARE the spaghetti according to the package directions.

MEANWHILE, heat a large nonstick skillet coated with cooking spray over medium-high heat. Add the garlic and ginger. Cook, stirring, for 2 minutes, or until fragrant. Stir in the pepper and onion. Cook, stirring, for 5 minutes, or until the onions are tender. Add the chicken. Cook, stirring, for 3 to 5 minutes, or until the chicken is no longer pink in the center. Add the snow peas, spaghetti, and the broth mixture. Cook, stirring occasionally, for 1 minute, or until the sauce thickens. Sprinkle with the scallions.

Makes 4 servings

Per serving: 241 calories, 19 g protein, 38 g carbohydrate, 1 g fat, 0.5 g saturated fat, 33 mg cholesterol, 635 mg sodium,* 2 g fiber

*Limit saturated fat to 10 percent of total calories—about 17 grams per day for most women—and sodium intake to less than 2,300 milligrams.

Chicken and Vegetable Pasta au Gratin

351 Calories

This hearty Midwestern harvest casserole makes a fast weeknight family meal. Plus, it can be doubled and the extras frozen for up to 1 month.

Total time: 50 minutes

- 8 ounces penne pasta
- 8 ounces boneless, skinless chicken thighs, cut into 1" pieces
- 1 cup chopped onions
- 1 cup reduced-sodium chicken broth
- 2 carrots, thinly sliced
- 2 parsnips, thinly sliced
- 1 tablespoon minced garlic
- 1 teaspoon Italian seasoning
- ¼ cup all-purpose flour
- 2 cups fat-free milk
- 1 cup shredded fat-free mozzarella cheese
- ¾ cup chopped tomatoes
- ¼ cup dry bread crumbs
- ¼ cup grated Parmesan cheese

PREHEAT the oven to 400°F. Prepare the pasta according to the package directions.

MEANWHILE, heat a Dutch oven coated with cooking spray over medium-high heat. Add the chicken, onions, and ¼ cup of the broth. Cook, stirring, for 5 minutes, or until the onions are tender. Add the carrots, parsnips, garlic, seasoning, and the remaining ¾ cup broth. Cover and cook for 5 to 8 minutes, or until the vegetables are tender.

STIR in the flour. Cook, stirring constantly, for 2 minutes. Gradually add the milk and mozzarella. Cook, stirring, for 4 minutes, or until the sauce thickens. Stir in the pasta and tomatoes, tossing to coat. Mix the bread crumbs and Parmesan; sprinkle over the pasta mixture. Bake for 20 minutes, or until the topping is golden brown.

Makes 6 servings

Per serving: 351 calories, 23 g protein, 57 g carbohydrate, 4 g fat, 1.5 g saturated fat, 28 mg cholesterol, 494 mg sodium, 5 g fiber

POULTRY
PORK
AND BEEF

Cajun Chicken with Sautéed Veggies

311 Calories

—Elena Dodge, Erie, Pennsylvania

This quick and easy dish actually employs stir-fry methods for fast results. Use a wok if you prefer. Serve over noodles, rice, or couscous.

Total time: 20 minutes

- 2 boneless, skinless chicken breast halves, cut into thin strips
- 1 tablespoon Cajun seasoning
- 2 tablespoons hot sauce
  Salt and ground black pepper
- 1 large red bell pepper, cut into thin strips
- 1 large orange bell pepper, cut into thin strips
- 1 large yellow bell pepper, cut into thin strips
- 1 large green bell pepper, cut into thin strips
- 1 large onion, cut into thin wedges

HEAT a large skillet coated with cooking spray over medium heat. Add the chicken, seasoning, and hot sauce. Season with salt and pepper. Cook, stirring, for 5 minutes, or until the chicken is no longer pink. Transfer to a plate; keep warm.

HEAT the same skillet coated with cooking spray over medium heat. Add the bell peppers and onion. Cook, stirring, for 10 minutes, or until the peppers are crisp-tender. Stir in the chicken and cook for 1 minute.

Makes 2 servings

Per serving: 311 calories, 44 g protein, 28 g carbohydrate, 3 g fat, 1 g saturated fat, 99 mg cholesterol, 900 mg sodium,* 6 g fiber

*Limit saturated fat to 10 percent of total calories—about 17 grams per day for most women—and sodium intake to less than 2,300 milligrams.

Crunchy Chicken Breasts

237 Calories

—Nancy Dentler, Greensboro, North Carolina

Flaxseeds are a rich source of omega-3s, but they're also vulnerable to going rancid quickly. Refrigerate for up to 6 months and grind just before using. Serve these breasts with baked french fries and low-fat cole slaw for a healthy down-home meal.

Total time: 20 minutes

- 2 **tablespoons milled flaxseeds**
- ¾ **cup Fiber One cereal, crushed to very fine crumbs**
- 1 **tablespoon crushed sliced almonds**
- 2 **teaspoons no-salt-added tomato-basil-garlic-herb seasoning**
- 1 **teaspoon smoked paprika**
- 1 **cup water**
- 4 **boneless, skinless chicken breast halves**

STIR together the flaxseeds, cereal, almonds, herb seasoning, and paprika on a large plate. Place the water in a small bowl. Dip the chicken into the water. Press both sides of the chicken into the crumb mixture.

HEAT a large skillet coated with cooking spray over medium heat. Cook the chicken for 8 to 12 minutes, turning once, until the chicken is golden brown, a thermometer inserted in the thickest portion registers 160°F, and the juices run clear.

Makes 4 servings

Per serving: 237 calories, 41 g protein, 11 g carbohydrate, 5 g fat, 1 g saturated fat, 99 mg cholesterol, 152 mg sodium, 6 g fiber

Chicken Roll-Ups

229 Calories

—Marilyn Miller, Ogunquit, Maine

Change up this simple meal by switching the cheese to Jarlsberg and the celery to celeriac or jícama. Serve with rice or roasted potatoes.

Total time: 30 minutes

- 4 boneless, skinless chicken breast halves
- 2 tablespoons spicy mustard
- 4 slices reduced-fat Cheddar or pepper Jack cheese
- 1 carrot, julienned
- 1 rib celery, julienned

  Italian or balsamic vinaigrette spray-on dressing

PREHEAT the oven to 400°F. Coat a baking sheet with cooking spray.

PLACE the chicken breasts between two sheets of wax paper. Flatten the breasts with a mallet until the breasts are $\frac{1}{4}$" thick. Spread each breast with $1\frac{1}{2}$ teaspoons of the mustard and top with the cheese, then the carrot and celery. Starting at a short side, roll each breast around the vegetables. Secure with toothpicks. Place on the prepared baking sheet. Spray the chicken with dressing.

BAKE for 20 minutes, or until a thermometer inserted in the thickest portion registers 160°F and the juices run clear.

Makes 4 servings

Per serving: 229 calories, 40 g protein, 3 g carbohydrate, 4.5 g fat, 2 g saturated fat, 88 mg cholesterol, 395 mg sodium, 1 g fiber

Crunchy Almond Chicken

405 Calories

—Maryalice Wood, Langley, British Columbia, Canada

"This is a delightful entrée that always gets 'compliments to the chef'! It has eye appeal and passes the taste test with flying colors for any age group."

Total time: 25 minutes

- 1 egg
- 1 egg white
- ⅓ cup fat-free milk
- ¼ cup all-purpose flour
- 1 teaspoon salt
- 2 teaspoons lemon pepper
- 1 cup sliced almonds
- 4 boneless, skinless chicken breast halves
- 2 tablespoons canola oil

PREHEAT the oven to 350°F. Coat a baking sheet with cooking spray.

BEAT the egg, egg white, and milk in a shallow bowl. Stir together the flour, salt, and lemon pepper on a plate. Spread the almonds on another plate.

DIP the chicken into the egg mixture. Dredge in the flour mixture. Dip again in the egg mixture. Dip into the almonds.

HEAT the oil in a large skillet over medium-high heat. Cook the chicken for 4 minutes, turning once, until browned. Transfer to the prepared baking sheet and bake for 10 minutes, or until a thermometer inserted in the thickest portion registers 160°F and the juices run clear.

Makes 4 servings

Per serving: 405 calories, 42 g protein, 12 g carbohydrate, 21 g fat, 2.5 g saturated fat, 136 mg cholesterol, 714 mg sodium,* 3 g fiber

*Limit saturated fat to 10 percent of total calories—about 17 grams per day for most women—and sodium intake to less than 2,300 milligrams.

Grilled Chicken with Bodacious Bean Relish

373 Calories

—Janice Elder, Charlotte, North Carolina

"One thing I have learned in my 30-pound weight loss odyssey is that big flavors tend to satisfy longer. This dish is bursting with great flavors."

Total time: 30 minutes

- ⅓ cup mango jam
  Juice of 1 lime
- 2 tablespoons soy sauce
- 2 teaspoons grated fresh ginger
- ¼ teaspoon ground red pepper
- 1 can (15.5 ounces) black beans, rinsed and drained
- 1 Asian pear, peeled and finely chopped
- 1 cucumber, peeled, seeded, and finely chopped
- ¼ cup thinly sliced scallions
- 1 red serrano or red jalapeño pepper, seeded and finely chopped (wear plastic gloves when handling)
- 2 tablespoons chopped almonds, toasted
- 2 tablespoons chopped fresh basil
- 4 boneless, skinless chicken breast halves
  Salt and ground black pepper

WHISK together the jam, lime juice, soy sauce, ginger, and ground red pepper in a small bowl.

STIR together the beans, pear, cucumber, scallions, serrano pepper, almonds, basil, and 3 tablespoons of the jam mixture.

PREHEAT the grill. Sprinkle the chicken with salt and pepper. Grill the chicken for 10 to 12 minutes, turning once, until a thermometer inserted in the thickest portion registers 160°F and the juices run clear; baste with the remaining jam mixture during the last 3 to 4 minutes of cooking. Serve the chicken with the bean mixture.

Makes 4 servings

Per serving: 373 calories, 46 g protein, 39 g carbohydrate, 4 g fat, 1 g saturated fat, 99 mg cholesterol, 777 mg sodium,* 8 g fiber

*Limit saturated fat to 10 percent of total calories—about 17 grams per day for most women—and sodium intake to less than 2,300 milligrams.

Smoky Grilled Chicken with Tomato Chutney

509 Calories

—Heather Kenney, Arlington, Virginia

Sweet and zesty, this chutney is delicious over chicken breasts. Try it on tacos, too.
If you like, make it ahead and refrigerate for up to 1 week. The flavors will only improve.

Total time: 25 minutes + marinating time

CHICKEN

- 2 cloves garlic, minced
  Grated zest and juice of 1 lemon
- 1 tablespoon olive oil
- 1 teaspoon dried oregano
- 1 teaspoon ground cumin
- ¾ teaspoon salt
- ½ teaspoon ground black pepper
- 4 boneless, skinless chicken breast halves

CHUTNEY

- 1 tablespoon olive oil
- 1 red onion, finely chopped
- 1 bell pepper, finely chopped
- 1 chipotle chile (canned, in adobo), seeded and minced
- 1 can (15 ounces) diced tomatoes, drained
- ½ cup pomegranate juice
- ⅓ cup honey
- ½ cup golden raisins
- ¼ cup dried cranberries
- ½ teaspoon salt
- ¼ cup slivered almonds

TO MAKE THE CHICKEN:

PLACE the garlic, lime zest and juice, oil, oregano, cumin, salt, and pepper in a resealable plastic bag. Add the chicken and seal. Refrigerate for up to 2 hours, turning occasionally.

TO MAKE THE CHUTNEY:

HEAT the oil in a medium saucepan over medium-high heat. Add the onion and bell pepper. Cook, stirring, for 5 minutes, or until the onion is tender. Add the chipotle, tomatoes, pomegranate juice, honey, raisins, cranberries, and salt. Reduce the heat to low, cover, and simmer for 10 minutes. Remove from the heat and stir in the almonds.

PREHEAT the grill. Remove the chicken from the marinade. Discard the marinade. Grill the chicken for 10 to 12 minutes, turning once, until a thermometer inserted in the thickest portion registers 160°F and the juices run clear. Serve with the chutney.

Makes 4 servings

Per serving: 509 calories, 43 g protein, 60 g carbohydrate, 11 g fat, 1.5 g saturated fat, 99 mg cholesterol, 672 mg sodium,* 4 g fiber

*Limit saturated fat to 10 percent of total calories—about 17 grams per day for most women—and sodium intake to less than 2,300 milligrams.

Heart-Healthy Tuscan Chicken and Shrimp Penne

400 Calories

—Ben Jones, Cataula, Georgia

For a last-minute dinner, this sauce can be prepared while the pasta cooks. Any whole wheat pasta will work, such as shells, rotini, or elbows.

Total time: 20 minutes

- 12 ounces whole wheat penne pasta
- 4 tablespoons extra-virgin olive oil, divided
- 1 boneless, skinless chicken breast half, chopped
- ½ green bell pepper, chopped
- ¼ onion, chopped
- 1 clove garlic, minced
- ¼ teaspoon ground black pepper
- 1 teaspoon salt
- 1 cup sliced mushrooms
- 1½ cups small peeled, deveined shrimp
- 1 tablespoon lemon juice
- 1 tomato, diced
- 1 cup baby spinach leaves
- 2 tablespoons pine nuts

PREPARE the pasta according to the package directions. Place in a large bowl and toss with 2 tablespoons of the oil.

HEAT the remaining 2 tablespoons oil in a medium saucepan over medium heat. Add the chicken, bell pepper, onion, garlic, black pepper, and salt. Cook, stirring, for 5 minutes, or until the chicken is no longer pink. Stir in the mushrooms and shrimp. Reduce the heat to low, cover, and simmer for 3 minutes, or until the shrimp are opaque. Stir in the lemon juice. Pour over the pasta and toss to coat. Top with the tomato, spinach, and pine nuts; toss to coat.

Makes 4 servings

Per serving: 400 calories, 24 g protein, 46 g carbohydrate, 14 g fat, 2 g saturated fat, 74 mg cholesterol, 295 mg sodium, 4 g fiber

Ham and Cheese Chicken Rolls

—Clayton Davis, USA

"I got to 345 pounds and had a hard time tying my shoes! Thanks to the Atkins diet and a slow and steady walking program, I am proud to say that I am down to 263 pounds after about a year. And I feel great! I came up with this recipe because I needed something that was terrific right out of the oven and could be warmed up the next day for lunch."

Total time: 45 minutes

- 4 boneless, skinless chicken breast halves
- 2 ounces very thinly sliced ham
- 1 small tomato, seeded and chopped
- 1 slice ($\frac{1}{2}$") part-skim mozzarella cheese, cut into 4 pieces
- 3 tablespoons fine dry bread crumbs
- 1 tablespoon grated Parmesan cheese
- 1 teaspoon dried parsley
- $\frac{1}{2}$ teaspoon dried oregano, crushed
- $\frac{1}{8}$ teaspoon garlic powder
- $\frac{1}{8}$ teaspoon ground black pepper
- 1 tablespoon fat-free milk

PREHEAT the oven to 350°F. Coat a baking dish with cooking spray.

PLACE the chicken breasts between two sheets of wax paper. Flatten the breasts with a mallet until the breasts are $\frac{1}{4}$" thick. Top each breast with $\frac{1}{4}$ of the ham, $\frac{1}{4}$ of the tomato, and 1 piece of the cheese. Roll up, jellyroll-style, tucking in the sides to seal well. Secure with toothpicks.

STIR together the bread crumbs, Parmesan, parsley, oregano, garlic powder, and pepper on a sheet of wax paper. Brush the chicken rolls with the milk. Roll in the crumb mixture to coat well.

PLACE in the prepared baking dish. Coat the rolls with cooking spray. Bake for 25 minutes, or until a thermometer inserted in the thickest portion registers 160°F and the juices run clear.

Makes 4 servings

Per serving: 252 calories, 45 g protein, 6 g carbohydrate, 4.5 g fat, 2 g saturated fat, 109 mg cholesterol, 335 mg sodium, 1 g fiber

Light Chicken Burritos

502 Calories

—Linda Croley, Hoover, Alabama

Cotija is a popular Mexican cheese; dry and aged, it has a robust flavor and is increasingly available in most supermarkets. You may substitute Parmesan or Romano cheese.

Total time: 50 minutes

- 1 can (15.5 ounces) black beans, rinsed and drained
- ½ cup chunky salsa
- 1 tablespoon vegetable oil
- 2 boneless, skinless chicken breast halves, finely chopped
- 2 scallions, thinly sliced
- ½ teaspoon ground cumin
- ½ teaspoon ground ancho chile
- ½ teaspoon chili powder
- ½ teaspoon ground black pepper
- 8 ounces fat-free cream cheese, softened
- 1 box (10 ounces) frozen chopped spinach, thawed and squeezed dry
- 2 tablespoons chopped fresh cilantro, divided
- 4 whole wheat flour tortillas (8" diameter)
- 4 ounces shredded Cheddar cheese
- 1 can (10 ounces) red enchilada sauce
- ½ cup light sour cream
- 2 ounces crumbled cotija cheese

PREHEAT the oven to 350°F. Coat a 13" × 9" baking dish with cooking spray.

COMBINE the beans and salsa in a small saucepan. Cook over medium heat for 5 minutes, or until warmed.

HEAT the oil in a medium skillet over medium-high heat. Add the chicken, scallions, cumin, ancho chile, chili powder, and black pepper. Cook, stirring, for 5 minutes, or until the chicken is no longer pink. Remove from the heat and stir in the cream cheese, spinach, and 1 tablespoon of the cilantro.

WRAP the tortillas in microwavable paper towels and microwave on high power for 20 seconds. Place the tortillas on the work surface and top each with ¼ of the chicken mixture, ¼ of the bean mixture, and ¼ of the Cheddar. Roll up the tortillas to cover the filling and then fold in the ends.

SPREAD ¼ cup of the enchilada sauce on the bottom of the baking dish. Place the burritos on the sauce and cover with the remaining enchilada sauce. Bake for 20 minutes, or until hot and bubbling. Combine the remaining 1 tablespoon cilantro with the sour cream. Serve the burritos with the cotija cheese and the sour cream.

Makes 4 servings

Per serving: 502 calories, 40 g protein, 41 g carbohydrate, 19 g fat, 8 g saturated fat,* 90 mg cholesterol, 1,095 mg sodium,* 9 g fiber

*Limit saturated fat to 10 percent of total calories—about 17 grams per day for most women—and sodium intake to less than 2,300 milligrams.

Chinese Barbecued Chicken in Lettuce Cups

397
Calories

—Nancy H. Elliott, Houston, Texas

Lettuce leaves make the perfect carrier for this sweet chicken mixture. Its light, refreshing crunch is a pleasant contrast to the rich, smoky flavors of the barbecue sauce.

Total time: 50 minutes

1½ pounds boneless, skinless chicken breasts, cut into 1½" pieces

1 large shallot, minced

1 can (8 ounces) sliced water chestnuts, drained and finely chopped

½ cup barbecue sauce

2 scallions, thinly sliced, green part only

½ cup water

1 teaspoon Chinese five-spice powder

1 teaspoon toasted sesame oil

2 cups cooked brown rice

8 large iceberg lettuce leaves

STIR together the chicken, shallot, water chestnuts, barbecue sauce, scallions, water, five-spice powder, and sesame oil in a medium saucepan. Bring to a boil over high heat. Reduce the heat to low, cover, and simmer for 30 minutes, or until the chicken is no longer pink. Increase the heat to high and boil until most of the liquid is evaporated, breaking up the chicken with a wooden spoon. Remove from the heat. Cool for 10 minutes.

TO serve, divide the rice among the lettuce leaves and top with the chicken. Roll to enclose the filling.

Makes 4 servings

Per serving: 397 calories, 43 g protein, 44 g carbohydrate, 5 g fat, 1 g saturated fat, 99 mg cholesterol, 519 mg sodium, 5 g fiber

Island Chicken with Pineapple Salsa

304 Calories

A favorite tropical fruit, pineapple is formed by the fusion of about 100 separate flowers recognizable as "eyes" on its thorny hide and yellow flesh. Serve this fast and flavorful dinner with a side dish of rice or orzo.

Total time: 25 minutes + marinating time

- 1 can (8 ounces) crushed pineapple packed in juice, drained, with juice reserved
- 1 tablespoon reduced-sodium soy sauce
- 1 tablespoon honey
- 2 cloves garlic, minced
- ½ teaspoon crushed red pepper flakes
- 4 boneless, skinless chicken breast halves
- ½ cup chopped onion
- ¼ cup packed brown sugar
- 2 tablespoons lime juice
- 1 teaspoon minced jalapeño pepper (wear plastic gloves when handling)
- 1 teaspoon minced fresh cilantro

PLACE the pineapple in a medium bowl. Cover and refrigerate. Place the pineapple juice in a shallow glass dish. Stir in the soy sauce, honey, garlic, and pepper flakes. Add the chicken, turning to coat. Cover and refrigerate for at least 4 hours or up to 24 hours, turning occasionally.

PREHEAT the grill or broiler. Remove the pineapple from the refrigerator. Stir in the onion, brown sugar, lime juice, jalapeño, and cilantro. Let stand at room temperature.

REMOVE the chicken from the marinade; reserve the marinade. Grill or broil 4" from the heat for 10 to 12 minutes, turning once, until a thermometer inserted in the thickest portion registers 160°F and the juices run clear.

MEANWHILE, transfer the marinade to a small saucepan. Bring to a boil over medium-high heat. Cook for 5 minutes, or until reduced by half. Pour over the chicken. Top with the pineapple mixture.

Makes 4 servings

Per serving: 304 calories, 40 g protein, 30 g carbohydrate, 2 g fat, 1 g saturated fat, 99 mg cholesterol, 268 mg sodium, 1 g fiber

Montreal Grilled Chicken with Spring Mix and Lemon Vinaigrette

361 Calories

—Charlene Chambers, Ormond Beach, Florida

The steak seasoning adds pungency to chicken breasts. Look for the seasoning mix in the supermarket spice section. This chicken is delicious atop the crisp salad.

Total time: 25 minutes

- 2 tablespoons Montreal steak seasoning
- 4 boneless, skinless chicken breast halves
- 1 tablespoon canola oil
- 2 tablespoons olive oil
- 2 tablespoons lemon juice
- 2 cloves garlic, minced
- ½ teaspoon salt
- ¼ teaspoon ground black pepper
- 2 bags (5 ounces each) spring lettuce mix
- ½ small red onion, thinly sliced
- 2 tomatoes, cut into thin wedges
- 2 ounces reduced-fat feta cheese, crumbled

SPRINKLE the seasoning on both sides of the chicken. Heat the canola oil in a large nonstick skillet over medium heat. Cook the chicken for 8 to 12 minutes, turning once, until a thermometer inserted in the thickest portion registers 160°F and the juices run clear. Transfer to a plate. Let stand for 5 minutes; slice.

MEANWHILE, whisk together the olive oil, lemon juice, garlic, salt, and pepper in a large bowl. Add the lettuce, onion, and tomatoes, tossing to coat well. Divide the salad among four plates. Divide the feta and chicken among the plates.

Makes 4 servings

Per serving: 361 calories, 46 g protein, 8 g carbohydrate, 16.5 g fat, 4 g saturated fat,* 110 mg cholesterol, 981 mg sodium,* 2 g fiber

*Limit saturated fat to 10 percent of total calories—about 17 grams per day for most women—and sodium intake to less than 2,300 milligrams.

Chicken Breasts with Mint Sauce

278 Calories

During the summer, you can substitute 1 tablespoon chopped fresh mint leaves for the jelly. Serve with basmati rice and green beans.

Total time: 40 minutes + marinating time

Juice of 1 lime
2 tablespoons reduced-sodium soy sauce
4 cloves garlic, minced
2 tablespoons honey or packed brown sugar
1 teaspoon olive oil
½ teaspoon ground coriander
4 boneless, skinless chicken breast halves
1 cup fat-free plain yogurt
1 tablespoon mint jelly

STIR together the lime juice, soy sauce, garlic, honey, oil, and coriander in an 8" × 8" glass baking dish. Add the chicken and turn to coat. Cover and refrigerate for 30 minutes, turning occasionally.

PREHEAT the oven to 375°F. Bake the chicken in the marinade for 30 minutes, or until a thermometer inserted in the thickest portion registers 160°F and the juices run clear. Place the chicken on a plate. Pour the pan juices into a medium saucepan. Bring to a boil over medium-high heat. Cook, stirring frequently, for 5 minutes, or until reduced by half. Remove from the heat. Stir in the yogurt and jelly. Serve over the chicken.

Makes 4 servings

Per serving: 278 calories, 43 g protein, 19 g carbohydrate, 3 g fat, 1 g saturated fat, 100 mg cholesterol, 448 mg sodium, 0 g fiber

Maureen Harris

VITAL STATS

WEIGHT LOST:
70 pounds

HEIGHT: 5'2"

WEIGHT NOW:
115 pounds

HEALTH BONUS:
Her cholesterol is
now within the
healthy range!

Within 3 years of being diagnosed with endometriosis, Maureen had packed on close to 75 pounds. "The pain of knowing I could never bear children combined with the physical discomfort was overwhelming," she says.

"The doctor said flat out that my blood pressure and cholesterol were off the charts and I'd die young if I didn't make changes," she says. "I felt powerless: My dad died of heart disease at age 52, and my brother had a triple bypass at 48—I was simply falling in line with my family history."

Then, in early 2006, Maureen saw a picture of herself that jolted her to reality. "Something finally clicked," she says. "I looked so large and unhappy—like someone I didn't even recognize. For the first time I clearly saw what I'd done to myself and realized I could choose not to let the fate of my relatives become my own." Three days later, she signed up for NutriSystem, a low-glycemic plan based on foods that don't spike blood sugar.

After 2 months of eating the program's prepackaged foods, Maureen lost 25 pounds. "I feared what would happen when I had to make my own meals," she says, "so I started printing out lists of low-glycemic foods." Overhauling her diet included replacing white bread with whole wheat and swapping fries or chips with veggies at restaurants. "My mantra was *I can choose*," she says. "My whole life changed once I realized that I controlled my eating decisions. Instead of having pie on Easter, for example, I asked for strawberries with fat-free half-and-half. I felt truly empowered."

She also worked out on a treadmill for 30 to 45 minutes, 4 or 5 days a week, while watching her favorite recorded TV shows. Meanwhile, she collected recipes from people she met on NutriSystem's message boards—and that's how Maureen became friends with fellow dieter Karen Glynn. "Karen motivated me to exercise, while I encouraged her to resist cravings," says Maureen. "I credit so much of my happiness now to her support," continues Maureen, who's on her way to becoming a registered dietitian. "Even though we've known each other less than a year, we've formed a friendship that will last a lifetime—and what a long, healthy life it will be!"

Lemon, Tomato, and Olive Chicken Pilaf

417 Calories

—Charlene Chambers, Ormond Beach, Florida

Mediterranean flavors take this chicken and rice combo to a whole new level. Niçoise olives are small and black. Feel free to substitute another type if they're not available.

Total time: 30 minutes

- 1 tablespoon canola oil
- 4 boneless, skinless chicken breast halves
- ¾ cup white rice
- 1 cup chopped onions
- ½ cup chopped green bell pepper
- 2 cups reduced-sodium chicken broth
- ½ cup dry white wine
- 1 tablespoon grated lemon zest
- 2 tablespoons lemon juice
- 2 large tomatoes, seeded and chopped
- 3 tablespoons pitted and chopped Niçoise olives
- 1 tablespoon fresh basil, cut into ribbons

HEAT the oil in a large skillet over medium-high heat. Add the chicken and cook for 4 minutes, turning once, until lightly browned. Transfer to a plate. Stir the rice, onions, pepper, broth, wine, lemon zest, and lemon juice into the skillet. Bring to a boil. Reduce the heat to medium and cook for 15 minutes. Stir in the tomatoes, olives, and basil. Top with the chicken. Cover and cook for 10 minutes, or until a thermometer inserted in the thickest portion of a breast registers 160°F and the juices run clear.

Makes 4 servings

Per serving: 417 calories, 44 g protein, 38 g carbohydrate, 7 g fat, 1 g saturated fat, 99 mg cholesterol, 392 mg sodium, 3 g fiber

Guiltless Chicken Française

351
Calories

—Tara Jakubik, Bedminster, New Jersey

Boneless, skinless chicken breasts are a dieter's best friend, but they always need a little flavor infusion. This recipe does the trick with a low-fat take on a classic chicken dish.

Total time: 20 minutes

¼ cup whole wheat flour
¼ cup egg substitute
2 boneless, skinless chicken breast halves
1 cup white wine
¼ cup lemon juice
Lemon slices (optional)

PLACE the flour in a shallow dish. Place the egg substitute in another shallow dish. Dredge the chicken in the flour. Dip into the egg and dredge in the flour again.

HEAT a large skillet coated with cooking spray over medium heat. Add the chicken. Cook for 10 minutes, turning once, until browned. Add the wine and lemon juice to the skillet and simmer for 5 minutes, or until the sauce thickens, a thermometer inserted in the thickest portion of a breast registers 160°F, and the juices run clear. Place the chicken on a plate and drizzle with the sauce. Garnish with the lemon slices, if using.

Makes 2 servings

Per serving: 351 calories, 44 g protein, 17 g carbohydrate, 2 g fat, 6 g saturated fat,* 99 mg cholesterol, 174 mg sodium, 2 g fiber

*Limit saturated fat to 10 percent of total calories—about 17 grams per day for most women—and sodium intake to less than 2,300 milligrams.

Spicy Chicken Dinner

205
Calories

—Heather Simone, Roswell, Georgia

"I like this dish served with mixed salad greens and low-fat Italian dressing."

Total time: 55 minutes

- 1 cup reduced-sodium soy sauce
- 2 tablespoons hot sauce
- 2 tablespoons ground black pepper
- 4 boneless, skinless chicken breast halves
- 1 pound green beans
- 1 pound baby carrots
- ½ cup water

PREHEAT the oven to 375°F. Coat a 13" × 9" baking dish with cooking spray.

STIR together the soy sauce, hot sauce, and pepper in a small bowl. Place the chicken in the prepared baking dish. Pour about half of the sauce over the chicken. Bake for 30 minutes. Remove from the oven. Arrange the beans and carrots around the chicken. Stir the water into the remaining soy sauce mixture. Pour around the chicken. Bake for 20 minutes, or until a thermometer inserted in the thickest portion registers 160°F and the juices run clear.

Makes 4 servings

Per serving: 205 calories, 35 g protein, 10 g carbohydrate, 2 g fat, 0.5 g saturated fat, 82 mg cholesterol, 835 mg sodium,* 4 g fiber

*Limit saturated fat to 10 percent of total calories—about 17 grams per day for most women—and sodium intake to less than 2,300 milligrams.

Northern-Style Mexican Lasagna

329
Calories

—Marla Hyatt, St. Paul, Minnesota

Just like Italian lasagna, this south-of-the-border counterpart is perfect served alongside a mixed green salad and fresh fruit. Use whole wheat tortillas to boost the fiber content ever further.

Total time: 50 minutes

- 1 **pound ground chicken breast**
- ½ **cup chopped onion**
- 1 **can (14.5 ounces) chopped no-salt-added tomatoes**
- 1 **can (8 ounces) tomato sauce with chiles**
- 1 **package (1 ounce) taco seasoning**
- 8 **large flour tortillas (10″ diameter)**
- 4 **cups shredded low-fat Mexican cheese**

PREHEAT the oven to 350°F. Coat a 13″ × 9″ glass baking dish with cooking spray.

COOK the chicken in a large nonstick skillet coated with cooking spray over medium-high heat for 5 minutes, or until no longer pink. Add the onion, tomatoes, tomato sauce, and taco seasoning. Reduce the heat to low and simmer for 8 minutes, or until the mixture thickens.

ARRANGE 2 tortillas in a single overlapping layer on the bottom of the prepared baking dish. Spoon ⅓ of the chicken mixture on the tortillas. Sprinkle 1 cup of the cheese over the chicken. Repeat the layers, ending with tortillas and cheese. Bake for 25 to 30 minutes, or until the cheese is melted.

Makes 8 servings

Per serving: 329 calories, 24 g protein, 31 g carbohydrate, 14 g fat, 5 g saturated fat,* 49 mg cholesterol, 983 mg sodium,* 3 g fiber

*Limit saturated fat to 10 percent of total calories—about 17 grams per day for most women—and sodium intake to less than 2,300 milligrams.

Roast Chicken Breasts with Chicken Gravy

216 Calories

Serve this easy roast chicken with baked potatoes and steamed green beans. Bake the potatoes at the same time as the chicken, giving them a head start of about 15 or 20 minutes.

Total time: 40 minutes

- 6 boneless, skinless chicken breast halves
- 2 teaspoons olive oil
- ¼ cup chopped onion
- 2 cloves garlic, minced
- 2 tablespoons all-purpose flour
- 2 cups reduced-sodium chicken broth
- ¼ teaspoon dried thyme
- ¼ teaspoon ground black pepper
- ¼ teaspoon salt

PREHEAT the oven to 400°F. Coat a large roasting pan with cooking spray and arrange the chicken in a single layer in the pan. Roast for 40 minutes, or until a thermometer inserted in the thickest portion registers 160°F and the juices run clear.

MEANWHILE, heat a large nonstick skillet coated with cooking spray over medium-high heat. Add the oil, onion, and garlic. Cook, stirring, for 5 minutes. Add the flour. Cook, stirring, for 2 minutes. Gradually stir in the broth. Bring to a boil. Reduce the heat to medium. Cook, stirring occasionally, for 10 minutes, or until the gravy thickens. Stir in the thyme, pepper, and salt. Serve over the chicken.

Makes 6 servings

Per serving: 216 calories, 40 g protein, 3 g carbohydrate, 4 g fat, 1 g saturated fat, 99 mg cholesterol, 358 mg sodium, 0 g fiber

Chicken and Spinach Burger

454 Calories

—Linda Croley, Hoover, Alabama

Whole nutmeg—the hard, egg-shaped seed of the nutmeg tree—is available in the spice aisle of the supermarket. Grind just as much of it as needed with a nutmeg grinder or the fine side of a box grater. Its warm, spicy flavor is far superior to the ready-ground variety.

Total time: 20 minutes

- 1 pound ground chicken
- 1 box (10 ounces) frozen chopped spinach, thawed and squeezed dry
- 2 cloves garlic, minced
- ¼ cup finely chopped onion
- ¼ teaspoon grated nutmeg
- 1 teaspoon ground black pepper
- ½ teaspoon salt
- ½ cup crumbled feta cheese
- 4 ciabatta or hamburger rolls, split
- 1 tablespoon olive oil
- ½ cup plain low-fat yogurt
- ½ cup chopped seedless cucumber
- 4 tomato slices

PREHEAT the grill. Stir together the chicken, spinach, garlic, onion, nutmeg, pepper, and salt in a large bowl. Stir in the cheese. Shape into 4 burgers.

GRILL the burgers for 10 to 12 minutes, turning once, until no longer pink. Brush the rolls with the oil and place on the grill 1 minute before the burgers are done.

STIR together the yogurt and cucumber in a small bowl.

DIVIDE the rolls among 4 plates. Top each with a burger, tomato, and the yogurt mixture.

Makes 4 servings

Per serving: 454 calories, 30 g protein, 40 g carbohydrate, 19 g fat, 6 g saturated fat,* 92 mg cholesterol, 1,000 mg sodium,* 4 g fiber

*Limit saturated fat to 10 percent of total calories—about 17 grams per day for most women—and sodium intake to less than 2,300 milligrams.

Thai-Dyed Turkey Burger

—Linda Croley, Hoover, Alabama

318 Calories

These burgers get their zest from garlic, ginger, and cilantro pastes. Look for these flavor-in-a-flash pastes in the produce section of the supermarket, or make your own with a food processor.

Total time: 20 minutes

- 1½ pounds ground turkey
- 3 scallions, thinly sliced
- 4 mushrooms, finely chopped
- ¼ cup chopped carrot
- 1 tablespoon garlic paste
- 1 tablespoon ginger paste
- 2 tablespoons cilantro paste
- 3 tablespoons soy sauce
- 1 tablespoon ground black pepper
- 1 teaspoon salt
- 6 ciabatta rolls, split
- 1 tablespoon olive oil
- ¼ cup Thai satay sauce
- 6 tomato slices
- ½ head napa cabbage, shredded

PREHEAT the grill. Stir together the turkey, scallions, mushrooms, carrot, pastes, soy sauce, pepper, and salt. Shape into 6 burgers.

GRILL the burgers for 10 to 12 minutes, turning once, until no longer pink. Brush the rolls with the oil and place on the grill 1 minute before the burgers are done. Divide the rolls among 6 plates. Spread 1 tablespoon satay sauce on each roll. Top each with a burger, tomato slice, and cabbage.

Makes 6 servings

Per serving: 318 calories, 24 g protein, 28 g carbohydrate, 13 g fat, 4.5 g saturated fat,* 75 mg cholesterol, 900 mg sodium,* 3 g fiber

*Limit saturated fat to 10 percent of total calories—about 17 grams per day for most women—and sodium intake to less than 2,300 milligrams.

Red Onion Turkey Burger with Peach-Ginger Teriyaki Relish

450 Calories

—Charlene Chambers, Ormond Beach, Florida

"I've recently lost 54 pounds (20 more to go), and my husband has reached his goal weight after a loss of 72 pounds. We love to grill, and this recipe allows us to still have burgers without the fat and calories of beef."

Total time: 25 minutes

RELISH

- 1 tablespoon olive or canola oil
- 3 peaches, peeled, pitted, and chopped
- 1 teaspoon minced fresh ginger
- 1 tablespoon teriyaki sauce
- 1 cup light or fat-free mayonnaise

BURGERS

- 2 pounds ground turkey breast
- 1 tablespoon teriyaki sauce
- ½ small red onion, chopped
- ½ teaspoon salt
- ½ teaspoon ground black pepper
- 6 whole-grain or whole wheat kaiser rolls, split

TO MAKE THE RELISH:

HEAT the oil in a medium skillet over medium-high heat. Add the peaches and ginger. Cook, stirring, for 5 minutes. Stir in the teriyaki sauce. Cook for 1 minute. Transfer to a bowl. Cool slightly. Stir in the mayonnaise.

TO MAKE THE BURGERS:

PREHEAT the grill. Stir together the turkey, teriyaki sauce, onion, salt, and pepper in a large bowl. Shape into 6 burgers.

GRILL the burgers for 10 to 12 minutes, turning once, until no longer pink. Coat the rolls with cooking spray and place on the grill 1 minute before the burgers are done. Divide the rolls among 6 plates. Top each with a burger and the relish.

Makes 6 servings

Per serving: 450 calories, 44 g protein, 40 g carbohydrate, 13.5 g fat, 2 g saturated fat, 67 mg cholesterol, 889 mg sodium,* 3 g fiber

*Limit saturated fat to 10 percent of total calories—about 17 grams per day for most women—and sodium intake to less than 2,300 milligrams.

Baked Italian-Style Stuffed Tomatoes

297 Calories

—DeAnna Piper, Rice Lake, Wisconsin

If you like stuffed peppers, give these a try. Serve these summer-fresh tomatoes with a whole-grain baguette and iced tea.

Total time: 55 minutes

- 1 pound lean ground turkey
- 1 teaspoon no-salt garlic and herb seasoning
- ¼ cup Marsala wine
- 2 fresh basil leaves, finely chopped
- 4 large beefsteak tomatoes
- 1 cup Italian-style bread crumbs
- ¼ cup grated Parmesan cheese

PREHEAT the oven to 350°F. Coat an 8" × 8" baking dish with cooking spray.

HEAT a large skillet coated with cooking spray over medium-high heat. Cook the turkey, stirring, for 10 minutes, or until no longer pink. Add the seasoning and wine and bring to a boil. Reduce the heat to low. Simmer for 5 minutes, or until the liquid is reduced by half. Stir in the basil. Remove the turkey mixture to a large bowl using a slotted spoon.

HOLLOW out the insides of the tomatoes, leaving a ¼" shell. Chop the tomato pieces and add to the turkey mixture. Stir the bread crumbs and cheese into the turkey mixture. Loosely stuff the tomato shells with the turkey mixture. Place in the prepared baking dish. Cover and bake for 30 minutes, or until the tomatoes are soft.

Makes 4 servings

Per serving: 297 calories, 35 g protein, 28 g carbohydrate, 5 g fat, 1 g saturated fat, 49 mg cholesterol, 872 mg sodium,* 3 g fiber

*Limit saturated fat to 10 percent of total calories—about 17 grams per day for most women—and sodium intake to less than 2,300 milligrams.

Turkey Packets

—Lori Schmerler, New Smyrna Beach, Florida

This is an easy recipe that's delicious eaten warm or cold and is a great way to get veggies into your meals. You can even make it without the turkey.

440 Calories

Total time: 25 minutes

- 1 onion, finely chopped
- 1 bell pepper, finely chopped
- ½ cup ketchup
- ½ pound cooked turkey or chicken, chopped
- 5 ounces broccoli, chopped
- 1 cup crumbled low-fat feta cheese
- 8 refrigerated egg roll wrappers
- 3 tablespoons canola oil

STIR together the onion, pepper, and ketchup in a small bowl. Cover and refrigerate until ready to serve.

STIR together the turkey, broccoli, and cheese in a large bowl. Working one at a time, set an egg roll wrapper on a clean work surface (cover the remaining wrappers with a damp cloth to prevent them from drying out) and place ⅛ of the turkey mixture just below the center. Dip a finger into a bowl of warm water and wipe the sides of the dough. Press half of the wrapper over the dough to seal. Repeat with the remaining wrappers and turkey.

HEAT the oil in a large skillet over medium-high heat. Add half of the packets and cook for 3 to 5 minutes, turning several times, until evenly browned. Transfer to paper towels to drain and keep warm. Repeat with the remaining packets.

PLACE 2 packets and 2 tablespoons of the ketchup mixture on each of 4 plates.

Makes 4 servings

Per serving: 440 calories, 26 g protein, 51 g carbohydrate, 16 g fat, 3 g saturated fat, 36 mg cholesterol, 1,100 mg sodium,* 3 g fiber

*Limit saturated fat to 10 percent of total calories—about 17 grams per day for most women—and sodium intake to less than 2,300 milligrams.

Julieanne's Chops 'n' Beans

349 Calories

—Julieanne Speciale, West Paterson, New Jersey

Tender pork chops are simmered in tomatoes, beans, and Italian herbs for a flavorful dish.

Total time: 30 minutes

- 2 center-cut pork chops (5 to 6 ounces each), trimmed

    Salt and ground black pepper

- 1 teaspoon olive oil

- 1 clove garlic, minced

- 1 can (14.5 ounces) stewed tomatoes

- 1 can (14.5 ounces) no-salt-added kidney beans, rinsed and drained

- 2 teaspoons dried Italian herbs

SEASON the pork chops with salt and pepper.

HEAT the oil in a large skillet over medium heat. Add the garlic. Cook for 1 minute. Add the pork chops and cook, turning once, for 4 to 6 minutes, or until browned. Transfer to a plate.

ADD the tomatoes, beans, and herbs to the skillet. Bring to a boil. Return the chops to the skillet. Reduce the heat to low, cover, and simmer for 20 minutes, turning the chops once.

Makes 2 servings

Per serving: 349 calories, 36 g protein, 33 g carbohydrate, 8 g fat, 2.5 g saturated fat, 71 mg cholesterol, 704 mg sodium,* 12 g fiber

*Limit saturated fat to 10 percent of total calories—about 17 grams per day for most women—and sodium intake to less than 2,300 milligrams.

Kimberly Justus

WEIGHT LOST:
68 pounds
HEIGHT: 5'5"
WEIGHT NOW:
152 pounds
HEALTH BONUS:
Her chronic
headaches are
gone.

By eighth grade, Kimberly Justus was 150 pounds and an easy target for teasing. "When all the girls were wearing cool jeans, I was taunted for my elastic-waist pants," she says. "I never tried to lose weight, though. I guess I just accepted that I was destined to be fat." This became a self-fulfilling prophecy: "I kept gaining. Years later, after I had my son, Beau, the pregnancy pounds stuck with me. When I reached my largest size, 22W, I hid my body under my then-husband's sweats."

Finally, in 2001, Kimberly realized she couldn't hide from the truth. "Beau was 10 and active in sports, and it was getting hard for me to keep up with him," she says. "One day when I bent over to pick up a ball he'd just thrown, I realized I had developed 'oomph syndrome': I couldn't pick it up without making a big *oomph* sound from the exertion! It hit me right then that I needed to slim down. If not, I'd be on the sidelines for the rest of my life."

Kimberly started eating more fruits, vegetables, and whole grains—and a lot less refined and artificial sugar. "I still enjoy organic honey and maple syrup, but I've eliminated everything else," she says. After losing 10 pounds on her own, Kimberly joined Weight Watchers for extra motivation. "I also started a food journal, which made me realize how much my emotions spurred my eating," she says.

Six months into the program, she took a job as an office manager at a gym. "Each day I watched the Spinning class. It looked fun, but I didn't think I'd be able to keep up," she says. "Then an instructor urged me to try it and after a couple of classes, I was hooked."

"Today, I'm proud to say I'm an athlete. In 2005, I ran my first half marathon, and I've since completed four triathlons. Exercise makes me feel alive and, best of all, happy," says Kimberly. "I'll always be pear-shaped— and I accept it! I focus on the positives of my figure, like how strong my legs are and how they've carried me across so many finish lines."

Apricot Pork Tenderloin

—Lisa Maltese, Prospect, Kentucky

262 Calories

"I was inspired to make this dish because I have a bit of a sweet tooth and any time I can add sweetness to a meal, I love it. This dish is very satisfying and tasty, and kids love it, too!"

Total time: 15 minutes

1½ cups chopped apricots

⅓ cup apricot preserves

1 tablespoon hoisin sauce

1 tablespoon reduced-sodium soy sauce

1 pound pork tenderloin, cut into 1" pieces

Salt and ground black pepper

2 teaspoons olive oil

Cooked rice (optional)

STIR together the apricots, preserves, hoisin sauce, and soy sauce in a small bowl.

SEASON the pork with salt and pepper. Heat the oil in a large skillet over medium-high heat. Add the pork and cook, stirring, until lightly browned, about 5 minutes. Stir in the apricot mixture. Bring to a boil, reduce the heat to low, cover, and simmer for 10 minutes, or until the pork is cooked through and the sauce is thick. Serve over rice, if using.

Makes 4 servings

Per serving: 262 calories, 25 g protein, 26 g carbohydrate, 7 g fat, 2 g saturated fat, 74 mg cholesterol, 349 mg sodium, 1 g fiber

Vietnamese Grilled Pork

371
Calories

—Susan Riley, Allen, Texas

Fresh herbs are a key ingredient in this classic Vietnamese dish. Be careful to avoid overcooking. Pork is bred to be very lean, so it's easy to overcook, resulting in dry meat.

Total time: 20 minutes + overnight marinating time

DIPPING SAUCE

- ½ cup water
- ¼ cup sugar
- ¼ cup reduced-sodium fish sauce
- 2½ tablespoons lime juice
- 2 teaspoons rice wine vinegar
- 1 teaspoon Asian chili sauce
- 1 clove garlic, minced

PORK

- 4 cloves garlic
- ¼ small onion
- 3 tablespoons reduced-sodium fish sauce
- 1 teaspoon grated lime zest
- 3 tablespoons lime juice
- 2 tablespoons soy sauce
- 1½ tablespoons sugar
- 1 tablespoon toasted sesame oil
- 1½ pounds pork loin, trimmed and sliced across the grain into ¼" pieces
- 1½ cups bean sprouts
- 1 small bunch fresh mint, chopped
- 1 bunch fresh basil, chopped
- 1 bunch fresh cilantro, chopped
- 4 cups hot cooked jasmine rice

TO MAKE THE DIPPING SAUCE:

STIR together the water, sugar, fish sauce, lime juice, vinegar, chili sauce, and garlic in a small bowl. Refrigerate overnight to combine the flavors.

TO MAKE THE PORK:

COMBINE the garlic, onion, fish sauce, lime zest and juice, soy sauce, sugar, and sesame oil in a blender or food processor and process until well blended. Transfer the mixture to a large resealable plastic bag, add the pork, and seal. Refrigerate for 1 hour.

COAT a stir-fry grill pan with cooking spray. Remove the pork from the marinade and discard the marinade. Cook the pork in the grill pan for 2 minutes, turning, until no longer pink. Transfer to a bowl. Stir in the bean sprouts, mint, basil, and cilantro.

DIVIDE the rice among 6 plates. Top each with the pork mixture. Serve with the dipping sauce.

Makes 6 servings

Per serving: 371 calories, 29 g protein, 45 g carbohydrate, 7 g fat, 2 g saturated fat, 71 mg cholesterol, 1,037 mg sodium,* 2 g fiber

*Limit saturated fat to 10 percent of total calories—about 17 grams per day for most women—and sodium intake to less than 2,300 milligrams.

Stuffed Pork Tenderloin

218 Calories

Stuffing the meat with herbs and spices is an easy way to infuse the dish from the inside out. Enjoy this down-home meal for Sunday supper or a special occasion.

Total time: 1 hour

- 2 cups reduced-sodium chicken broth, divided
- ¼ cup chopped onion
- 2 tablespoons raisins
- 1½ cups dry cornbread stuffing
- 1 teaspoon poultry seasoning
- 2 pork tenderloins (12 ounces each), trimmed of fat
- 1 teaspoon chopped fresh rosemary
- ½ teaspoon ground allspice
- ¼ teaspoon ground black pepper
- 2 tablespoons balsamic vinegar
- 1 teaspoon cornstarch
- 1 tablespoon water

BRING 1 cup of the broth to a boil in a large nonstick skillet over medium-high heat. Add the onion and raisins. Cook, stirring frequently, for 5 minutes, or until the onions are tender. Remove from the heat. Add the stuffing and poultry seasoning. Mix well.

PREHEAT the oven to 425°F. Slice a lengthwise cut in each pork tenderloin almost, but not completely, through with a sharp knife. Open 1 tenderloin like a book and place between 2 sheets of wax paper. Pound to ½" thickness with a meat mallet. Repeat with the second tenderloin. Spoon the stuffing onto each pork tenderloin and roll carefully to enclose the filling. Tie in several places with kitchen twine or secure with small skewers.

STIR together the rosemary, allspice, and pepper in a small bowl. Rub over the outside of the tenderloins. Heat a large nonstick skillet coated with cooking spray over medium-high heat until hot. Add the pork. Cook for 5 minutes, turning, until browned. Add the remaining 1 cup broth. Reduce the heat to low. Cover and simmer for 25 minutes, or until the pork is tender and cooked through.

PLACE the pork on a serving platter. Remove the twine or skewers. Slice the pork into ½" slices. Cover to keep warm. Add the vinegar to the skillet. Bring to a boil, scraping to loosen any browned bits from the bottom. Mix the cornstarch and water in a cup until smooth. Add to the skillet. Cook, stirring, until the gravy has thickened. Pour over the pork.

Makes 6 servings

Per serving: 218 calories, 26 g protein, 16 g carbohydrate, 6 g fat, 2 g saturated fat, 73 mg cholesterol, 333 mg sodium, 1 g fiber

Beef and Cabbage Stir-Fry

278
Calories

This stir-fry makes an appealing meal served over noodles or rice. For easier slicing of the raw beef, cut with a serrated knife while still partially frozen.

Total time: 20 minutes + marinating time

- 2 tablespoons reduced-sodium soy sauce
- 2 cloves garlic, minced
- 1 tablespoon sugar
- 2 teaspoons toasted sesame oil
- 1 teaspoon hot sauce
- 1 teaspoon cornstarch
- 1 pound beef top sirloin or round steak, trimmed
- ¼ cup apple juice
- 1 cup chopped onions
- 1 cup frozen corn
- 3 cups shredded green cabbage
- 1 cup sliced carrots

STIR together the soy sauce, garlic, sugar, sesame oil, hot sauce, and cornstarch in a shallow glass dish. Slice the beef across the grain into thin strips. Stir into the soy mixture. Cover and refrigerate for 30 minutes, stirring occasionally.

HEAT a large nonstick skillet coated with cooking spray over medium-high heat until hot. Add the beef; reserve the marinade. Cook, stirring, for 5 minutes, or until browned and just lightly pink in the center. Transfer to a plate; cover to keep warm.

ADD the apple juice to the skillet. Bring to a boil and scrape the bottom to loosen any browned bits. Add the onions and corn. Cook, stirring, for 3 minutes, or until the onions are tender. Add the cabbage and carrots. Cook, stirring, for 3 to 4 minutes, or until the vegetables are tender. Return the beef and the reserved marinade to the skillet. Bring to a boil. Cook, stirring, for 1 minute, or until the sauce thickens slightly.

Makes 4 servings

Per serving: 278 calories, 28 g protein, 25 g carbohydrate, 8 g fat, 2.5 g saturated fat, 50 mg cholesterol, 397 mg sodium, 4 g fiber

Thai Beef Kabobs with Garden Vegetable Sauté

255 Calories

A lemony sweet-and-sour marinade works flavor magic on lean beef as it waits for the grill. The kabobs are perfect served on top of a colorful fresh vegetable medley.

Total time: 30 minutes + 2 hours chilling time

- 2 tablespoons lemon juice
- 1 tablespoon reduced-sodium soy sauce
- 1 tablespoon packed brown sugar
- 1 tablespoon minced garlic
- 1 teaspoon red pepper flakes
- 1 teaspoon ground black pepper
- 1 pound beef chuck, trimmed of fat and cut into 2″ cubes
- 1 cup julienned zucchini
- ½ cup sliced scallions
- ½ cup corn kernels
- ½ cup sliced green beans
- 1 tablespoon olive oil
- ½ pint cherry tomatoes, halved (1 cup)
- 1 tablespoon minced fresh parsley or cilantro

MIX the lemon juice, soy sauce, brown sugar, garlic, pepper flakes, black pepper, and beef in a resealable plastic bag. Refrigerate for 2 hours.

PREHEAT the grill or broiler. Drain the beef, reserving the marinade. Thread the beef onto 8 skewers. Grill or broil the kabobs 4″ from the heat for 12 to 15 minutes, or until the beef is lightly browned on all sides and no longer pink in the center (check by inserting the tip of a sharp knife into 1 beef cube).

MEANWHILE, coat a large nonstick skillet with cooking spray and place over medium-high heat. Add the zucchini, scallions, corn, beans, and oil. Cook, stirring, for 5 minutes, or until the beans are crisp-tender. Add the tomatoes and 2 tablespoons of the reserved marinade (discard any remaining marinade); cook, stirring occasionally, for 2 minutes. Add the parsley. Serve with the beef.

Makes 4 servings

Per serving: 255 calories, 27 g protein, 14 g carbohydrate, 10 g fat, 3 g saturated fat, 61 mg cholesterol, 246 mg sodium, 2 g fiber

Tangy Flank Steak with Onions

301 Calories

Scoring the surface of the flank steak before marinating allows more of the flavors to penetrate the beef better. The sugar in the balsamic vinegar helps caramelize the onions.

Total time: 25 minutes + marinating time

- ½ cup frozen apple juice concentrate, thawed
- 1 tablespoon packed brown sugar
- 1 teaspoon dry mustard
- ½ teaspoon paprika
- ¾ cup balsamic vinegar, divided
- 1 pound beef flank steak, trimmed of fat
- 2 cups sliced onions
- 1 teaspoon minced garlic
- ¼ cup reduced-sodium beef broth

STIR together the apple juice concentrate, brown sugar, mustard, paprika, and ½ cup of the vinegar in a shallow glass dish. Score the surface of the steak several times on both sides with a sharp knife. Place it in the dish, turning to coat. Cover and refrigerate for at least 3 hours or overnight, turning occasionally.

HEAT a large nonstick skillet coated with cooking spray over medium-high heat. Add the onions and garlic. Cook, stirring, for 5 minutes, or until the onions are lightly browned. Add the broth and the remaining ¼ cup vinegar. Cook, stirring, for 8 to 10 minutes, or until the liquid has almost evaporated.

PREHEAT the broiler. Coat the rack of a broiler pan with cooking spray. Remove the steak from the marinade and place it on the rack. Discard the marinade. Broil the steak 4" from the heat for 8 minutes, turning once, until a thermometer inserted in the center registers 145°F for medium-rare. Serve with the onions.

Makes 4 servings

Per serving: 301 calories, 26 g protein, 31 g carbohydrate, 7 g fat, 2.5 g saturated fat, 37 mg cholesterol, 113 mg sodium, 2 g fiber

Beef Brisket in Chile Pepper Sauce

208
Calories

This recipe serves 12, which makes it a great make-ahead main dish for a party.
Or prepare it for a family dinner and freeze the leftovers for terrific sandwiches.

Total time: 3 hours 35 minutes

- ½ cup apple juice or red wine
- ½ cup no-salt-added tomato sauce
- ½ cup chopped onion
- 1 tablespoon packed brown sugar
- ½ teaspoon ground black pepper
- ¼ teaspoon salt
- 4 pounds beef brisket, trimmed
- 1 teaspoon cornstarch
- 2 tablespoons water
- 1 tablespoon minced jalapeño pepper (wear plastic gloves when handling)
- ¼ teaspoon paprika

PREHEAT the oven to 350°F. Coat a 13" × 9" baking dish with cooking spray. Stir in the apple juice, tomato sauce, onion, brown sugar, black pepper, and salt. Add the beef and turn to coat all sides. Cover and bake for 3 hours. Uncover and bake for 20 minutes, or until the beef is tender. Transfer to a plate.

WHISK together the cornstarch and water in a small saucepan. Pour the cooking liquid from the baking dish into the saucepan. Add the jalapeño and paprika. Bring to a boil over medium-high heat. Cook, stirring, for 3 to 5 minutes, or until the sauce thickens. Serve with the brisket.

Makes 12 servings

Per serving: 208 calories, 33 g protein, 4 g carbohydrate, 6 g fat, 2.5 g saturated fat, 62 mg cholesterol, 163 mg sodium, 0 g fiber

Garlic Beef Burgers on Toasted Buns

306 Calories

Adding a small amount of grated Parmesan and garlic to burgers lifts them above the ordinary. To match the nutrition facts in this recipe, look for whole wheat hamburger buns that offer at least 3 grams of fiber per serving.

Total time: 20 minutes

- 1 **pound extra-lean beef ground round**
- ¼ **cup soft bread crumbs**
- 2 **tablespoons grated Parmesan cheese**
- 1 **tablespoon minced garlic**
- ½ **teaspoon ground black pepper**
- 1 **tablespoon fat-free mayonnaise**
- 1 **teaspoon Dijon mustard**
- 4 **whole wheat hamburger buns, split and toasted**
- 4 **large lettuce leaves**
- 4 **tomato slices**

PREHEAT the grill or broiler. Mix the beef, bread crumbs, cheese, garlic, and pepper in a large bowl. Form into 4 burgers. Grill or broil 4" from the heat for 4 minutes; turn and cook for 5 to 8 minutes more, or until a thermometer inserted in the center registers 160°F.

SPREAD the mayonnaise and mustard on the buns. Top the burgers with lettuce and tomato slices.

Makes 4 servings

Per serving: 306 calories, 29 g protein, 26 g carbohydrate, 9 g fat, 3.5 g saturated fat,* 73 mg cholesterol, 399 mg sodium, 4 g fiber

*Limit saturated fat to 10 percent of total calories—about 17 grams per day for most women—and sodium intake to less than 2,300 milligrams.

Sloppy Joes

230 Calories

Ground beef has been popular for ages. If you prefer ground turkey, look for extra lean. Cumin and ground red pepper add zest to this classic meal.

Total time: 30 minutes

- 1 cup chopped onions
- ½ cup chopped green bell pepper
- ½ cup chopped carrots
- 2 tablespoons minced garlic
- 12 ounces extra-lean ground beef round
- ¼ cup reduced-sodium ketchup
- 1 tablespoon reduced-sodium Worcestershire sauce
- 1 can (8 ounces) no-salt-added tomato sauce
- ½ teaspoon ground cumin
- ¼ teaspoon ground red pepper
- 6 hamburger buns, split and toasted

HEAT a large nonstick skillet coated with cooking spray over medium-high heat. Add the onions, bell pepper, carrots, and garlic. Cook, stirring, for 1 minute. Add the beef. Cook, stirring, for 3 minutes, or until the beef begins to brown. Add the ketchup, Worcestershire sauce, tomato sauce, cumin, and red pepper. Cover and cook, stirring occasionally, for 20 minutes, or until thick. Serve on the buns.

Makes 6 servings

Per serving: 230 calories, 16 g protein, 32 g carbohydrate, 4 g fat, 1.5 g saturated fat, 30 mg cholesterol, 258 mg sodium, 3 g fiber

Mexicali Meat Loaf

Guaranteed to be different from your mother's version of meatloaf, spicy salsa gives this version character, and corn adds sweetness.

150 Calories

Total time: 1 hour 30 minutes

- 1 pound extra-lean ground beef
- 8 ounces ground turkey breast
- ¾ cup salsa
- ¾ cup soft bread crumbs
- 1 cup chopped onions
- ½ cup corn
- 1 egg, lightly beaten
- 2 cloves garlic, minced
- 1½ teaspoons chili powder
- ½ teaspoon ground cumin
- ¼ teaspoon ground black pepper
- ⅛ teaspoon salt
- ¼ cup reduced-sodium tomato sauce
- 1 tablespoon reduced-sodium ketchup
- 1 teaspoon sugar

PREHEAT the oven to 350°F. Coat a 9" × 5" nonstick loaf pan with cooking spray.

STIR together the beef, turkey, salsa, bread crumbs, onions, corn, egg, garlic, chili powder, cumin, pepper, and salt in a large bowl. Press into the prepared pan.

STIR together the tomato sauce, ketchup, and sugar in a small bowl. Spread over the top of the meat loaf. Cover with foil and bake for 1 hour, or until a thermometer inserted into the center of the loaf reads 160°F. Uncover and bake for 5 minutes, or until the top browns slightly. Let stand for 10 minutes before slicing.

Makes 8 servings

Per serving: 150 calories, 20 g protein, 10 g carbohydrate, 4 g fat, 1 g saturated fat, 74 mg cholesterol, 268 mg sodium, 2 g fiber

DESSERTS

Luscious Blueberry Creme

—Glee Ann Erdelbrock, Toutle, Washington

"I love this rich, elegant dessert. It's a feast for both the eyes and mouth!"

Total time: 35 minutes + freezing time

- ½ cup hazelnuts
- 1 cup crushed low-fat honey graham crackers
- 2 tablespoons packed reduced-calorie brown sugar blend
- ½ teaspoon ground cinnamon
- 5 tablespoons butter, melted
- 1 can (14 ounces) low-fat sweetened condensed milk
- 2 tablespoons pineapple juice
- 1 tablespoon lemon juice
- 1 teaspoon vanilla extract
- 1 package (10 ounces) frozen blueberries, thawed
- 1 container (8 ounces) light frozen whipped topping, thawed
  Fresh blueberries, strawberries, mint sprigs, and additional whipped topping (optional)

PREHEAT the oven to 375°F. Coat a 9-inch springform pan with cooking spray.

COARSELY chop the nuts in a food processor. Add the graham crackers, sugar blend, cinnamon, and butter. Pulse until moist crumbs form. Press onto the bottom of the prepared pan. Bake for 10 minutes, or until golden brown. Cool on a rack.

WHISK together the milk, pineapple juice, lemon juice, and vanilla in a large bowl. Stir in the blueberries; fold in the whipped topping. Spoon over the crust; cover. Freeze for 3 hours, or until set.

REMOVE from the freezer 15 minutes before serving. Carefully run a knife around the edge of the pan. Garnish with blueberries, strawberries, mint sprigs, and topping, if using.

Makes 12 servings

Per serving: 282 calories, 4 g protein, 38 g carbohydrate, 12 g fat, 6 g saturated fat,* 17 mg cholesterol, 111 mg sodium, 1 g fiber

*Limit saturated fat to 10 percent of total calories—about 17 grams per day for most women—and sodium intake to less than 2,300 milligrams.

Cream Cheese Apricot Kisses

—Lillian Julow, Gainesville, Florida

Whenever you need a sweet little pick-me-up, these treats are just the ticket. When covered and refrigerated, they'll keep for up to 4 days. When covered and refrigerated, they'll keep for up to 4 days.

Total time: 10 minutes

- 6 tablespoons pistachios, very finely chopped
- 8 ounces reduced-fat cream cheese, softened
- 10 soft-dried apricots, cut into quarters

LINE a baking sheet with wax paper. Place the nuts in a shallow dish. Scoop a heaping $\frac{1}{2}$ teaspoon of the cream cheese. Press a piece of apricot into the center of the cheese, forming a ball.

ROLL the ball in the chopped nuts to create a crust; set on the prepared baking sheet. Repeat with the remaining cream cheese, apricots, and nuts.

Makes 40 servings (2 kisses each)

Per serving: 46 calories, 2 g protein, 4 g carbohydrate, 3 g fat, 1 g saturated fat, 3 mg cholesterol, 44 mg sodium, 1 g fiber

Chocolate-Covered-Strawberry Shake

160 Calories

—Lauren Klak, Playa del Rey, California

"This recipe is filling and great when you crave a frozen dessert. I've always struggled with weight, but these shakes have made it much easier to manage."

Total time: 5 minutes

1 cup frozen strawberries

1½ cups ice

½ cup light silk soy milk

1 cup water

2 scoops chocolate whey protein powder

½–1 tablespoon Splenda or other granular sugar substitute

BLEND the strawberries, ice, soy milk, water, protein powder, and Splenda in a blender until smooth.

Makes 2 servings

Per serving: 160 calories, 26 g protein, 14 g carbohydrate, 0.5 g fat, 0 g saturated fat, 5 mg cholesterol, 86 mg sodium, 2 g fiber

SHOPPING SAVVY

Get Juiced

Starting the day with a metabolism-revving breakfast is crucial for weight loss success. But if your morning meal's become ho-hum, wake it up with an exotic juice such as Mountain Sun Grape & Açai juice. From a tall plant that grows in the Amazon basin, the açai (pronounced "ah-sigh-ee") is the size of a blueberry and infused with almost four times the antioxidants of red grapes—namely,

anthocyanins, which may help lower artery-clogging LDL cholesterol levels. Mountain Sun Pure Juice has also teamed up with Celestial Seasonings to create two other antioxidant-rich sips, Mountain Sun Blueberry Green Tea Blend and Pomegranate Roobios Juice Tea Blend. For more information, visit mountainsun.com.

Oreo Delight

—April Dudgeon, Campbellsville, Kentucky

341 Calories

Who needs fancy, calorie-dense mix-ins from a high-end ice cream store? Instead, you can have your own delicious version with this leaner treat.

Total time: 5 minutes

- 1 **cup light vanilla ice cream**
- 1 **package (100-calorie) Oreo crisps**
  Fat-free whipped cream

PLACE the ice cream in a shallow bowl. Crumble the Oreos in the package before opening. Spread over the ice cream and mix together. Top with a dollop of the whipped cream.

Makes 1 serving

Per serving: 341 calories, 8 g protein, 57 g carbohydrate, 9 g fat, 4 g saturated fat,* 23 mg cholesterol, 107 mg sodium, 1 g fiber

*Limit saturated fat to 10 percent of total calories—about 17 grams per day for most women—and sodium intake to less than 2,300 milligrams.

Mandarin Cream Delight

269 Calories

—Mary Ann Martinko, Youngstown, Ohio

"I love this dessert because it is refreshing and low in calories but tastes like it's sinful! I take this to picnics or other social functions, and people cannot believe it's low in calories."

Total time: 15 minutes + chilling time

- 2 cups crushed vanilla wafers
- ¼ cup light butter, melted
- 2 cans (11 ounces each) mandarin oranges in light syrup, drained, reserving ½ cup juice
- ¼ cup Splenda or other granular sugar substitute
- 1 carton (16 ounces) fat-free sour cream
- 1 carton (8 ounces) low-fat sour cream
- 2 packages (3.4 ounces each) fat-free instant vanilla pudding mix
- 1 container (8 ounces) fat-free whipped topping

STIR together the wafer crumbs and butter in a large bowl. Pat into a 13" × 9" baking pan.

STIR together the reserved juice, Splenda, sour creams, and pudding mix in a large bowl. Stir in the oranges. Spoon the orange mixture over the crust, spreading evenly. Top with whipped topping. Chill for at least 1 hour.

Makes 12 servings

Per serving: 269 calories, 3 g protein, 44 g carbohydrate, 8 g fat, 3 g saturated fat, 18 mg cholesterol, 358 mg sodium, 0 g fiber

PB&C Oatmeal Snack

—Cristen Dutcher, Marietta, Georgia

"This recipe was developed to satisfy my nighttime sweet tooth cravings. I wanted something filling and sweet, but not full of empty calories. The half-serving of oatmeal is enough to fill my hunger, and the peanut butter and chocolate remind me of my favorite candy treats, without all the processed sugar."

Total time: 5 minutes

- ¼ cup quick-cooking oats
- ½ cup light vanilla soy milk
- 1 tablespoon creamy peanut butter
- 1 tablespoon mini semisweet chocolate chips

STIR together the oats and milk in a microwavable bowl and microwave on high at 30-second intervals, stirring in between, until the oatmeal reaches your desired consistency. Stir in the peanut butter and chocolate chips.

Makes 1 serving

Per serving: 283 calories, 9 g protein, 34 g carbohydrate, 14 g fat, 4 g saturated fat,* 0 mg cholesterol, 122 mg sodium, 4 g fiber

*Limit saturated fat to 10 percent of total calories—about 17 grams per day for most women—and sodium intake to less than 2,300 milligrams.

SHOPPING SAVVY

Great Straight Off the Spoon

Calling peanut butter a diet food, with about 210 calories per serving, might seem counterintuitive. But the classic sandwich spread has the enviable combination of fiber (2 grams per serving) and protein (about 8 grams) that fills you up and keeps you full longer, so you eat less overall. Smucker's Natural and Organic Peanut Butters offer plenty of peanut flavor and delightful stickiness, but with less than half the sugar of familiar mass-market brands—just 1 gram per 2-tablespoon serving. The 16 grams of fat is the heart-healthy monounsaturated variety—a recent study found that insulin-resistant adults who ate a diet high in monos had less belly fat than people who ate more carbohydrates or saturated fat. And think beyond PB&J: Stir a smidgen of warmed Smucker's into yogurt, oatmeal, or even hot cocoa. Check supermarkets for Smucker's Natural or Organic Peanut Butter (both in creamy and chunky versions) or shop online at smuckers. com.

Banana Chocolate Chip Muffins

119 Calories

—Seanna Wesley, Petawawa, Ontario, Canada

Banana and chocolate come together beautifully in these tender whole-grain muffins. No one will notice they're good for you, too.

Total time: 20 minutes + cooling time

- ½ cup bran cereal
- ¼ cup Sucanat sweetener
- 2 tablespoons vegetable oil
- 2 tablespoons applesauce
- 1 cup mashed bananas (about 3)
- 1 egg
- 1 teaspoon vanilla extract
- ½ cup whole wheat flour
- ¼ cup wheat germ
- 2 tablespoons ground flaxseed
- 2 tablespoons bran
- 1 teaspoon baking powder
- 1 teaspoon baking soda
- ½ teaspoon salt
- ¼ cup chocolate chips

PREHEAT the oven to 400°F. Coat a 12-muffin pan with cooking spray.

STIR together the bran cereal, Sucanat, oil, applesauce, bananas, egg, and vanilla in a medium bowl. Let stand for 5 minutes.

STIR together the flour, wheat germ, flaxseed, bran, baking powder, baking soda, and salt in a large bowl. Stir in the banana mixture just until blended. Stir in the chocolate chips. Spoon into the prepared pan.

BAKE for 12 to 15 minutes, or until a toothpick inserted in the center comes out clean. Cool on a rack in the pan for 2 minutes. Transfer to the rack; cool completely.

Makes 12 servings

Per serving: 119 calories, 3 g protein, 18 g carbohydrate, 5 g fat, 1 g saturated fat, 18 mg cholesterol, 251 mg sodium, 3 g fiber

Hidden-Health Mississippi Mud Cake

—Susan Riley, Allen, Texas

Adding canned pumpkin to a cake mix eliminates the need for added fat while keeping the rich chocolate flavor and texture. Plus, it adds a fiber boost, too.

Total time: 45 minutes + cooling time

- 1 box (18.25 ounces) chocolate fudge cake mix
- 1 can (15 ounces) pumpkin
- 1½ cups coarsely chopped pecans, toasted
- 1 box (16 ounces) confectioners' sugar
- ½ cup fat-free milk
- ⅓ cup unsweetened cocoa powder
- ½ teaspoon vanilla extract
- 1 bag (10.5 ounces) miniature marshmallows

PREHEAT the oven to 350°F. Coat a 15" × 10" jelly roll pan with cooking spray.

STIR together the cake mix and pumpkin in a large bowl until well blended. Stir in the nuts. Spread evenly in the prepared pan.

BAKE for 25 to 30 minutes, or until a toothpick inserted in the center comes out clean.

WHISK together the sugar, milk, cocoa, and vanilla in a large bowl.

REMOVE the cake from the oven and sprinkle with the marshmallows. Bake for 5 minutes, or until lightly browned. Remove to a rack. Drizzle with the cocoa mixture. Cool completely.

Makes 20 servings

Per serving: 312 calories, 3 g protein, 60 g carbohydrate, 8 g fat, 1 g saturated fat, 0 mg cholesterol, 215 mg sodium, 3 g fiber

Chocolate Angel Food Cake

Angel food cake rises to new heights with this chocolate-rich recipe. Serve it with your choice of fresh berries or low-fat vanilla yogurt for a delicious, low-fat treat.

125 Calories

Total time: 55 minutes + cooling time

- 1 cup all-purpose flour
- 1 cup sugar
- ⅓ cup unsweetened cocoa powder
- ½ teaspoon ground cinnamon
- 10 egg whites, at room temperature
- 1¼ teaspoons cream of tartar
- 1½ teaspoons vanilla extract

PREHEAT the oven to 350°F. Sift the flour and ½ cup of the sugar into a medium bowl. Stir in the cocoa and cinnamon.

PLACE the egg whites in a large bowl. Beat with an electric mixer on medium speed until foamy. Add the cream of tartar and beat until soft peaks form. Gradually beat in the remaining ½ cup sugar and the vanilla; continue beating until stiff peaks form. Fold in the flour mixture ½ cup at a time.

POUR into a 10" tube pan, spreading evenly and deflating any large air pockets with a knife. Bake for 40 minutes, or until a toothpick inserted in the center comes out clean. Cool upside down for 40 minutes before removing the cake from the pan.

Makes 12 servings

Per serving: 125 calories, 5 g protein, 27 g carbohydrate, 1 g fat, 0 g saturated fat, 0 mg cholesterol, 47 mg sodium, 1 g fiber

Banana Walnut Torte

—Jean Gottfried, Upper Sandusky, Ohio

"This recipe was created for a family gathering. Lower in calories, fat, and carbohydrates than more traditional dessert choices, it's a great option for those who are counting calories or cutting carbohydrates and fat from their diet."

Total time: 45 minutes + cooling and chilling time

- 2 cups walnut halves or pieces, toasted, divided
- 2 containers (6 ounces each) light banana cream pie flavor yogurt
- 1 cup mashed bananas (about 3)
- ½ cup graham cracker crumbs
- 1 teaspoon grated lemon zest
- ¼ teaspoon ground cinnamon
- 4 egg whites
- ¼ teaspoon cream of tartar
- ¾ cup dark chocolate chips
- 3 tablespoons fat-free half-and-h

PREHEAT the oven to 350°F. Lightly spray the bottom of a 9" round cake pan with cooking spray. Line the pan bottom with parchment paper, then lightly coat the paper and the sides of the pan with cooking spray.

CHOP ⅓ cup of the walnuts and set aside for garnish. Pulse the remaining nuts in a food processor or blender until finely ground.

STIR together the yogurt, bananas, crumbs, lemon zest, cinnamon, and ground walnuts in a large bowl.

BEAT the egg whites in a bowl with an electric mixer on medium speed until foamy. Add the

cream of tartar and continue beating on high until stiff peaks form. Stir a small amount of whites into the yogurt mixture with a rubber spatula. Fold in the remaining egg whites just until incorporated.

POUR the mixture into the prepared pan, smoothing the top. Bake for 30 to 35 minutes, or until the top is firm to the touch and a toothpick inserted in the center comes out clean. Cool in the pan on a rack for 20 minutes. Cut around the sides of the pan and invert the torte onto the rack. Remove the parchment paper and refrigerate for 1 hour.

MELT the chocolate and half-and-half in a small microwavable bowl in the microwave on high at 30-second increments, stirring after each, until the chips are melted. Cool for 2 minutes.

PLACE the cake on the rack over a baking sheet to catch drips. Brush loose crumbs from the torte. Cover the sides and top of the cake with the chocolate mixture using a cake spatula. To garnish, press reserved walnuts on sides of torte. Refrigerate for 30 minutes, or until the chocolate is set. Slide the torte onto a serving plate.

Makes 12 servings

Per serving: 217 calories, 5 g protein, 20 g carbohydrate, 14 g fat, 3 g saturated fat, 1 mg cholesterol, 61 mg sodium, 2 g fiber

Low-Fat Carrot Cake

194
Calories

—Tina Whyte, Coquitlam, British Columbia, Canada

"I love carrot cake but could never find a low-fat version. This one is so fabulous.
Everyone loves it, and no one knows that it is healthy."

Total time: 1 hour 15 minutes +
cooling time

CAKE

6 egg whites

¾ cup applesauce

½ cup fat-free milk

¼ cup packed brown sugar

3 tablespoons Splenda or other granular
sugar substitute

¼ cup fat-free vanilla yogurt

1½ teaspoons vanilla extract

2 cups whole wheat flour

2 teaspoons baking soda

2½ teaspoons ground cinnamon

½ teaspoon ground nutmeg

½ teaspoon ground cloves

2 cups grated carrots

½ cup raisins

1 can (8 ounces) crushed pineapple
packed in juice

FROSTING

1 cup 1% cottage cheese

1 tablespoon fat-free vanilla yogurt

2 teaspoons vanilla extract

1 package (8 ounces) 97% fat-free cream
cheese, softened

2 tablespoons Splenda or other granular
sugar substitute

PREHEAT the oven to 350°F. Coat a 13" × 9"
baking pan with cooking spray.

TO MAKE THE CAKE:

STIR together the egg whites, applesauce,
milk, brown sugar, Splenda, yogurt, and
vanilla in a large bowl. Stir together the flour,
baking soda, cinnamon, nutmeg, and cloves in
a medium bowl. Stir the flour mixture into the
egg white mixture until well blended. Stir in
the carrots, raisins, and pineapple with juice
until well blended. Spread in the prepared
baking pan.

BAKE for 1 hour, or until a toothpick inserted
in the center comes out clean. Cool for 10
minutes on a rack. Remove from the pan and
cool completely.

TO MAKE THE FROSTING:

PUREE the cottage cheese, yogurt, and vanilla
in a food processor. Add the cream cheese and
Splenda and blend until creamy. Refrigerate
until the cake cools. Spread over the cake.

Makes 16 servings

Per serving: 194 calories, 11 g protein,
37 g carbohydrate, 1 g fat, 0.5 g saturated fat,
3 mg cholesterol, 444 mg sodium, 4 g fiber

Strawberry-Grapefruit Parfaits

261 Calories

—Maryalice Wood, Langley, British Columbia, Canada

"Nobody thinks this is lower in calories because it looks so rich and tastes so good! I created this delightful dessert to enable everyone to enjoy the treat—my diabetic children, as well as many of us who are trying to keep extra pounds at bay!"

Total time: 25 minutes

- 1 cup low-fat milk
- 2 envelopes unflavored gelatin
- ½ cup sugar
- ½ cup Splenda or other granular sugar substitute
- 1 cup light whipped topping
- 2 red grapefruit, halved, seeded, and pulp scooped out
- 1 tablespoon lemon juice
- 1 cup cracked ice
- 2 cups frozen unsweetened sliced strawberries (partially thawed)
- 1 cup chocolate cookie crumbs

  Low-calorie whipped topping and whole strawberries (optional)

PLACE ½ cup of the milk in a large bowl and sprinkle with the gelatin. Let stand for 1 minute to soften.

PLACE the remaining ½ cup milk in a small saucepan and heat until hot but not boiling. Whisk the hot milk into the bowl until the gelatin is dissolved. Stir in the sugar, Splenda, and whipped topping. Stir in the grapefruit pulp and lemon juice. Place the mixture in a blender or food processor. Add the ice, about 2 tablespoons at a time, and process until the mixture is smooth. Return to the bowl and fold in the strawberries. The mixture should be slightly thickened. (If not, chill until partially set.)

SPOON alternate layers of the grapefruit mixture and chocolate crumbs into dessert parfait glasses. Garnish with a dollop of whipped topping and a whole strawberry, if using. Sprinkle with any remaining crumbs.

Makes 6 servings

Per serving: 261 calories, 5 g protein, 53 g carbohydrate, 5 g fat, 2 g saturated fat, 2 mg cholesterol, 133 mg sodium, 3 g fiber

Kiwi-Strawberry Parfaits

364 Calories

The ingredients for this easy dessert are both fresh and frozen. You assemble it in minutes, then pop it back into the freezer until serving time. What a wonderful way to get 5 grams of fiber!

Total time: 10 minutes + freezing time

- 6 cups frozen sliced strawberries
- ½ cup frozen raspberries
- 1 cup low-fat vanilla frozen yogurt
- ½ cup sugar
- 4 kiwifruits, sliced

PROCESS the strawberries, raspberries, frozen yogurt, and sugar in a blender or food processor until smooth.

DIVIDE half of the kiwifruit among 4 parfait glasses. Fill each glass halfway with the strawberry mixture. Repeat with the remaining kiwifruit and strawberry mixture. Freeze for 30 minutes, or until the mixture is slushy.

Makes 4 servings

Per serving: 364 calories, 6 g protein, 81 g carbohydrate, 3 g fat, 1 g saturated fat, 33 mg cholesterol, 41 mg sodium, 5 g fiber

SHOPPING SAVVY

A Healthier Granola

Heard about hemp? This little seed—a relative of the marijuana plant, without the psychedelic effects—has grown into a hot new ingredient, thanks to its healthful properties: Hemp is loaded with good-for-you but hard-to-get omega-3 fatty acids, as well as fiber, B vitamins, iron, and vitamin E. For an easy, tasty way to include this superfood in your diet, try Nature's Path HempPlus Granola. This just-sweet-enough cereal combines hemp seeds with rolled oats and flaxseed to create a granola that has half the calories (140) of regular granola, plus 3 grams each of protein and fiber—and 600 milligrams of heart-healthy omega-3s. All ingredients are third-party-certified organic, which also means they're grown and processed without genetically engineered ingredients. For more information, visit naturespath.com.

Summer Fruit Tart

—Linda J. Bottjer, Myrtle Beach, South Carolina

214 Calories

"This dessert helps me keep on track during the summer months, when the ice cream truck threatens my good works of losing over 100 pounds."

Total time: 50 minutes

- 6 strawberries, halved
- 1 peach, peeled and chopped
- 2 tablespoons water
- ½ sourdough Wasa cracker, finely crushed
- 6 pecan halves, finely crushed
- ½ teaspoon unsweetened applesauce
- 1 teaspoon honey, divided
- ¼ cup low-fat plain yogurt

PREHEAT the oven to 350°F. Bring the strawberries, peach, and water to a simmer in a small saucepan over medium-high heat. Simmer for 20 minutes, or until the fruit is soft and a thick syrup has formed. Let cool.

MEANWHILE, stir together the cracker crumbs, pecans, applesauce, and ½ teaspoon honey in a small bowl. Press into a thin cracker shape on an ungreased baking sheet and bake for 5 minutes. (Cracker cake should not be browned or crispy—just solid.) Remove from the oven and cool slightly.

STIR together the yogurt and the remaining ½ teaspoon honey. Place the cracker on a plate and top with the yogurt mixture. Pour the fruit over the yogurt.

Makes 1 serving

Per serving: 214 calories, 6 g protein, 38 g carbohydrate, 7 g fat, 1 g saturated fat, 1 mg cholesterol, 55 mg sodium, 6 g fiber

Light Peach and Summer Berry Strata

366 Calories

—Wolfgang Hanau, West Palm Beach, Florida

The perfect finale to a summer barbecue or pool party, fresh fruit becomes even more juicy and delicious baked between slices of hearty bread.

Total time: 35 minutes

- 1 cup sugar
- ½ teaspoon ground cinnamon
- 10 slices 7-grain bread, crusts removed and cut in half
- 2 tablespoons extra-virgin olive oil, divided
- ¾ cup shredded reduced-fat Cheddar cheese
- 2 pounds peaches, peeled, pitted, and sliced
- 2 cups blueberries
- 2 cups sliced strawberries
- 1 cup raspberries
- 1 cup blackberries
- ¼ cup sliced mint leaves
- 12 ounces thinly sliced mozzarella

PREHEAT the oven to 425°F. Coat a 13" × 9" baking dish with cooking spray. Combine the sugar and cinnamon in a small bowl.

ARRANGE half of the bread in the prepared baking dish. Brush with 1 tablespoon of the oil. Sprinkle with half of the sugar mixture. Sprinkle with the Cheddar and bake for 10 minutes, or until the cheese melts.

REMOVE from the oven and reduce the temperature to 350°F. Arrange the peaches, berries, and mint on top of the bread. Top with the remaining bread slices. Cover with the mozzarella and sprinkle with the remaining cinnamon sugar.

BAKE for 15 minutes, or until the sugar on top begins to caramelize.

Makes 10 servings

Per serving: 366 calories, 15 g protein, 52 g carbohydrate, 13 g fat, 6 g saturated fat,* 22 mg cholesterol, 429 mg sodium, 6 g fiber

*Limit saturated fat to 10 percent of total calories—about 17 grams per day for most women—and sodium intake to less than 2,300 milligrams.

Crunchy Cranapple Crisp

250 Calories

—Maryalice Wood, Langley, British Columbia, Canada

Nothing smells like "Mom's kitchen" more than this dessert baking in the oven. Plus, it's easy to put together in about 15 minutes. Then the oven does the rest of the work!

Total time: 45 minutes

FILLING

- 5 firm apples, peeled and sliced
- 1 cup chopped fresh or frozen cranberries
- 2 tablespoons sugar
- 2 tablespoons Splenda or other granular sugar substitute
- ½ teaspoon ground cinnamon

TOPPING

- ⅓ cup all-purpose flour
- ⅓ cup packed brown sugar
- ¼ cup trans-free margarine
- ½ teaspoon almond extract
- ½ cup ground almonds
- ½ teaspoon ground cinnamon

  Light whipped topping (optional)

PREHEAT the oven to 350°F. Coat an 8" × 8" baking dish with cooking spray.

TO MAKE THE FILLING

PLACE the apples and cranberries in the prepared baking dish. Sprinkle with the sugar, Splenda, and cinnamon.

TO MAKE THE TOPPING:

COMBINE the flour, brown sugar, butter, and almond extract in a medium bowl. Mix with a pastry blender until crumbly. Stir in the almonds and cinnamon. Spread the mixture on top of the apples and cranberries.

BAKE for 30 minutes, or until the fruit is soft and the top is browned. Serve warm with a dollop of whipped topping, if using.

Makes 6 servings

Per serving: 250 calories, 3 g protein, 40 g carbohydrate, 9 g fat, 1 g saturated fat, 0 mg cholesterol, 59 mg sodium, 3 g fiber

Fruit Salsa and Cinnamon Chips

135 Calories

—Hazel Hunt, Foley, Alabama

"I love Mexican food, and here's a great way to enjoy a Mexican-inspired dessert without all the fat. I like to use butter-flavored cooking spray for this."

Total time: 50 minutes

SALSA

- 2 kiwifruit, peeled and diced
- 2 Golden Delicious apples, peeled and chopped
- 2 cups raspberries
- 3 cups strawberries, halved
- 2 tablespoons granulated sugar
- 1 tablespoon packed brown sugar
- 3 tablespoons fruit preserves, any flavor

CHIPS

- 6 flour tortillas (10" diameter)
- ½ cup granulated sugar
- 2 teaspoons ground cinnamon

TO MAKE THE SALSA:

STIR together the kiwifruit, apples, raspberries, strawberries, sugars, and fruit preserves in a large bowl. Cover and refrigerate for at least 15 minutes.

TO MAKE THE CHIPS:

PREHEAT the oven to 350°F. Coat 2 large baking sheets with cooking spray.

COAT one side of each tortilla with cooking spray. Cut each tortilla into 6 wedges and arrange in a single layer on the baking sheets. Mix the sugar and cinnamon in a cup; lightly sprinkle over the tortillas. Spray again with cooking spray.

BAKE for 8 to 10 minutes, or until lightly browned. Cool on a rack. Serve with the chilled fruit mixture.

Makes 12 servings

Per serving: 135 calories, 2 g protein, 30 g carbohydrate, 2 g fat, 1 g saturated fat, 0 mg cholesterol, 114 mg sodium, 3 g fiber

Apple-Berry Buckle

331 Calories

—Mary Shivers, Ada, Oklahoma

"With fresh apples in abundance in late summer and early fall, I am always trying to create recipes to use them. We also gather fresh wild blackberries, and I think the flavor combination of the two fruits makes this recipe a perfect dessert."

Total time: 50 minutes

FILLING

- 4 cups peeled and thinly sliced red apples
- 2 tablespoons lemon juice
- 2 cups blackberries
- ¾ cup packed brown sugar
- ⅓ cup granulated sugar
- 3 tablespoons all-purpose flour
- ½ teaspoon ground cinnamon

TOPPING

- 1 cup rolled oats
- ¼ cup all-purpose flour
- ¼ cup packed brown sugar
- ¼ teaspoon baking soda
- ½ cup trans-free margarine, softened

PREHEAT the oven to 350°F. Coat a 13" × 9" baking dish with cooking spray.

TO MAKE THE FILLING:

STIR together the apples and lemon juice in a large bowl. Gently stir in the blackberries. Stir together the sugars, flour, and cinnamon in a small bowl. Stir into the apple mixture. Spoon into the prepared baking dish.

TO MAKE THE TOPPING:

STIR together the oats, flour, brown sugar, and baking soda in a medium bowl. Add the margarine and work the margarine into the mixture with a fork until crumbly. Sprinkle over the apple mixture.

BAKE for 35 to 45 minutes, or until the apples are tender and the top is golden. Serve warm.

Makes 8 servings

Per serving: 331 calories, 4 g protein, 59 g carbohydrate, 10 g fat, 3 g saturated fat, 0 mg cholesterol, 142 mg sodium, 4 g fiber

Apple Brown Betty

290
Calories

You can serve this dessert everyday-style by simply spooning it into bowls.
Or for fancier occasions, try inverting the entire dessert onto a pretty serving plate.

Total time: 50 minutes

- 4 tart apples, peeled and sliced
- 2 tablespoons lemon juice
- 2 tablespoons honey
- 2 cups soft bread crumbs
- ¼ cup trans-free margarine, softened
- ¼ cup packed brown sugar
- ½ teaspoon ground cinnamon
- ¼ teaspoon ground allspice

NUTRITION NEWS TO USE

Eat the peel—the bulk of an apple's benefit lies in its skin. In a recent lab experiment, more than a dozen chemicals in the peels of Red Delicious apples inhibited the growth of breast, liver, and colon cancer cells. Researchers suspect that the peels of other apple varieties are also extra potent. Buy organic if you're concerned about exposure to pesticides.

PREHEAT the oven to 375°F. Coat a 9" × 5" loaf pan with cooking spray. Lightly flour the pan and shake off any excess.

STIR together the apples, lemon juice, and honey in a medium bowl. Transfer to the prepared pan.

STIR together the bread crumbs, butter, brown sugar, cinnamon, and allspice in the same bowl. Sprinkle on top of the apples.

BAKE for 40 minutes, or until the apples are soft and the topping is crisp.

Makes 4 servings

Per serving: 290 calories, 2 g protein, 51 g carbohydrate, 9 g fat, 1 g saturated fat, 350 mg cholesterol, 240 mg sodium, 3 g fiber

Raspberry Crisp

This unusual combination of raspberries and peaches makes a vivid and delicious crisp. Delicious all year round, frozen fruits may be substituted for the fresh.

270
Calories

Total time: 50 minutes

- 1 navel orange
- 3 cups sliced peaches
- 3 cups raspberries
- ½ cup packed light brown sugar, divided
- 1 cup all-purpose flour
- ½ cup rolled oats
- ½ teaspoon ground cinnamon
- 2 tablespoons trans-free margarine
- ⅓ cup low-fat buttermilk

PREHEAT the oven to 350°F. Coat an 8" × 8" baking dish with cooking spray.

GRATE the zest of the orange into a medium bowl. Squeeze the orange juice into the bowl. Stir in the peaches, raspberries, and ¼ cup of the brown sugar. Spoon into the prepared baking dish.

STIR together the flour, oats, and cinnamon in a large nonstick skillet. Cook, stirring, over medium heat for 3 to 5 minutes, or until light brown. Remove from the heat. Stir in the butter, buttermilk, and the remaining ¼ cup brown sugar. Spoon over the fruit. Bake for 45 minutes, or until the topping is golden and the fruit is bubbling.

Makes 6 servings

Per serving: 270 calories, 5 g protein, 56 g carbohydrate, 4 g fat, 0 g saturated fat, 0 mg cholesterol, 50 mg sodium, 7 g fiber

Pumpkin Brulee

126 Calories

Dazzle your dinner guests with this easy-to-make dessert that tastes just as good as a restaurant version, with a good amount of fiber and far less fat.

Total time: 45 minutes

- 1 **can (15 ounces) solid-pack pumpkin**
- ½ **cup brown sugar**
- 1½ **teaspoons ground cinnamon**
- ½ **teaspoon ground ginger**
- ¼ **teaspoon ground nutmeg**
- ¼ **teaspoon ground cloves**
- ¼ **teaspoon salt**
- 2 **eggs**
- 1 **cup fat-free evaporated milk**
- 2 **tablespoons turbinado sugar**
- 1 **tablespoon orange zest**

PREHEAT oven to 325°F. Coat eight 4-ounce ramekins with cooking spray and set aside.

COMBINE the pumpkin and brown sugar in a large bowl. Add the cinnamon, ginger, nutmeg, cloves, and salt, and stir until well combined. Add the eggs and milk and mix until thoroughly combined. Divide pumpkin mixture equally among ramekins.

ARRANGE ramekins on a baking sheet and bake for 30 minutes. Remove from oven and sprinkle ¾ teaspoon turbinado sugar over each dish. Broil for 2 to 4 minutes until sugar melts. Serve warm. Garnish with orange zest.

Makes 8 servings

Per serving: 126 calories, 5 g protein, 25 g carbohydrate, 1.5 g fat, 0.5 g saturated fat, 54 mg cholesterol, 134 mg sodium, 2 g fiber

Cherry Pudding Cake

189
Calories

In France, soft cakes like this are called clafouti, and they're often made with tart cherries harvested during July and August. Instead of traditional heavy cream, we substituted yogurt to lighten the batter.

Total time: 30 minutes

- 2 cups frozen dark sweet cherries, thawed
- 1 cup fat-free plain yogurt
- ½ cup part-skim ricotta cheese
- ¼ cup all-purpose flour
- ¼ cup sugar
- 2 eggs
- ¼ teaspoon ground nutmeg
- ¼ cup raisins
- 2 tablespoons packed brown sugar

PREHEAT the oven to 400°F. Coat a 12" quiche dish with cooking spray. Place the cherries in the dish. Process the yogurt, ricotta, flour, sugar, eggs, and nutmeg in a blender or food processor until smooth. Pour over the cherries. Sprinkle with the raisins.

BAKE for 12 minutes, or until the cake begins to set. Sprinkle with the brown sugar. Bake for 8 minutes, or until the cake is firm and golden brown.

Makes 6 servings

Per serving: 189 calories, 8 g protein, 34 g carbohydrate, 4 g fat, 2 g saturated fat, 78 mg cholesterol, 74 mg sodium, 1 g fiber

Healthy Chocolate Chip Cookies

—Katherine J. Bright, Austin, Texas

94 Calories

You'll never miss the butter in these rich and delicious cookies—so tasty with a hint of banana and milk chocolate chips.

Total time: 35 minutes

- 1 banana, mashed
- ½ cup cinnamon applesauce
- ¼ cup granulated sugar
- ¼ cup packed brown sugar
- 1 teaspoon vanilla extract
- 2 cups whole wheat flour
- 1 teaspoon salt
- 1 teaspoon baking soda
- ½ cup chopped pecans
- ½ cup milk chocolate chips

PREHEAT the oven to 325°F. Coat 2 baking sheets with cooking spray.

STIR together the banana, applesauce, sugars, and vanilla in a large bowl. Stir in the flour, salt, and baking soda until well blended. Stir in the pecans and chocolate chips.

DROP by tablespoonfuls onto the prepared baking sheets, leaving 2" space between cookies. Bake for 20 minutes, or until lightly browned.

Makes 24 cookies

Per cookie: 94 calories, 2 g protein, 16 g carbohydrate, 3 g fat, 1 g saturated fat, 1 mg cholesterol, 154 mg sodium, 2 g fiber

Chocolate Almond Orange Cookies

196 Calories

—Nancy Dentler, Greensboro, North Carolina

"My family loves these rich and delicious cookies for breakfast as well as an afternoon pick-me-up."

1 box (20.5 ounces) low-fat chocolate brownie mix

1 box (16.2 ounces) Original Fiber One cereal, crushed into very fine crumbs

⅓ cup sliced almonds

10 pitted orange-flavored soft dried plums

4 cups water

1 teaspoon almond extract

1 teaspoon vanilla extract

1 tablespoon grated orange zest

PREHEAT the oven to 350°F. Coat 2 baking sheets with cooking spray.

STIR together the brownie mix, cereal crumbs, and almonds in a large bowl.

PUREE the plums and 1 cup of the water in a blender until smooth. Add the plum mixture and the remaining water to the brownie mixture, stirring until well blended. Stir in the almond extract, vanilla, and orange zest. The mixture will be stiff.

DROP the batter by scant ½ cupfuls onto the prepared sheets and flatten cookies with the bottom of a glass sprayed with cooking spray. Each cookie should be about 4".

BAKE for 22 to 26 minutes, or until a toothpick inserted in center of the cookies comes out clean. Cookies will be slightly firm and springy to the touch when they are fully baked. Remove the cookies to cooling racks.

Makes 18 cookies

Per cookie: 196 calories, 4 g protein, 53 g carbohydrate, 2 g fat, 1 g saturated fat, 0 mg cholesterol, 275 mg sodium, 13 g fiber

Oatmeal Bran Cookies

97 Calories

—Becky Weber, USA

"These cookies take the edge off my sweet tooth. And they're great crumbled into a bowl of cereal. Toasting the oats adds a nutty flavor. To toast, place on a baking sheet and toast in a 300°F oven for 4 minutes, or until lightly browned."

Total time: 35 minutes

- ³⁄₄ cup packed brown sugar
- ¹⁄₃ cup olive oil
- ¹⁄₃ cup fat-free milk
- 1 egg
- 2 teaspoons vanilla extract
- 1 cup whole wheat flour
- 1 cup bran flakes cereal (crushed down to ¹⁄₂ cup)
- 1 teaspoon baking soda
- 1 teaspoon ground cinnamon
- ¹⁄₂ teaspoon salt
- 3 cups rolled oats, toasted

PREHEAT the oven to 350°F. Coat 2 baking sheets with cooking spray.

BEAT the brown sugar, oil, milk, egg, and vanilla with an electric mixer on medium speed in a large bowl. Stir in the flour, cereal, baking soda, cinnamon, and salt until well blended. Stir in the oats.

SHAPE into 1" balls and place on the prepared baking sheets, leaving 1" space between cookies. Bake for 8 to 10 minutes, or until browned. Let cool on a wire rack.

Makes 30 cookies

Per cookie: 97 calories, 2 g protein, 15 g carbohydrate, 3 g fat, 1 g saturated fat, 7 mg cholesterol, 96 mg sodium, 2 g fiber

Ginger Cookies

These cookies are tasty for school lunches or holiday gifts. The distinct blend of spices is truly heart-warming. In a pinch, light and dark molasses can be used interchangeably, but the light molasses will have a less robust flavor.

Total time: 25 minutes + chilling and cooling time

 2 cups all-purpose flour
3/4 teaspoon baking soda
1/2 teaspoon ground ginger
1/2 teaspoon ground cinnamon
1/4 teaspoon ground cloves
1/2 cup packed brown sugar
1/4 cup molasses
1/4 cup trans-free margarine, softened

STIR together the flour, baking soda, ginger, cinnamon, and cloves in a large bowl. Process the brown sugar, molasses, and butter in a blender or food processor until smooth. Stir into the flour mixture. Form the dough into a log. Wrap in plastic wrap and refrigerate for 30 minutes.

PREHEAT the oven to 375°F. Line 2 large baking sheets with foil or parchment paper.

WITH a sharp knife, cut the log into 1/4"-thick slices. Place on the prepared baking sheets, leaving 1" space between cookies. Bake for 7 minutes, or until lightly browned. Let cool on a wire rack. Continue until all cookies are baked.

Makes 36 cookies

Per cookie: 50 calories, 1 g protein, 10 g carbohydrate, 1 g fat, 0 g saturated fat, 0 mg cholesterol, 37 mg sodium, 0 g fiber

Chewy Chocolate Toffee Soy Nut Bar

—Susan Riley, Allen, Texas

"I love this recipe because it is chocolaty, chewy, and sweet. It also provides some fiber and protein. It makes me feel like I'm eating a very high-calorie dessert, when I'm not."

Total time: 10 minutes + cooling time

- 2½ cups mini marshmallows
- 1½ tablespoons butter
- 1½ cups toasted whole wheat flakes cereal
- 1½ cups crispy rice cereal
- 1 cup soy nuts
- ⅔ cup semisweet chocolate chips, melted
- ⅓ cup toffee bits

COAT an 8" × 8" baking dish with cooking spray. Place the marshmallows and butter in a large microwavable bowl and microwave on high for 50 seconds, stirring once, until smooth. Stir in the cereals and nuts, tossing to coat. Press into the prepared baking dish. Spread the melted chocolate on top. Sprinkle with the toffee bits. Cool for 1 hour.

Makes 16 servings

Per serving: 207 calories, 5 g protein, 31 g carbohydrate, 8 g fat, 4 g saturated fat,* 6 mg cholesterol, 89 mg sodium, 2 g fiber

*Limit saturated fat to 10 percent of total calories—about 17 grams per day for most women—and sodium intake to less than 2,300 milligrams.

Bonne Marano

VITAL STATS

WEIGHT LOST:
52 pounds

HEIGHT: 5'2"

WEIGHT NOW:
116 pounds

HEALTH BONUS:
Exercising reduced post-accident pain.

Bonne Marano had struggled with her weight since her teen years but finally hit her all-time high—168 pounds—her freshman year of college. "That was when a friend invited me to join a gym with her and said she'd pay the $19-a-month fee if I'd drive. Sold!" says Bonne.

That same day, Bonne found herself in a 30-minute aerobics class. "I was exhausted by the end, but I adored the group energy," she says. "After 9 months, I'd lost 35 pounds and was even offered a job at the gym that included teaching class myself." As an instructor, Bonne felt self-imposed pressure to slim down further. "I worried no one would want exercise advice from a chubby girl, so I taught up to seven classes a day, skipped meals, and drank a lot of coffee," she says. "I maintained this extreme pace for 6 years and I was considered one of the best instructors in the area, which fed my inner perfectionist. There was no way I was going to slack off."

Then in 1992, on her 25th birthday, a car accident left her with two herniated disks. "Sidelined for 8 months, I gained 15 pounds and became depressed," says Bonne. The silver lining: "Once I returned to the gym, I was physically unable to go back to my excessive schedule. Instead of teaching 'no pain, no gain,' I understood that if something doesn't feel good, you shouldn't do it." She stopped over-dosing on exercise and began taking off 2 days a week to allow her muscles to recover.

To help compensate, she finally paid attention to her diet. "I ate satisfying, balanced meals," she says. "I'd go online to calories.net to look up the junk food I was craving. When I saw how many calories and grams of fat were in a bucket of chicken, I'd stop and think, *I can make a chicken breast for myself.*" She eats more veggies and turns a salad into a meal by adding chicken, tuna, turkey, or eggs, with a sprinkle of Parmesan replacing a glob of dressing. "I won't deprive myself—I still indulge my sweet tooth these days, only now I eat a bite of Snickers rather than the whole bar," she says.

"I used to constantly compare myself with the person on the next treadmill. Now I feel comfortable in my own skin."

MENUS FOR
SPECIAL
TIMES

Watching your weight doesn't mean the end of sharing a great food with family and friends. In fact, there's probably never been a better time for you to introduce loved ones to your favorite weight loss dishes. The key to success is a bit of advance planning. Whether you're having a family supper or a casual party, the following menus are designed to offer inspiration for using many of the recipes in this book

Try them as they are, or pick and choose from other recipes to create your favorite combination. To make meal time even easier, some menus include side-dish servings of foods that don't really require recipes. You'll also find that each menu includes total nutrition analyses for one-serving nutrition And because

Prevention recommends that you limit saturated fat intake to 10 percent of total calories—about 17 grams per day for most women—and sodium intake to less than 2,300 milligrams, we've noted with an asterisk (*) which menus are slightly high in these nutrients so you can remember to be mindful of your choices for the rest of the day.

So what do these menus really offer you? In a nutshell, great food. Whether you're planning a weekend brunch or having the gang over to watch an upcoming football game, you'll be able to enjoy food that's worth celebrating. And, we bet, no one will guess that you're keeping an eye on your portion size and calories. How do we know? They'll be too busy asking you for the recipes!

Rise and Shine Breakfast

Zesty Spinach Omelet, page 46

2 slices of thin sliced whole-grain toast with 2 teaspoons jam

½ cup nonfat vanilla yogurt topped with ½ cup melon cubes

Coffee or tea

> **Per serving:** 370 calories, 21 g protein, 71 g carbohydrate, 3 g fat, 1 g saturated fat, 10 mg cholesterol, 450 mg sodium, 13 g fiber

Weekend Brunch

Protein Waffle One-Two-Three, page 55

Topped with ½ cup blueberries

1 ounce extra-lean turkey sausage

½ cup fresh squeezed orange juice

Coffee or tea

> **Per serving:** 343 calories, 30 g protein, 32 g carbohydrates, 10 g fat, 4 saturated fat,* 47 mg cholesterol, 450 mg sodium 4 g fiber

Morning on the Go

Breakfast in a Muffin, page 59

1 teaspoon trans free margarine or jam

½ cup skim milk

1 medium banana

> Per serving: 343 calories, 9 g protein,
> 63 g carbohydrates, 10 g fat, 2 saturated fat,
> 47 mg cholesterol, 430 mg sodium, 5 g fiber

A Summer Luncheon

Summer Wheat Berry Salad, page 81

Chilled Beet Soup with Orange, page 102

Herbal iced tea

> Per serving: 423 calories, 17 g protein,
> 86 g carbohydrate, 5.5 g fat, 1 g saturated fat;
> 0 mg cholesterol, 1,380 mg sodium,* 16 g fiber

Family Game Night

Italian Meatball Sandwiches, page 149

Healthy Spinach Artichoke Dip, page 128

¼ cup fruit juice mixed with seltzer

> **Per serving:** 460 calories, 31 g protein,
> 53 g carbohydrate, 14 g fat, 7 g saturated fat*,
> 70 mg cholesterol, 990 mg sodium,* 4 g fiber

Late Summer Picnic

Curried Chicken and Peach Wraps, page 144

Broccoli-Tomato Salad, page 90

Iced tea with lemon

> **Per serving:** 510 calories, 31 g protein,
> 52 g carbohydrate, 21 g fat, 3 g saturated fat,
> 45 mg cholesterol, 310 mg sodium, 10 g fiber

Dinner with Friends

**Grapefruit Spinach Salad
with Creamy Dressing,** page 85

Guiltless Chicken Française, page 248

Fennel Bake with Parmesan, page 161

Sparkling water with mint and lemon

> **Per serving:** 560 calories, 53 g protein,
> 61 g carbohydrate, 4.5 g fat, 1.5 g saturated fat,
> 105 mg cholesterol, 700 mg sodium,* 12 g fiber

Sunday Night Football

White Chicken Chili, page 118

Fruit salsa & cinnamon chips

Sugar-free soda

> **Per serving:** 430 calories, 32 g protein,
> 54 g carbohydrate, 10 g fat, 3 g saturated fat,
> 60 mg cholesterol, 1,010 mg sodium,* 11 g fiber

Better Than Takeout

Shrimp Toasts, page 132

Vietnamese Grilled Pork, page 264

Green tea

Fresh oranges

> **Per serving:** 530 calories, 40 g protein,
> 75 g carbohydrate, 7 g fat, 2 g saturated fat,
> 120 mg cholesterol, 1,280 mg sodium,*
> 7 g fiber

Easy Italian Night

Creamy Spinach Parmesan Orzo, page 172

Baked Italian-Style Stuffed Tomatoes,
page 256

Italian Ice

> **Pper serving:** 530 calories, 44 g protein,
> 66 g carbohydrate, 10g fat, 3 g saturated fat,
> 60 mg cholesterol, 1,030 mg sodium,* 5 g fiber

Southern Comfort

Buttermilk Dinner Rolls, page 173

Roast Chicken Breasts with Chicken Gravy, page 252

Simple Succotash, page 160

½ baked sweet potato

> **Per serving:** 540 calories, 49 g protein, 67 g carbohydrate, 8 g fat, 1.5 g saturated fat, 67 mg cholesterol, 630 mg sodium,* 8 g fiber

Harvest Dinner

Roasted Garlic Soup with Turkey, page 113

Butternut Squash Risotto, page 178

> **Per serving:** 425 calories, 16 g protein, 80 g carbohydrate, 5 g fat, 1 g saturated fat, 3 mg cholesterol, 818 mg sodium,* 8 g fiber

Spring Fling

Minted Pea Soup, page 104

Montreal Grilled Chicken with Spring Mix and Lemon Vinaigrette, page 242

Seltzer with lemon

> **Per serving:** 470 calories, 53 g protein, 27 g carbohydrate, 17 g fat, 4.5 g saturated fat,* 110 mg cholesterol, 1,570 mg sodium,* 9 g fiber

Cinco De Mayo

Northern Style Mexican Lasagna, page 251

Zesty Zucchini, page 163

1 cup fresh melon

> **Per serving:** 470 calories, 27 g protein, 56 g carbohydrate, 18 g fat, 6 g saturated fat,* 50 mg cholesterol, 1,580 mg sodium,* 7 g fiber

CALORIE AND NUTRIENTS CHART OF COMMON FOODS

There's no better way to upset your weight-loss goals than to not have the right foods to eat on hand. But with the sheer number of foods available in the average market, making the best choices isn't always as easy as it would seem. That's why we've gathered all the nutrition facts you need to consider in the following list of common foods. Use this handy chart as your guide to determine which of your favorite fresh fruits and vegetables offer the most fiber, learn which cuts of meat are leaner than others, and make sure you're not overloading on too much sodium or saturated fat in your cheese choices.

You can also use this chart to get a grasp on exactly what you're eating so you can find out where the bulk of your calories comes from. Then you can make simple substitutions that shave off calories without sacrificing taste or satisfaction. For example, consider trading a handful of pretzels for 3 cups of air-popped popcorn sprinkled with 1 tablespoon of grated Parmesan cheese—you'll save about 115 calories and enjoy loads more flavor while tripling your portion size. Need some more motivation? Just remember that when you're guessing how many calories you can eat, being off by just 100 calories a day can keep you 6 to 10 pounds overweight.

CALORIE AND NUTRIENTS CHART OF COMMON FOODS

BEANS AND LEGUMES

Food Item	Serving Size	Calories	Protein (g)	Carb (g)
Baked beans	1/3 c	126	5	18
Baked beans, vegetarian	1/3 c	79	4	18
Bean sprouts (mung beans)	1/2 c	13	1	3
Black beans, cooked with salt	1/2 c	114	8	20
Black-eyed peas (cowpeas), cooked with salt	1/2 c	99	6.6	18
Butter beans (lima), cooked with salt	1/2 c	105	6	20
Cannellini beans, cooked without salt	1/2 c	100	6	17
Chickpeas (garbanzo beans), cooked with salt	1/2 c	134	7	22
Edamame (immature green soybeans), frozen, prepared	1/2 c	95	8	8
Edamame, out of shell, cooked without salt	1/2 c	100	10	9
Falafel, cooked	2.25 in patty	57	2	5
French beans, cooked with salt	1/2 c	114	6	21
Hummus	1/8 c	54	1	6
Kidney beans, red, cooked with salt	1/2 c	112	8	20
Lentils, brown, cooked with salt	1/2 c	115	9	20
Navy beans, cooked with salt	1/2 c	127	7	24
Pinto beans, cooked with salt	1/2 c	122	8	22
Refried beans, canned	1/2 c	118	7	20
Refried beans, fat-free	1/2 c	130	6	18
Refried beans, vegetarian	1/2 c	100	6	17
Soybeans, dry-roasted, salted	1/4 c	194	17	14
White beans, small, cooked with salt	1/2 c	127	8	23

Fiber (g)	Sugar (g)	Fat (g)	Sat Fat (g)	Sodium (mg)
5	0	4	2	352
3	7	1	0	288
1	2	0	0	6
8	0	1	0	204
6	3	½	0	205
5	1	0	0	215
5	1	1	0	40
6	4	2	0	199
4	2	4	0	5
1	2	2.5	0	70
0	0	3	0	50
8	0	1	0	214
1	0	3	0	74
7	0	0	0	211
8	2	0	0	236
10	0	1	0	216
8	0	1	0	203
7	0	2	1	379
6	1	0	0	580
6	2	1	0	560
4	0	9	1	70
9	0	1	0	213

CHEESE

Food Item	Serving Size	Calories	Protein (g)	Carb (g)
American, pasteurized process, fat-free	1 in cube	24	4	2
American, pasteurized process, low-fat	1 in cube	32	4	1
American cheese food	1 oz	93	6	2
American cheese food, low-fat	1 in cube	32	4	1
Blue, crumbled	1 Tbsp	30	2	0
Brie	1 in cube	57	4	0
Cheddar	1 in cube	69	4	0
Cheddar, fat-free	1 in cube	40	8	1
Cheddar, low-fat	1 in cube	30	4	0
Cottage cheese, low-fat 1%	4 oz	81	14	3
Cottage cheese, fat-free, large curd, dry	½ c	96	20	2
Cottage cheese, low-fat 2%	¼ c	51	8	2
Cream cheese	2 Tbsp	101	2	1
Cream cheese, fat-free	2 Tbsp	28	4	2
Cream cheese, low-fat	2 Tbsp	69	3	2
Feta	1 in cube	45	2	1
Monterey Jack, fat-free	1 in cube	40	8	1
Monterey Jack, low-fat	1 in cube	53	5	0
Mozzarella, fat-free, shredded	¼ oz	42	9	1
Mozzarella, low-sodium	1 in cube	50	5	1
Mozzarella, part-skim, low moisture	1 oz	86	7	1
Mozzarella, string	1 (1 oz)	80	8	1
Muenster	1 in cube	66	4	0
Muenster, low-fat	1 in cube	49	4	1
Parmesan, grated	2 Tbsp	43	4	0
Parmesan, hard	1 in cube	40	4	0
Provolone	1 in cube	60	4	0
Ricotta	¼ c	107	7	2
Ricotta, low-fat	¼ c	85	7	3

Fiber (g)	Sugar (g)	Fat (g)	Sat Fat (g)	Sodium (mg)
0	2	0	0	244
0	0	1	1	257
0	2	7	4	452
0	0	1	1	257
0	0	2.5	1.5	118
0	0	5	3	107
0	0	6	4	106
0	1	0	0	220
0	0	1	1	106
0	3	1	1	459
0	2	0	0	15
0	0	1	1	229
0	0	10	6	86
0	0	0	0	158
0	0	5	3	89
0	1	4	3	190
0	1	0	0	220
0	0	4	2	96
1	0	0	0	210
0	0	3	2	3
0	0	6	4	150
0	0	6	3	240
0	0	5	3	113
0	1	3	2	108
0	0	3	2	153
0	0	3	2	165
0	0	5	3	149
0	0	8	5	52
0	0	5	3	77

Food Item	Serving Size	Calories	Protein (g)	Carb (g)
Swiss	1 in cube	57	4	1
Swiss, low-fat	1 in cube	27	4	1
Swiss, low-fat, singles	1 slice	50	8	1

OTHER DAIRY

Food Item	Serving Size	Calories	Protein (g)	Carb (g)
Sour cream	1 Tbsp	31	0	1
Yogurt, banana, low-fat	4 oz	120	5	21
Yogurt, blueberry–French vanilla, low-fat	4 oz	120	5	24
Yogurt, coffee, fat-free	4 oz	103	6	20
Yogurt, plain, fat-free	4 oz	63	6	9
Yogurt, plain, low-fat	4 oz	71	6	8
Yogurt, plain, whole milk	4 oz	69	4	5
Yogurt, strawberry, fat-free, Breyer's	4 oz	62	4	11
Yogurt, strawberry, low-fat, Breyer's	4 oz	109	4	21
Yogurt, vanilla, low-fat	4 oz	96	6	16

EGGS

Food Item	Serving Size	Calories	Protein (g)	Carb (g)
Egg, hard-cooked	1 large	78	6	1
Egg, poached	1 large	71	6	0
Egg, scrambled	1 large	102	7	1
Egg white, cooked	1 large	17	4	0
Egg white, Egg Beaters	¼ c	30	6	1

Fiber (g)	Sugar (g)	Fat (g)	Sat Fat (g)	Sodium (mg)
0	0	4	3	29
0	0	1	1	39
0	0	1	1	73

Fiber (g)	Sugar (g)	Fat (g)	Sat Fat (g)	Sodium (mg)
0	0	3	2	8
0	18	2	2	60
0	21	1	0	70
0	20	0	0	78
0	9	0	0	87
0	8	2	1	79
0	5	4	2	52
0	9	0	0	51
0	20	1	1	59
0	16	1	1	75

Fiber (g)	Sugar (g)	Fat (g)	Sat Fat (g)	Sodium (mg)
0	1	5	2	62
0	0	5	2	147
0	1	7	2	171
0	0	0	0	55
0	0	0	0	115

FATS AND OILS

Food Item	Serving Size	Calories	Protein (g)	Carb (g)
Butter, with salt	1 tsp	34	0	0
Butter, without salt	1 tsp	34	0	0
Butter-margarine blend, stick, without salt	1 tsp	33	0	0
Flaxseed oil	1 tsp	40	0	0
Margarine, hard, corn and soybean oils	1 tsp	33	0	0
Margarine, hard, corn oil	1 tsp	34	0	0
Margarine, hard, soybean oil	1 tsp	34	0	0
Margarine, regular, with salt	1 tsp	34	0	0
Margarine, regular, without salt	1 tsp	34	0	0
Oil, canola	1 tsp	40	0	0
Oil, olive	1 tsp	40	0	0
Oil, safflower	1 tsp	40	0	0
Oil, sesame	1 tsp	40	0	0
Oil, walnut	1 tsp	40	0	0

FISH

Food Item	Serving Size	Calories	Protein (g)	Carb (g)
Cod, Atlantic, baked	3 oz	89	19	0
Flounder, baked	3 oz	99	21	0
Grouper, baked	3 oz	100	21	0
Halibut, Atlantic and Pacific, baked	3 oz	119	23	0
Mahi mahi, baked	3 oz	93	20	0
Salmon, Alaskan chinook, smoked, canned	3 oz	128	20	1
Salmon, pink, canned, drained	3 oz	116	20	0
Swordfish, baked	3 oz	132	22	0
Tilapia, baked or broiled	3 oz	109	22	0
Tuna, bluefin, baked	3 oz	156	25	0

Fiber (g)	Sugar (g)	Fat (g)	Sat Fat (g)	Sodium (mg)
0	0	4	2	27
0	0	4	2	1
0	0	4	1	1
0	0	5	0	0
0	0	4	1	30
0	0	4	1	44
0	0	4	1	44
0	0	4	1	44
0	0	4	1	0
0	0	5	0	0
0	0	5	1	0
0	0	5	0	0
0	0	5	1	0
0	0	5	0	0

Fiber (g)	Sugar (g)	Fat (g)	Sat Fat (g)	Sodium (mg)
0	0	1	0	66
0	0	1	0	89
0	0	1	0	45
0	0	3	0	59
0	0	1	0	96
0	0	5	n/a	n/a
0	0	4	1	339
0	0	4	1	98
0	0	2	1	48
0	0	5	1	42

Food Item	Serving Size	Calories	Protein (g)	Carb (g)
Tuna, StarKist Chunk Light, canned in water, drained	2 oz	70	15	0
Tuna, white, canned in water, drained	3 oz	109	20	0
Tuna, yellowfin, baked	3 oz	118	25	0

FRUIT

Food Item	Serving Size	Calories	Protein (g)	Carb (g)
Apple	1 medium (2¾ in. dia)	72	0	19
Apricot	1	17	0	4
Avocado	¼ c	58	1	3
Banana	1 large (8 in)	121	1	31
Blackberries	1 c	62	2	14
Blueberries	½ c	42	1	11
Cantaloupe, wedged	⅛ medium	23	1	6
Cranberries	1 c	44	0	12
Grapefruit, pink, red, white	½ medium	41	1	10
Grapes, green or red	½ c	52	1	14
Lemon	1 medium (2⅛ in)	17	1	5
Nectarine	1 medium (2¾ in)	69	2	16
Orange	1 large (3¹⁄₁₆ in)	86	2	22
Peach	1 medium	58	1	14
Pear	½ medium	52	0	14
Pineapple	¼	57	1	15
Plum	1 (2⅛ in)	30	0	8
Raspberries, red	¾ c	48	1	11
Strawberry	1 medium	4	0	1
Watermelon, sliced	1 wedge (¹⁄₁₆ of melon)	86	2	22

Fiber (g)	Sugar (g)	Fat (g)	Sat Fat (g)	Sodium (mg)
0	0	0	0	230
0	0	3	1	320
0	0	1	0	40

Fiber (g)	Sugar (g)	Fat (g)	Sat Fat (g)	Sodium (mg)
3	14	0	0	1
1	3	0	0	0
2	0	5	1	3
4	17	0	0	1
8	7	1	0	1
2	7	0	0	1
1	5	0	0	11
4	4	0	0	2
1	9	0	0	0
1	12	0	0	2
2	1	0	0	1
3	12	1	0	0
4	17	0	0	0
2	13	0	0	0
3	9	0	0	1
2	11	0	0	1
1	7	0	0	0
6	4	1	0	1
0	1	0	0	2
1	18	0	0	3

GRAINS AND RICES

Food Item	Serving Size	Calories	Protein (g)	Carb (g)
Couscous, cooked	⅓ c	59	2	12
Oat bran, cooked	⅓ c	29	2	8
Oats, rolled, dry	2 Tbsp	37	1	7
Quinoa, dry	2 Tbsp	79	3	15
Rice, brown, long-grain, cooked	¼ c	54	1	11
Rice, brown, medium-grain, cooked	¼ c	55	1	11
Rice, brown, short-grain, dry	1½ Tbsp	66	1	15
Rice, whole grain, brown, Uncle Ben's 10-minute, dry	¼ c	170	1	35
Rice, white, long-grain, cooked	¼ c	51	1	11
Rice, wild, cooked	⅓ c	55	2	12

MEATS

Food Item	Serving Size	Calories	Protein (g)	Carb (g)
Beef				
Bottom round, all lean, roasted, boneless	3 oz	144	24	0
Filet mignon, lean, broiled	3 oz	164	24	0
Flank steak, lean, braised	3 oz	201	24	0
Ground patty, 10% fat, raw	4 oz	199	23	0
Ground, extra lean, raw (5% fat)	4 oz	155	24	0
Hot dog, beef, fat-free	1 frank	62	7	3
Roast beef, lunchmeat, medium-rare	1 oz	30	6	1
Steak, top sirloin, lean, broiled	3 oz	160	26	0
Pork				
Bacon, medium slice, cooked	1 slice	43	3	0
Canadian bacon, grilled	1 slice	43	6	0
Chop, center lean, with bone, braised	3 oz	172	25	0
Chop sirloin, lean, with bone, braised	1 chop	142	19	0
Ground, cooked	3 oz	252	22	0

Fiber (g)	Sugar (g)	Fat (g)	Sat Fat (g)	Sodium (mg)
1	0	0	0	3
2	n/a	1	0	1
1	0	1	0	0
1	n/a	1	0	4
1	0	0	0	2
1	n/a	0	0	0
1	0	1	0	2
2	0	1.5	0	0
0	0	0	0	0
1	0	0	0	2

Fiber (g)	Sugar (g)	Fat (g)	Sat Fat (g)	Sodium (mg)
0	0	5	2	32
0	0	7	3	50
0	0	11	5	61
0	0	11	5	75
0	0	6	3	75
0	0	1	0	455
0	1	1	1	235
0	0	6	2	54
0	0	3	1	185
0	0	2	1	363
0	0	7	3	53
0	0	6	2	38
0	0	18	7	62

Food Item	Serving Size	Calories	Protein (g)	Carb (g)
Ham, low-sodium, 96% fat-free, roasted, boneless	1 oz	47	6	0
Hot dog, pork	1 frank	204	10	0
Ribs, country-style, lean, braised	3 oz	199	22	0
Sausage, pork, cooked	1 oz (1 each)	82	4	0
Tenderloin, roasted, lean	3 oz	139	24	0
Veal				
Breast, braised, boneless, lean	3 oz	185	26	0
Ground, broiled	3 oz	146	21	0
Loin, roasted, lean	3 oz	149	22	0

NUTS, SEEDS, AND BUTTERS

Food Item	Serving Size	Calories	Protein (g)	Carb (g)
Almond butter, plain, with salt	1 Tbsp	101	2	3
Almonds, dry-roasted, with salt	½ oz (11 nuts)	85	3	3
Almonds, natural, sliced	½ oz	82	3	3
Brazil nuts, dried	1 nut	33	1	1
Brazil nuts, dried	½ oz (3 nuts)	93	2	2
Cashew butter, plain, with salt	1 Tbsp	94	3	4
Cashew nuts, dry-roasted, with salt	½ oz	81	2	5
Cashew nuts, raw	½ oz	78	3	4
Flaxseed, ground	1 Tbsp	37	1	2
Macadamia nuts, dry-roasted, with salt	½ oz (5–6 nuts)	101	1	2
Mixed nuts, dry-roasted, with peanuts, with salt	½ oz	84	2	4
Peanut butter, creamy, with salt	1 Tbsp	94	4	3
Peanut butter, with salt, reduced-fat	1 Tbsp	83	4	6
Peanut butter, crunchy, with salt	1 Tbsp	95	4	3

Fiber (g)	Sugar (g)	Fat (g)	Sat Fat (g)	Sodium (mg)
0	0	2	1	275
0	0	18	7	620
0	0	12	4	54
0	0	7.5	3	200
0	0	4	1	48
n/a	n/a	8	3	58
0	0	6	3	71
0	0	6	2	82

Fiber (g)	Sugar (g)	Fat (g)	Sat Fat (g)	Sodium (mg)
1	1	9	1	72
2	1	7	1	48
2	1	7	1	0
0	0	3	1	0
1	0	9	2	0
0	1	8	2	98
0	1	7	1	91
1	1	6	1	2
2	0	3	0	2
1	1	11	2	38
1	1	7	1	95
1	1	8	2	73
1	1	5	1	86
1	1	8	1	78

Food Item	Serving Size	Calories	Protein (g)	Carb (g)
Peanut butter, natural	1 Tbsp	100	4	4
Peanuts, dry-roasted, with salt	½ oz	83	3	3
Peanuts, shelled, cooked, with salt	1 Tbsp	36	2	2
Pecans, dried, chopped	⅛ c	94	1	2
Pecans, dried, halved	⅛ c	86	1	2
Pecans, dry-roasted, with salt	½ oz	101	1	2
Pistachios, dry-roasted, with salt	½ oz	81	3	4
Walnuts, dried, black	1 Tbsp	48	2	1
Walnuts, English, ground	⅛ c	65	2	1
Walnuts, dried, halved	½ oz	93	2	2

PASTA

Food Item	Serving Size	Calories	Protein (g)	Carb (g)
Note: For most pasta shapes, 1 ounce of dry pasta makes approximately ½ cup cooked.				
Angel hair, whole wheat, dry	1 oz	106	4	21
Bow ties, semolina, dry	1 oz	103	4	21
Fettuccine (tagliatelle), semolina, dry	1 oz	102	4	21
Fettuccine (tagliatelle), spinach, dry	1 oz	98	4	20
Lasagna, semolina, dry	1 oz	102	4	21
Linguine, semolina, dry	1 oz	102	4	21
Penne, semolina, dry	1 oz	106	4	22
Penne, whole wheat, dry	1 oz	106	4	21
Spaghetti, whole wheat, dry	1 oz	99	4	21

POULTRY

Food Item	Serving Size	Calories	Protein (g)	Carb (g)
Chicken				
Chicken, breast, boneless, without skin, stewed	½ breast	143	23	0
Chicken, drumstick, without skin, roasted	½ drumstick	76	12	0

Fiber (g)	Sugar (g)	Fat (g)	Sat Fat (g)	Sodium (mg)
1	1	8	1	60
1	1	7	1	115
1	0	2.5	.5	84
1	1	10	0	0
1	1	9	1	0
1	1	11	1	54
2	1	7	1	57
1	0	5	0	0
1	0	7	1	0
1	0	9	0	0

Fiber (g)	Sugar (g)	Fat (g)	Sat Fat (g)	Sodium (mg)
3	1	1	0	5
1	1	0	0	1
1	1	1	0	2
1	1	1	0	9
1	1	1	0	1
1	1	1	0	2
1	1	.5	0	3
3	1	1	0	5
4	1	.5	0	2

Fiber (g)	Sugar (g)	Fat (g)	Sat Fat (g)	Sodium (mg)
0	0	3	1	77
0	0	2	1	42

Food Item	Serving Size	Calories	Protein (g)	Carb (g)
Chicken, thigh, boneless, without skin, roasted	1 thigh	109	13	0
Chicken frankfurter	1 frank	116	6	3
Chicken lunchmeat, deli	1 oz	23	5	0
Turkey				
Turkey, breast, with skin, roasted	from 1 lb turkey	150	28	0
Turkey, dark meat, with skin, roasted	from 1 lb turkey	230	29	0
Turkey, ground, cooked	3 oz	145	17	0
Turkey, light meat, with skin, roasted	from 1 lb turkey	134	19	0
Turkey frankfurter	1	102	6	1
Turkey sausage, smoked, hot	1 oz	44	4	1

SEAFOOD

Food Item	Serving Size	Calories	Protein (g)	Carb (g)
Crab, Alaskan, king crab, steamed	3 oz	82	16	0
Crab, baked or broiled	3 oz	117	16	0
Crab, imitation (surimi)	3 oz	81	6	13
Crab, sautéed	3 oz	117	16	0
Lobster, Northern steamed	3 oz	83	17	1
Shrimp, cooked	3 oz	84	17	0
Shrimp, steamed	1 large	5	1	0

VEGETABLES

Food Item	Serving Size	Calories	Protein (g)	Carb (g)
Alfalfa sprouts	½ c	4	1	0
Artichoke	1 medium	60	4	13
Asparagus, cooked	8 spears	26	3	5
Bell pepper, chopped	1 c	30	1	7

Fiber (g)	Sugar (g)	Fat (g)	Sat Fat (g)	Sodium (mg)
0	0	6	2	46
0	0	9	2	616
0	0	0	0	210
0	0	3	1	52
0	0	12	4	79
0	0	8	2	66
0	0	6	2	43
0	0	8	3	642
0	1	2	1	260

Fiber (g)	Sugar (g)	Fat (g)	Sat Fat (g)	Sodium (mg)
0	0	1	0	911
0	n/a	5.5	1	270
0	5	0	0	715
0	0	5	1	270
0	0	1	0	323
0	0	1	0	190
0	0	0	0	12

Fiber (g)	Sugar (g)	Fat (g)	Sat Fat (g)	Sodium (mg)
0	0	0	0	1
7	1	0	0	397
2	2	0	0	17
3	4	0	0	4

Food Item	Serving Size	Calories	Protein (g)	Carb (g)
Bell pepper, boiled	1 c	38	1	9
Broccoli, chopped, boiled	1 c	55	4	11
Broccoli, florets, fresh	1 c	20	2	4
Brussels sprouts, raw	1 c	38	3	8
Cabbage, raw	1 medium leaf	6	0	1
Carrot	1 medium	25	1	6
Carrot, baby	1 medium	4	0	1
Cauliflower	¼ medium head	36	3	8
Celery	1 medium stalk	6	0	1
Celery, chopped	1 c	16	1	3
Cherry tomatoes, red	1 c	27	1	6
Corn, sweet white or yellow	½ c	66	2	15
Corn, sweet white or yellow	1 large ear	123	5	27
Cucumber with peel, raw	1 (8¼ in)	45	2	11
Garlic	1 clove	4	0	1
Green beans, snap, raw	1 c	34	2	8
Green beans, with almonds, frozen, Green Giant	1 c	91	3	8
Lettuce, iceberg	5 large leaves	10	1	2
Lettuce, romaine	4 leaves	19	1	4
Mushrooms, brown Italian	5	27	3	4
Onion, green (scallions), tops and bulbs, chopped	½ c	16	1	4
Onion, red or yellow	1 medium	44	1	10
Peas, green, raw	½ c	59	4	10
Peas, snow, whole, raw	½ c	13	1	2
Potato, baked, with skin, without salt	1 medium	161	4	37

Fiber (g)	Sugar (g)	Fat (g)	Sat Fat (g)	Sodium (mg)
2	3	0	0	3
5	2	1	0	64
2	0	0	0	19
3	2	0	0	22
1	1	0	0	4
2	3	0	0	42
0	0	0	0	8
4	4	0	0	43
1	1	0	0	32
2	2	0	0	81
2	4	0	0	7
2	2	1	0	12
4	5	2	0	21
2	5	0	0	6
0	0	0	0	1
4	2	0	0	7
3	3	4.5	0	144
1	1	0	0	8
2	1	0	0	9
1	2	0	0	6
1	1	0	0	8
2	5	0	0	4
4	4	0	0	4
1	1	0	0	1
4	2	0	0	17

Food Item	Serving Size	Calories	Protein (g)	Carb (g)
Sauerkraut, canned, low-sodium	1 c	31	1	6
Spinach	3 oz	20	2	3
Spinach, cooked, with salt	1 c	41	5	7
Spinach, cooked, without salt	1 c	41	5	7
Squash, summer	1 medium	31	2	7
Sweet potato, baked, with skin, without salt	1 small	54	1	12
Tomato, red	1 medium	22	1	5
Zucchini, with skin, raw	1 medium	31	2	7

Fiber (g)	Sugar (g)	Fat (g)	Sat Fat (g)	Sodium (mg)
4	3	0	0	437
2	0	0	0	67
4	1	0	0	551
4	1	0	0	126
2	4	0	0	4
2	4	0	0	22
1	3	0	0	0
2	3	0	0	20

PHOTO CREDITS

INDEX

Underscored page references indicate boxed text. **Boldfaced** page references indicate photographs.

Conversion Chart

These equivalents have been slightly rounded to make measuring easier.

Volume Measurements

U.S.	Imperial	Metric
¼ tsp	–	1 ml
½ tsp	–	2 ml
1 tsp	–	5 ml
1 Tbsp	–	15 ml
2 Tbsp (1 oz)	1 fl oz	30 ml
¼ cup (2 oz)	2 fl oz	60 ml
⅓ cup (3 oz)	3 fl oz	80 ml
½ cup (4 oz)	4 fl oz	120 ml
⅔ cup (5 oz)	5 fl oz	160 ml
¾ cup (6 oz)	6 fl oz	180 ml
1 cup (8 oz)	8 fl oz	240 ml

Weight Measurements

U.S.	Metric
1 oz	30 g
2 oz	60 g
4 oz (¼ lb)	115 g
5 oz (⅓ lb)	145 g
6 oz	170 g
7 oz	200 g
8 oz (½ lb)	230 g
10 oz	285 g
12 oz (¾ lb)	340 g
14 oz	400 g
16 oz (1 lb)	455 g
2.2 lb	1 kg

Length Measurements

U.S.	Metric
¼"	0.6 cm
½"	1.25 cm
1"	2.5 cm
2"	5 cm
4"	11 cm
6"	15 cm
8"	20 cm
10"	25 cm
12" (1')	30 cm

Pan Sizes

U.S.	Metric
8" cake pan	20 × 4 cm sandwich or cake tin
9" cake pan	23 × 3.5 cm sandwich or cake tin
11" × 7" baking pan	28 × 18 cm baking tin
13" × 9" baking pan	32.5 × 23 cm baking tin
15" × 10" baking pan	38 × 25.5 cm baking tin (Swiss roll tin)
1½ qt baking dish	1.5 liter baking dish
2 qt baking dish	2 liter baking dish
2 qt rectangular baking dish	30 × 19 cm baking dish
9" pie plate	22 × 4 or 23 × 4 cm pie plate
7" or 8" springform pan	18 or 20 cm springform or loose-bottom cake tin
9" × 5" loaf pan	23 × 13 cm or 2 lb narrow loaf tin or pâté tin

Temperatures

Fahrenheit	Centigrade	Gas
140°	60°	–
160°	70°	–
180°	80°	–
225°	105°	¼
250°	120°	½
275°	135°	1
300°	150°	2
325°	160°	3
350°	180°	4
375°	190°	5
400°	200°	6
425°	220°	7
450°	230°	8
475°	245°	9
500°	260°	–